The Digital Matte Painting Handbook

For Meghan —

Let's talk about bring
my class to Parsons!

David B. Mattingly

The Digital Matte Painting Handbook

David B. Mattingly

WILEY

Wiley Publishing, Inc.

Acquisitions Editor: Mariann Barsolo
Development Editor: Gary Schwartz
Technical Editor: Jon McFarland
Production Editor: Eric Charbonneau
Copy Editor: Tiffany Taylor
Editorial Manager: Pete Gaughan
Production Manager: Tim Tate
Vice President and Executive Group Publisher: Richard Swadley
Vice President and Publisher: Neil Edde
Media Assistant Project Manager: Jenny Swisher
Media Associate Producer: Marilyn Hummel
Media Quality Assurance: Doug Kuhn
Book Designer: Mark Ong, Side by Side Studios
Compositor: Craig W. Johnson, Happenstance Type-O-Rama
Proofreader: Jen Larsen, Word One
Indexer: Ted Laux
Project Coordinator, Cover: Katherine Crocker
Cover Designer: Ryan Sneed
Cover Image: David B. Mattingly

Copyright © 2011 by Wiley Publishing, Inc., Indianapolis, Indiana

Published simultaneously in Canada

ISBN: 978-0-470-92242-2 (pbk)
ISBN: 978-1-118-07802-0 (ebk)
ISBN: 978-1-118-07804-4 (ebk)
ISBN: 978-1-118-07803-7 (ebk)

Dear Reader,

Thank you for choosing *The Digital Matte Painting Handbook*. This book is part of a family of premium-quality Sybex books, all of which are written by outstanding authors who combine practical experience with a gift for teaching.

Sybex was founded in 1976. More than 30 years later, we're still committed to producing consistently exceptional books. With each of our titles, we're working hard to set a new standard for the industry. From the paper we print on, to the authors we work with, our goal is to bring you the best books available.

I hope you see all that reflected in these pages. I'd be very interested to hear your comments and get your feedback on how we're doing. Feel free to let me know what you think about this or any other Sybex book by sending me an email at nedde@wiley.com. If you think you've found a technical error in this book, please visit http://sybex.custhelp.com. Customer feedback is critical to our efforts at Sybex.

Best regards,

Neil Edde
Vice President and Publisher
Sybex, an Imprint of Wiley

To Cathleen, with my love.

Acknowledgments

This is my first technical book, and I am grateful for all the professional guidance and support I received from the amazing Sybex team: Mariann Barsolo, acquisitions editor, for believing in the concept and helping to define the content of this book; Gary Schwartz, development editor, for his expert editorial direction, patience, and encouragement throughout the project; Jon McFarland, technical editor, for his uncanny ability to ferret out and correct my mistakes; Tiffany Taylor, copy editor; and the numerous unsung heroes behind the scenes at Sybex. My thanks to Sue Olinsky for making the introductions at Wiley that led to this project—I still owe you a dinner!

This book would not have been possible without the devotion and support of my wife Cathleen, who gave up many weekends to help me clarify concepts and wrestle my ungainly writing into readable prose.

I also extend my gratitude to three faithful readers who gave me feedback throughout the process: Lawrence Kaplan, Barclay Shaw, and Stephen Youll. Devoting the time to slog through a buddy's book is a test of friendship, and you are all true friends.

I want to acknowledge people who read individual chapters and provided their expert feedback: Craig Barron, Harrison Ellenshaw, and Eric Reinfeld.

Also, thanks to the individuals and companies that provided photographs and reference materials included on the DVD: Walton Dornisch, Ron Lyons Jr. of great-castles.com, Tomas Babinec of environment-textures.com, Simon Morse of 3dtotal.com, and Marcel Vijfwinkel of cgtextures.com.

Big thanks to Michele Moen, Eric Chauvin, and Dylan Cole for agreeing to be profiled in this book.

Finally, my deepest gratitude to the matte painting students at the School of Visual Arts and Pratt Institute—you make every semester an adventure!

About the Author

David B. Mattingly lives in Hoboken, New Jersey, right across the Hudson River from New York City. He teaches matte painting at the School of Visual Arts and at Pratt Institute. He has worked on major motion pictures and TV miniseries for the last 30 years, including *The Black Hole* (1979), *Tron* (1982), *Dick Tracy* (1990), *The Stand* (1994), *I, Robot* (2004), and *A Muppets Christmas: Letters to Santa* (2008). He has contributed matte shots and special effects to hundreds of commercial projects.

David worked at Walt Disney Studios for seven years in the 1980s and became head of the matte department in 1984. He moved to New York City in the late 1980s to pursue a career as a book illustrator.

David has produced more than 1,200 covers for major publishers of science fiction and fantasy, including Baen, Bantam, DAW, Del Rey, Dell, Marvel, Omni, Playboy, Signet, and Tor. For Scholastic Inc., David painted 54 covers for K. A. Applegate's blockbuster young adult series *Animorphs* and *Everworld*. He illustrated David Weber's space epic *Honor Harrington*, a *New York Times* best-seller. A compilation of his traditionally painted artwork, *Alternate Views, Alternate Universes: The Art of David B. Mattingly* was published in 1996.

David is a two-time winner of the Magazine and Booksellers "Best Cover of the Year" award, and he is also the winner of the Association of Science Fiction Artists "Chesley" award. David's other clients have included Michael Jackson, Lucasfilm, Universal Studios, Totco Oil, Galloob Toys, R/Greenberg Associates, Click 3X, and Spontaneous Combustion.

Contents

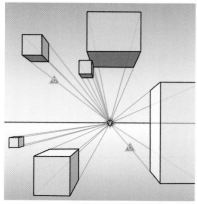

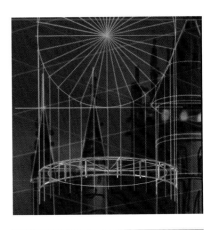

Chapter 6   Form   97

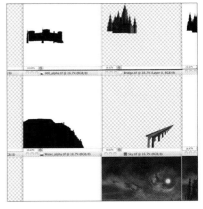

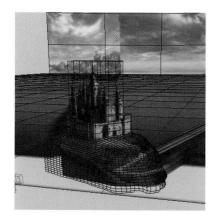

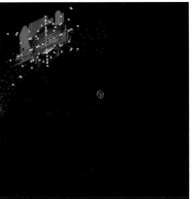

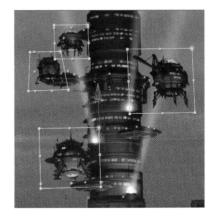

Foreword

Matte painting is all about storytelling. Every good movie tells the audience something relatable—something they already know, but in a way that is new and different. To be a great matte artist is to be a great storyteller. Certainly, there may be only one or two matte shots in a film, or perhaps dozens, but each individual shot has a responsibility to move the story forward. It isn't about how beautifully the artist renders a tree or a rock or a space-ship; it's about the collaborative process of continuing an emotional response.

I was fortunate enough to get a job as an apprentice matte artist in the early 1970s at a Hollywood film studio, long before a little film called *Star Wars* began to make special (visual) effects special. It was a time when studios had understaffed matte painting departments and were frustrated that art school students weren't interested in becoming matte artists because "painting like a photograph," wasn't the work of a "true artist."

It turned out to be somewhat ironic that I was hired for *Star Wars* not because I was good, but because I was one of the few matte artists in the industry. It was a turning point in my life.

I've seen bad matte shots in great movies and great matte shots in bad movies. So, often it's difficult for matte painters to know if they're any good. Movie success isn't about how good the matte paintings are—it's a gestalt about the whole, not the parts.

The Digital Matte Painting Handbook isn't necessarily just about technique. It will also show you how to touch your viewers' collective emotions: how to make each of them feel that there is meaning in their lives, over and above the mundane.

Matte painting is mystifying; you'll never fully understand the process, the techniques, or the final product. I never have, and neither will you. However, like Buddhism, it's the seeking of enlightenment—something you can never achieve, but still you must try. Frustration is part of the process; and whether you've an artist or not, here is insight into communication through the visual image in a most important way. Pay attention.

Harrison Ellenshaw

—Harrison Ellenshaw (Matte Artist: *Star Wars*, *The Black Hole*, *The Empire Strikes Back*; Visual Effects Supervisor: *Tron*, *Dick Tracy*, *Dave*); Los Angeles, California; 2011

Introduction

From an early age, I wanted to be an artist. I was drawn first to comic books and then to science-fiction literature because of the wondrous images that fed my artistic imagination. When I read Edgar Rice Burroughs, Robert Heinlein, and Isaac Asimov as an adolescent, I would spend as much time studying the covers as I did reading the books, and I began to compose pictures to go along with the narrative. Movies brought these pictures to life. I became an avid fan of fantasy and science-fiction films as much for the visuals as for the stories. I was acutely attuned to special effects and how moviemakers made the fantastic real on screen. With cinema's magical combination of fantastic imagery and motion, is it any wonder I became a matte artist? In fact, I distinctly remember the first time I became aware of a matte painting in a feature film.

My Story

It was 1968, and my father took me to see *Planet of the Apes*. It was my kind of movie: at 12 years of age, I put myself in the place of the protagonist, Charlton Heston, fearlessly challenging a society ruled by sentient apes. The two hours flew by.

In the film's final shot, the camera pulls back to reveal the Statue of Liberty, three-quarters of which is buried in sand at the ocean's edge. This iconic shot still packs a wallop to this day! In dumbstruck awe, I wondered aloud how the scene was done. My father, an inventor and college professor, suggested that it was a model. I couldn't believe a model could look that real.

I lived in a small town in Colorado, and not many people were knowledgeable about the then-arcane art of special effects. Nevertheless, an older friend who was active in community theater informed me that it was a "matte shot." What exactly that was remained a mystery until I made a visit to Denver.

In a well-stocked bookstore, I happened upon a book on special effects called *The Technique of Special Effects Cinematography*, by Raymond Fielding. I bought the book, and it answered many of my questions, including what a matte shot was.

In those days, artists who created matte paintings were given scant credit; and without the Internet or a DVD you could rewind, it took some sleuthing to find out who did the mattes on a movie. All through my childhood, I sat through effects films to the final frame, hoping to discover who did the mattes. I felt special, knowing about the invisible painted creations of Peter Ellenshaw, Albert Whitlock, and Matthew Yuricich. These artists, along with Frank Frazetta, James Steranko, and Jack Kirby, were my heroes.

I got my first job as a matte artist through pure happenstance. I was a student at the Art Center College of Design in Pasadena, CA when the first *Stars Wars* movie came out. As the end titles flashed by, I noted that the mattes were credited to P. S. Ellenshaw. Naturally, I assumed they were done by my idol, Peter Ellenshaw. This misinformation was corrected when I read an article about the film in *Starlog Magazine*, one of the first publications to cover special-effects movies in depth for a popular audience. The paintings were actually done by

Peter Ellenshaw's son, then known as P. S. Ellenshaw. P. S. Ellenshaw, whose birth name is Peter, later changed his name to Harrison to avoid confusion with his father. The article also revealed that he worked at Disney Studios.

On a crazy impulse, I called the switchboard at Disney Studios and asked for P. S. Ellenshaw. Much to my shock, I was put through directly, and he answered the phone. Overcoming my surprise, I told him I was a long-time admirer of both his and his father's work, and that I aspired to be a matte painter. He invited me to come to the studio for an interview. Two days later, he offered me a job. Ignoring my parents' apprehension and alarm, I quit school mid-semester and started working at Disney.

When I joined Disney, the studio was ramping up for one of the biggest and most expensive pictures in its history: *The Black Hole* (1979). Harrison trained and mentored me during the production of this film. His father, Peter Ellenshaw, served as production designer on *The Black Hole*, and I personally benefited from his comments and advice. I also had the priceless opportunity to watch him and Harrison paint.

After working at Disney Studios for seven years, I became the head of the matte department after Harrison left to set up the ILM matte department. While working at Disney, I began freelancing in my spare time as a science-fiction book cover illustrator. Although I love movies, cover art gives an artist more freedom to explore their personal vision. When Ballantine Books offered me a two-year contract, it was with the provision that I move to New York City. This was a very difficult decision, but I ultimately saw the offer as too good to refuse. To date, I have done more than 1,200 science-fiction and other book covers.

Even with the switch in my career focus, my love of matte painting and films never waned. Although most effects-heavy films are still made in California, I took assignments as a matte artist whenever I got the chance, primarily for commercials and independent films.

Seven years ago, I heard that the School of Visual Art wanted to add a matte painting course to its class offerings, and I applied for the job. I had no idea how much I would enjoy teaching, especially a subject I'm passionate about. When I was offered a second teaching position at Pratt Institute, I jumped at it. Every semester is a journey, with smart, challenging, and wildly talented students. I expand the syllabus yearly to embrace new ideas and emerging technologies. This book is the product of seven years of classroom experimentation to define and communicate the essential skill set for becoming a matte artist.

How This Book Came About

When I began teaching digital matte painting, I searched for a good textbook. Books were available on digital painting, but nothing specifically dealt with the art of digital matte painting. In the intervening years, some excellent resources have come out, including DVDs by Dylan Cole, Yannick Dusso, and Chris Stoski, yet all of them assume a fairly advanced knowledge of painting.

What I wanted was a book that would take students step by step through the process of making a matte painting, and one that didn't assume knowledge of the software or tools up front. Because my classes at the School of Visual Arts and Pratt Institute are electives, I have students enrolled from many different disciplines. Some students have never painted on the computer; others have never painted with anything other than a computer; and some, like my film majors, have never painted at all. The one thing that unifies them is an interest in matte painting. My challenge has been to design coursework that all of them can do, while giving a comprehensive introduction to the craft of matte painting.

Three years ago, I added camera projection to the class using Maya, a 3D modeling and rendering program. This important matte painting technique is a complex process consisting of many discrete steps. Again, I looked for a how-to manual that all my students could understand and use, without assuming any preexisting knowledge of Maya. I observed that many of my students became frustrated with the process because it is laborious and unforgiving. If you miss one step, the camera projection won't work. After years of teaching this class without a textbook, I decided to write it myself.

Who Should Read This Book

This book is written for a general audience, including anyone who wants to know more about matte painting or desires to be a matte artist.

You must have a basic understanding of how a computer works, but knowledge of the programs—Photoshop, Maya, and After Effects—isn't required. Even if you've never used the programs before, you should be able to follow the steps in this book and satisfactorily complete the projects. I'll teach you how to use the tools as you encounter them. If you're an advanced user with in-depth knowledge of Photoshop and After Effects, you can skip over the more basic material in this book and concentrate on the projects.

If you're working on your own, you don't have to purchase the software to try it. Most of the programs are available as demo versions on a time-limited basis. Colleges and universities with a software library usually include these industry-standard programs.

In my experience, if I can complete one project successfully using a new program, I can figure out a lot of the finer details as I continue to work. Much of the material in this book can be found in books covering specific topics in greater depth. When appropriate, I recommend books where you can find additional information that I didn't have the time or space to include. For instance, after Chapter 4, "Perspective Basics," I list three books that can give you commanding knowledge of this important component in the matte artist's toolbox.

This book will take an average computer user through a series of matte paintings by breaking down the process into easy-to-follow steps and manageable chunks. Checklists, screen shots, and illustrations provide guideposts so that no one will get lost doing the assignments. The level of technical knowledge and competency builds throughout the book in a logical progression. Each successfully completed project leads to the next chapter, which offers a more difficult exercise.

My goal is to give you basic knowledge of the building blocks of a good matte painting. In the first stationary matte painting, you'll learn about concept, perspective, tone, and texturing. In the following projects, you'll get a taste of three advanced techniques: camera projection, 2D compositing, and 3D compositing. Your final matte will incorporate live actors in a 3D universe.

This book will introduce you to the basic tools a matte artist will use, but there is much more that could be covered. I hope to write a follow-up book devoted to advanced matte painting topics: shot structure, camera motivation, and more elaborate effects.

There's a lot to learn, so let's get started with Chapter 1: "What Is a Matte Painting?"

How to Contact the Author

I would be happy to review and critique projects completed by readers of this book. Feel free to contact me through my personal website for the book at www .digitalmattepaintinghandbook.com.

Sybex strives to keep you supplied with the latest tools and information you need for your work. Please check the book's website at www.sybex.com/go/digitalmattepainting, where we'll post additional content and updates should the need arise.

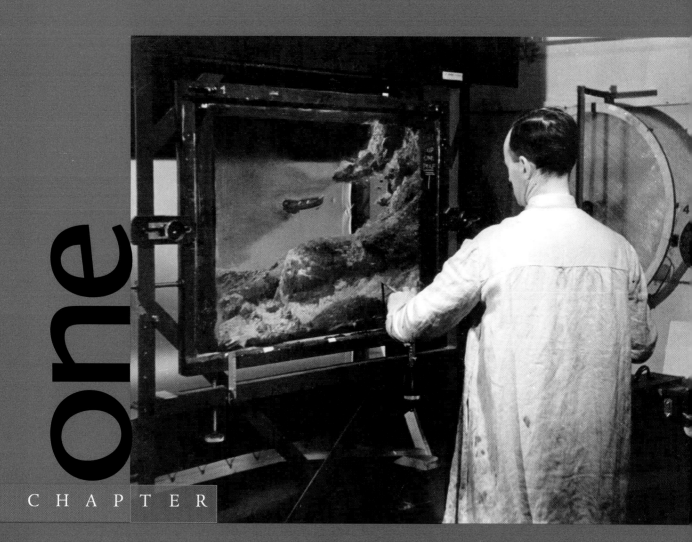

one

What Is a Matte Painting?

You just bought a book *on matte painting, so obviously you're interested in the craft. However, before you dive into the technical exercises, I'd like to invite you to take advantage of this chapter to learn about the history and evolution of matte painting and the giants who shaped the industry.*

This exploration begins with a simple question: To what does the word matte in matte painting refer? If you're stumped, I believe you'll find the historical information in this opening chapter illuminating. You don't really need to know how matte paintings were done prior to the computer age. But by studying and appreciating the contributions of the pioneers in this field, you'll deepen your understanding of this 100-year-old art form.

Matte Painting Defined

The *matte* in *matte painting* refers to the section of the filmed image that's blocked, or *matted out*. These blocking techniques have been abandoned with the advent of digital special effects, but for nearly 80 years some amazing work was done using these tools.

The Glass Shot

The earliest way of producing a matte painting was to place a sheet of glass between the camera and the scene to be filmed. An artist would then paint an image on the glass that blocked and replaced that part of the scene. Instead of building a set or carting in a mountain range, the needed elements were painted on the glass on location (Figure 1.1).

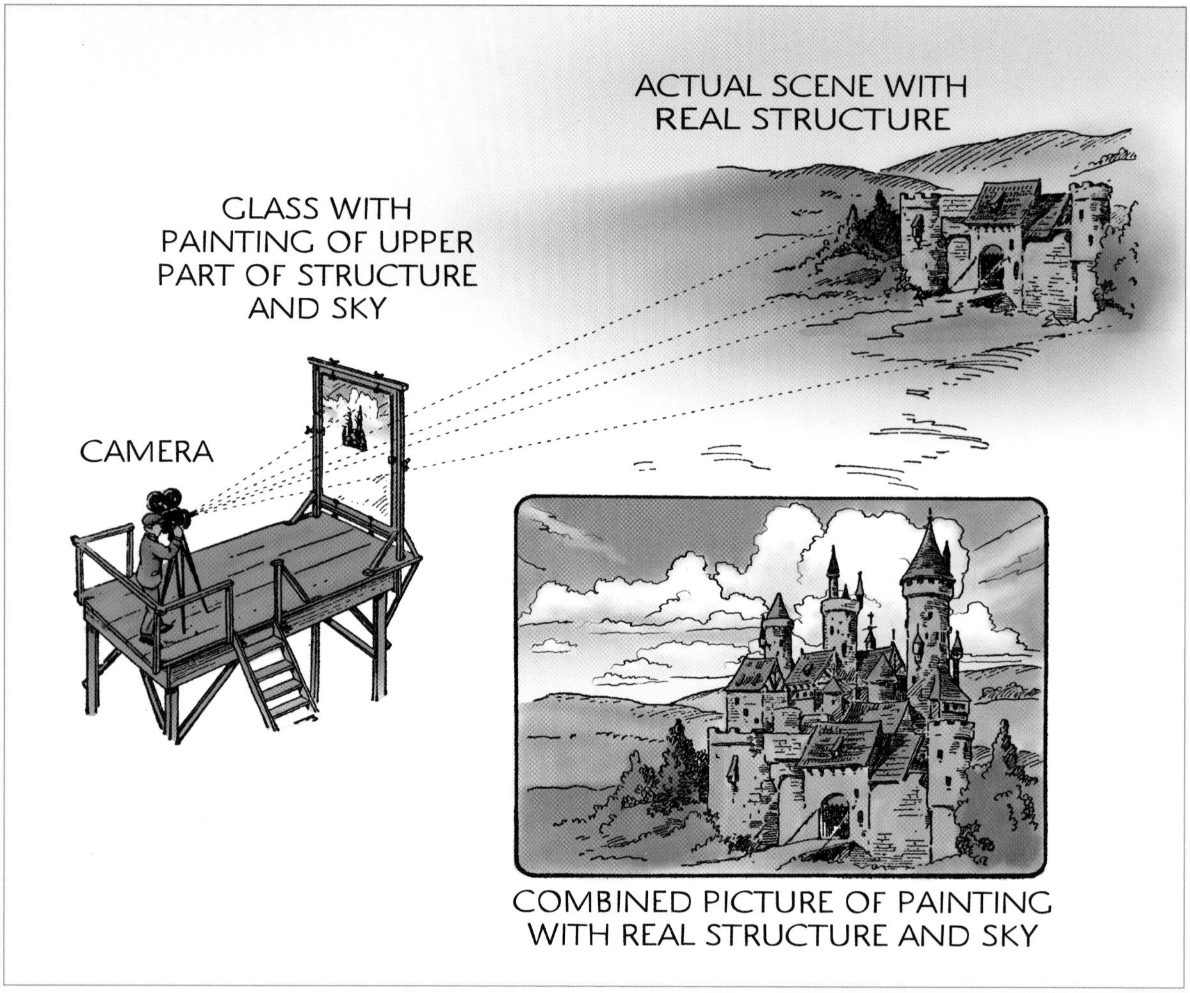
ACTUAL SCENE WITH
REAL STRUCTURE
GLASS WITH
PAINTING OF UPPER
PART OF STRUCTURE
AND SKY
CAMERA
COMBINED PICTURE OF PAINTING
WITH REAL STRUCTURE AND SKY

Credit: Based on a diagram in *The Motion Picture Cameraman* by E. G. Lutz (1927, Scribner).

Figure 1.1 *Diagram of a glass painting setup*

This approach presented some serious disadvantages. The artist and cameraman were at the mercy of the elements, disrupted by changing weather conditions, gusts of wind, and shifting light throughout the day. Also, the shot couldn't always be filmed when the actors and director were ready: it could be filmed only after the matte artist had completed the painting. As a consequence, the matte artist was often under pressure to produce the painting quickly.

The Original-Negative Matte

A second technique for creating matte paintings required cutting a black mask, or *matte*, and suspending it in front of the camera while shooting the live action footage. Later, back in the studio, a single frame of the footage was placed in a camera that had been locked down and secured to avoid any vibrations or movement. A light was placed behind the lens so that the camera acted both as camera and projector, and the frame of film was projected onto the surface on which the matte artist painted. The artist blacked out the areas on the matte painting where the film was exposed and painted only in the matted-out areas of the original exposure. Subsequent tests were run to ensure a perfect match between the painting and the footage, and then a second exposure was made to add the painted section to the film.

The great advantage of this technique was that the scene could be filmed when the production was ready, because it didn't require the matte artist to complete the painting on the spot. Using this technique, the painting could be completed after the filming, at the matte artist's convenience (Figure 1.2).

Figure 1.2 *Diagram of an original-negative matte setup*

The Rear-Projection Matte

A third way of shooting a matte allowed the director to shoot the plate normally without worrying about the matte, and add the matte and the painting later.

The film was developed normally, and then the reel was loaded into a rear projector. A sheet of glass in a sturdy frame was placed on a stand in front of the rear projector. A sheet of frosted projection material was positioned on the back of the glass facing the projector. The matte artist then plotted out the area where the painting was to be added. With the filmed and painted images aligned, the painting was executed. The matte artist ran multiple tests photographed from a camera on the opposite side of the projector to ensure a seamless match. With the camera and the rear projector carefully synchronized, the scene was filmed again, this time with the painting blocking out the matted areas of the original footage (Figure 1.3).

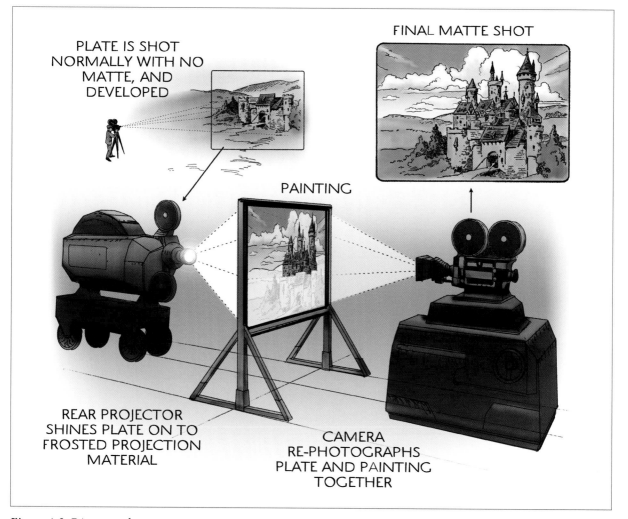

Figure 1.3 Diagram of a rear-projection matte setup

Digital Matte Painting

The advent of digital imaging made these techniques obsolete. In the past, mattes were limited by the available technology. Most were created with just a few elements: often only the plate and the painting. Today, most matte painting is done in Photoshop; it encompasses advanced compositing techniques that could never have been achieved without computers.

With digital compositing, it isn't uncommon for a shot to be created out of hundreds of different elements. Two-dimensional artwork can now be combined with 3D geometry to produce mattes that move and change perspective. But always remember that whether it's achieved with a camera and a piece of glass or by the most advanced computer system with the latest compositing software, the matte shot starts with the skills of the artist who creates the illusion of reality.

A Brief History of Matte Painting

Matte painting has been around since the dawn of filmmaking. It's been continuously used since the first example debuted in 1907. The history of matte painting begins with one man, a camera, and a sheet of glass in the bright sunlight of California.

Norman Dawn and the Invention of Matte Painting

Norman Dawn (1884–1975) was the first person to use a *glass shot* in a motion picture. Dawn was taught this technique while employed as a still photographer in Los Angeles in 1905. Glass shots were used to avoid costly retouching of photographic images. Assigned to photograph a building that had an unsightly pole in front of it, Dawn placed a sheet of glass in front of the camera and painted a tree on the glass to block out the pole.

A year later, while on a trip to Paris, Dawn met George Méliès, the French magician known as the "father of special effects." Méliès was already famous for his sci-fi film spectacle *A Trip to the Moon* (1902), which introduced surprisingly complex special-effects shots. Some of Méliès innovations included multiple exposures of film; the *stop trick*, where the camera was stopped and one item replaced with another; and time-lapse photography. Inspired by what he saw in Méliès' studio, Dawn bought a motion-picture camera while still in Paris: he was determined to try his hand at movie special effects.

When Dawn returned to the United States in 1907, he embarked on his first film. He made film history by applying the glass technique he used as a still photographer. He shot the crumbling Spanish colonial missions scattered along the California coast, restoring them on film to their former glory using matte paintings. His breakthrough film, *The Missions of California* (1907), stands as the first instance of the use of matte painting in motion pictures. Dawn also developed the original-negative matte technique, and he patented the process in 1918.

Although most moviegoers of the time were unaware that the process existed, matte painting became a studio mainstay in the 1930s and 40s; many of the larger studios set up dedicated matte departments. Under a shroud of secrecy, the MGM matte department produced scores of paintings for *The Wizard of Oz* (1939). David Selznick set up an independent matte department that provided nearly 100 matte shots for the epic *Gone With the Wind* (1939). No one in the wider public knew that in many shots, Tara was created by a matte artist. RKO's matte department produced a succession of matte paintings for the opening sequence of *Citizen Kane* (1941). In fact, the iconic scene of Kane in front of a huge campaign poster bearing his likeness is a matte shot.

In the late 1960s and early 1970s, matte painting fell out of favor, and many studios closed their matte departments. George Lucas, with the release of the first *Star Wars* film, is credited with reviving interest in matte painting. With Industrial Light & Magic, the groundbreaking visual effects company he created, Lucas shepherded special effects into the modern era, funding and encouraging the development of the digital techniques used today.

Paint vs. Pixels

Digital imaging has taken over the world of matte painting. Few can deny that the quality of matte paintings, and special-effects shots in general, improve each year. Matte shots today are much tighter than they were in the past, and they can bear the scrutiny of an informed audience that demands HD quality and who will rewatch a particularly juicy matte shot over and over again. When a contemporary viewer looks at the matte shots of the past, many of the shots look rather painterly and wouldn't pass muster in a modern production. However, they were state of the art when *Gone With the Wind*, *The Wizard of Oz*, and *Citizen Kane* premiered, and they hold their own timeless charm.

In this book, you'll learn an arsenal of digital tricks, and I'll encourage you to use in your workflow photographic references that purists may consider cheating. This is a common practice: matte artists today don't do "pure" painting as they did in the past. But there is no replacement for painting skills—so, these lessons aside, take time to do paintings yourself, whether physical or digital.

If you have an opportunity to see some of the original matte paintings created in the pre-digital era, I encourage you to seek them out. In addition to being skillful matte work, many of them are great paintings in their own right, with crispness and directness of paint application that is a wonder to behold.

It's appropriate to end this chapter by featuring the lives and work of two matte artists: Peter Ellenshaw and Albert Whitlock. They're considered among the most influential artists to work in this field.

Photo credit: Harrison Ellenshaw

Figure 1.4 *Peter Ellenshaw observing Percy "Pop" Day at work*

Peter Ellenshaw

Peter Ellenshaw (1913–2007) grew up in a small village in England. His chances of becoming a matte artist were highly unlikely until fate played a hand. In 1934, when Ellenshaw was 21, an artist named Percy "Pop" Day (1878–1965) moved in across the street from the Ellenshaw family. Day was a noted matte painter whose work appeared in Abel Gance's *Napoléon* (1927) and Alfred Hitchcock's *The Ring* (1927). He later went on to contribute the matte paintings for a number of English feature films, including *The Thief of Bagdad* (1940) and *Black Narcissus* (1947).

Ellenshaw had aspirations to be an artist, and he took samples of his work across the street to Day in the hope of getting some advice and encouragement. The meeting proved fortuitous. Day approved of the young man's work, and he later offered Ellenshaw a job as an assistant matte painter (Figure 1.4).

Ellenshaw's widowed mother worked for Pop Day as a housekeeper, and over time, they fell in love and married. Ellenshaw worked in his stepfather's studio for a total of 10 years. After striking out on his own, he painted mattes for four Walt Disney productions produced in England: *Treasure Island* (1950), *The Story of Robin Hood* (1952), *The Sword and the Rose* (1953), and *Rob Roy, the Highland Rogue* (1954). *The Sword and the Rose* was a high-water mark in Peter's energy and productivity: he managed to complete 62 highly detailed mattes in 27 weeks!

Ellenshaw's association with Walt Disney strengthened when he and his young family moved to California. He set up the first Walt Disney matte department and provided the matte paintings for *20,000 Leagues Under the Sea* (1954) while also overseeing the photography of the miniature Nautilus submarine. He won an Academy Award for Best Special Visual Effects for his work on *Mary Poppins*. He was nominated for an Academy Award three more times: for his production design on *Bedknobs and Broomsticks* (1971), for visual effects on *The Island at the Top of the World* (1974), and for *The Black Hole* (1979).

One of Ellenshaw's few non-Disney matte paintings was produced for Stanley Kubrick's epic *Spartacus* (1960). In Figure 1.5, the black areas on the painting are where live action was added.

On a personal note, Ellenshaw was one of the most amazing painters I had the privilege of watching work. I met him while I was working as a matte artist at Disney. During the production of *The Black Hole*, on which Ellenshaw was the production designer, I sat in his office on the Disney lot during breaks and watched him paint. His technique involved keeping the painting extraordinarily loose until he'd worked out all the compositional problems. Then, in a very short time, he painted in the final details that made the entire piece come together and look totally real.

One of my fondest memories of Ellenshaw was working with him on the opening shot for *Dick Tracy* (1990). The picture in Figure 1.6 shows Ellenshaw in the foreground. I'm directly behind him, and artist Leon Harris appears to the left.

Photo credit: Harrison Ellenshaw

Figure 1.5 Peter Ellenshaw matte painting for Stanley Kubrick's Spartacus

Ellenshaw's son, Harrison, is also a noted matte artist and effects director. He provided all the matte paintings in the 1977 release of the first *Star Wars* film. He set up the matte department at Industrial Light & Magic during the production of *Star Wars: The Empire Strikes Back* (1980). He was also the associate producer and visual effects supervisor on *Tron* (1982). Harrison Ellenshaw was my boss and mentor at Disney, and he's not only a talented artist but also a fine and patient teacher.

Figure 1.6 *Peter Ellenshaw working on the opening shot for* Dick Tracy

Photo credit: Harrison Ellenshaw

Albert Whitlock

Albert Whitlock (1915–2000) got his start in the film industry working as a sign painter and scenic artist on early English productions, including Alfred Hitchcock's *The Man Who Knew Too Much* (1934), *Sabotage* (1936), and *The Lady Vanishes* (1938). Whitlock moved to America in 1954 and worked with Peter Ellenshaw at Walt Disney Studios, where he honed his skills as a matte artist. In 1961, Whitlock left Disney to head up the matte department at Universal. He became known as "Universal's secret weapon" for his ability to deliver seemingly impossible shots. Robert Wise only agreed to direct *The Hindenburg* (1975) if Whitlock signed on to take charge of the effects; Wise was convinced that only Whitlock could recreate the world of the giant airship. Whitlock resumed his lifelong association with Alfred Hitchcock at Universal; he played a key part in the creation of many of Hitchcock's late classics, including *The Birds* (1963), *Marnie* (1964), *Torn Curtain* (1966), and *Frenzy (1972)*. Whitlock won back-to-back Oscars for *Earthquake* (1974) and *The Hindenburg*.

Many of Whitlock's solutions for creating complex effects were elegant as well as economical. To create a photorealistic dust storm rolling over a town in *Bound for Glory* (1976), he used large rolls of cotton rotating slowly on a rod. To destroy a hotel in *The Blues Brothers* (1980), he constructed the hotel out of cardboard and demolished it using compressed air.

Whitlock was legendary for his directness and speed. Like a modern Monet, he completed many of his mattes in less than a day. Up close, his paintings are loose and sketchy; but when you step back a few feet, they appear completely photographic. Part of Whitlock's prodigious skill was his ability to capture the impression of a scene without rendering the fine details. One of his most famous quotes is, "Paint is the effect of light, not the object itself" (Figure 1.7).

The photo of Albert Whitlock (Figure 1.7) shows a mirror on his left that he used to check his painting while he worked. Because the mirror reversed the image, he could check for perspective errors and get a fresh look at the painting. Digital artists do the equivalent when they flip their compositions horizontally while working on an image.

Figure 1.7 *Albert Whitlock in front of a matte shot for Mel Brooks'* The History of the World: Part 1 *(1981)*

It's my hope that this brief examination of matte painting's history and its towering figures has inspired you. In any field of endeavor, you quickly move beyond the ways things were done in the past as you embrace today's technologies. Yet all of us owe an incredible debt to these pioneers, who conceived and continually innovated the craft.

Where to Learn More

The Invisible Art: The Legends of Movie Matte Painting by Craig Barron and Mark Cotta Vaz is the ultimate resource on the history of matte painting. Richly illustrated and exhaustive, it's the must-have book for anyone who loves matte painting. This book is out of print, but it's often available at Amazon for a premium. A new edition is expected in 2012.

Ellenshaw Under Glass: Going to the Matte for Disney by Peter Ellenshaw, Bruce Gordon, and David Mumford is an autobiographical journey with the master matte artist. The narrative covers his entire career and provides numerous examples of his great work, including his post-Disney career as a fine artist. The collector's edition is covered in glass. Although the book is out of print, it's available at www.ellenshaw.com/bk_Under_Glass.htm.

Albert Whitlock: A Master of Illusion is a full-length documentary about Whitlock and his work, produced by Walton Dornisch and directed by Mark Horowitz. It contains unique footage of Whitlock painting and filmed interviews with many of the great directors with whom he collaborated. The original version is available on Amazon. You can purchase a new expanded DVD version at http://albertwhitlockamasterofillusion.com.

two

CHAPTER

Photoshop Workspace, Tools, and Custom Brushes

Photoshop is an extremely powerful

image-editing program. It has become the industry standard among matte artists. A few matte artists use a competing paint program, Corel Painter, but the main emphasis of that program is imitating natural media, or reproducing the look of painting with physical brushes and paint. Because the goal in most matte painting is to produce a photo-realistic scene and not a "painterly" work, I rarely use these tools. There is a lot of overlap between the two programs. The latest version of Photoshop, Creative Suite 5, has an entirely new natural media brush tool that is much more like Corel Painter, so even an aspiring digital Vincent Van Gogh will be satisfied.

Photoshop's powerful tools, including color correction, image distortion, and custom brushes, are well suited to matte painting, and they will be the focus of the lessons in next six chapters in this book.

The Digitizing Tablet

Before we go any further, we must pay attention to an indispensable tool for a digital-matte artist. After a computer, a copy of Photoshop, and a monitor, the one other tool you *must* have is a digitizing tablet. Although the mouse has revolutionized navigation on the computer, painting with a mouse is like painting with a brick.

What is a digitizing tablet? It's the digital equivalent of a brush and canvas that allows you to paint on the computer screen with a pressure-sensitive pen. The brand I use is Wacom. With the release of each new generation of Wacom tablet, the tool gets increasingly sensitive to the touch. When I bought my first tablet 16 years ago, it had 512 levels of sensitivity. That may sound like a lot, but the holy grail of pressure sensitivity is that of the B2 pencil. The levels of responsiveness you get from a pencil and your hand are 10 times greater than you could achieve with the original tablet. The early tablets were crude, especially at the lighter, more subtle end of the sensitivity range. The newest generation, the Wacom Intuos4, has 2,048 levels of sensitivity, and it's beginning to approach the range of a pencil.

Tablets come in an assortment of sizes and costs, depending on your budget and painting style. I have a preference for the 6″ × 8″ tablet. That may seem small, but you can zoom in to the image to add more detail.

For more information on Wacom tablets, go to www.wacom.com.

Setting Up Your Workspace

Photoshop has many different tools that meet a wide range of image-editing needs. As a matte artist, you'll use a select set of these tools. You turn panels on and off by going to the top menu and choosing Window and then the panel name. The Photoshop interface changes with each new version, and the version I'm using is CS5. Your interface may be slightly different depending on the version of Photoshop you're running and your computer platform.

Take a moment to configure your workspace as shown in Figure 2.1, the recommended setup for matte painting. You can consult Photoshop's documentation on how to dock and iconize panels. As you progress through these chapters, you may want to personalize your workspace to suit your habits and preferences. This setup is a good starting place for all the lessons to come.

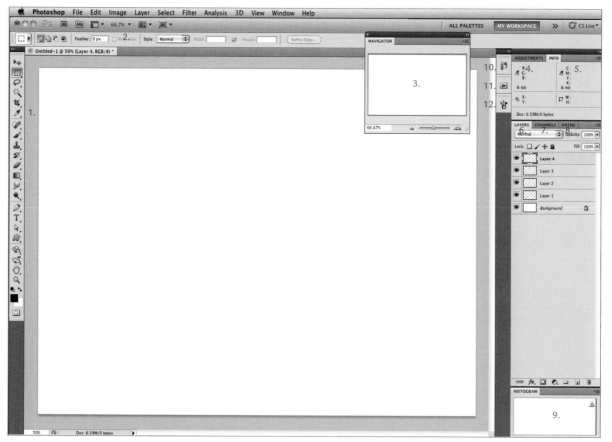

Figure 2.1 Matte painting workspace setup

Photoshop Panels

Let's look at the icons, panels, and tools in the workspace that contribute to your work as a matte painter.

Toolbar

Much of Photoshop's versatility resides in its robust set of tools. The following section lists a select set of the tools that a matte artist will regularly use. For information on any tool not covered here, refer to Photoshop's documentation.

Any tool with a triangle in the lower-right corner has subtools that you can view and select by clicking and holding the icon. The keyboard shortcut is indicated after the main tool on the list, and the subtools are indented below the main tool. Pressing Shift and the keyboard shortcut sequences through the subtools. For example, if you select the Lasso tool and press Shift+L, you'll cycle through the Polygonal Lasso tool and the Magnetic Lasso tool. Thus one keyboard command serves the main tool and all of its subtools.

All of the following tools are available in the toolbar, shown as item #1 in Figure 2.1:

- The Move tool (V) moves layers, selections, and guides. With the Move tool selected, hold down Option on the Mac or Alt on the PC to duplicate the selection and move it.
- The Rectangular Marquee tool (M) draws rectangular selections or square selections when you hold down the Shift key.
  - The Elliptical Marquee tool draws elliptical and circular selections.
- The Lasso tool (L) lets you draw freehand selections.
  - The Polygonal Lasso tool draws straight-edge selections, and the Magnetic Lasso tool snaps to the edge of an image to help you draw around the natural borders quickly.
- The Crop tool (C) crops and straightens images.
- The Eyedropper tool (I) selects colors from an image.
- The Brush tool (B) paints brush strokes.
- The Clone Stamp tool (S) clones the pixels from a specified point in an image to another location. This is particularly useful for duplicating objects or for touching up defects.
- The Eraser tool (E) deletes pixels on the current layer.
- The Gradient tool (G) creates a gradient between colors and/or transparency.
- The Blur tool allows you to blur an image using brushes from the Brush Preset Picker.
- The Dodge tool (O) lightens highlights, midtones, and shadows in your image.
  - The Burn tool darkens highlights, midtones, and shadows in your image. The Sponge tool either saturates or desaturates colors in your image.
- The Pen tool (P) draws smooth-edged vector paths that you can save in the Paths panel. Vector shapes are based on a mathematical description of a shape, rather than composed of pixel data. As a consequence, they're resolution-independent and can be enlarged or reduced without any loss of resolution or image quality.
  - The Freeform Pen tool allows you to draw freely with the anchor points added automatically. *Anchor points* are the building blocks of vector shapes: they describe the shape's curves and corners. The Add Anchor Point tool adds more anchor points to an existing path. The Delete Anchor Point tool deletes anchor points from an existing path. The Convert Point tool lets you convert an anchor point from curve to corner, as well as adjust the angle of the curve.
- The Path Selection tool (A) selects an entire path or shape to copy, move, or scale.

- The Direct Selection tool [⬚] selects the anchor points that form a path or shape to copy, move, or scale.
- The Hand tool (H) [✋] moves an image within your work area. You can hold down the spacebar for quick access to the Hand tool.
    - The Rotate View tool (R) [⟳] rotates your canvas to facilitate easier painting without compromising image quality. This important subtool that has its own special keyboard shortcut (Figure 2.2).

Figure 2.2 Rotate View tool

- The Zoom tool (Z) [🔍] zooms in and out of your image. There are many ways to zoom in Photoshop. To jump in to an image in set increments, click in your image with the Zoom tool. To jump out, Option/Alt+click in the image. To zoom in to a specific area, click+drag in the image with the Zoom tool to create an outline of the area you want to examine. This is called a *marquee window.* When you release the mouse button, the outlined area fills the screen. You can also use the keyboard shortcuts Command/Ctrl+ and Command/Ctrl- to zoom in and zoom out of your image.
- The Reset Colors to Default tool (D) ▪ resets your foreground and background colors to black and white.
- Switch Foreground/Background Colors (X) ↳ switches whatever color you have in the foreground to the background color and vice versa.
- Set Foreground/Background Color [◼] shows the two colors Photoshop remembers for you. The foreground color is used when you paint, fill, or stroke selections; the background color is used to make gradients and fill in the erased areas of an image. If you click either the foreground or background color, the Color Picker pops up so you can select a new color (Figure 2.3).

New in Photoshop CS5 is the ability to call up a heads-up display (HUD) color picker under your cursor any time you have a painting tool selected. With your cursor anywhere inside of your image area, use the shortcut Control+Option+Command+right-click/Shift+Alt+right-click to access the color picker (Figure 2.4).

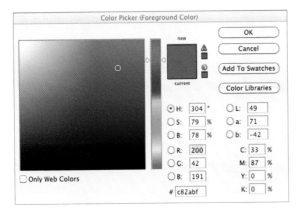

Figure 2.3 *Color Picker*

Figure 2.4 *Heads-up display color picker*

Selected Panels

Working in conjunction with the tools in the toolbar is a select set of panels that you'll rely on for matte painting. These give you the ability to modify the properties of the tools, help you manage and organize your project, and provide information about the image on which you're working. To find the location of each panel, refer to the item numbers in Figure 2.1:

2. Control Panel   The basic properties of a selected tool are automatically displayed in the Control panel (Figure 2.5). Think of the Control panel as a dashboard for driving each tool. The displayed options are specific to the tool in use. For instance, with the Brush tool selected, the Control panel gives you the ability to control the size, opacity, transfer mode, and flow of the brush. With the Text tool in use, you can select the font, type size, text alignment, and other variables.

Figure 2.5 *Control panel*

3. Navigator Panel   This "picture within a picture" displays the entire composition on which you're working, regardless of what appears on the screen. Notice how a red outline in the Navigator panel shows the zoomed-in portion of the painting (Figure 2.6). This is invaluable when you're zooming in and out, because you never lose sight of the overall image. When you're blocking in a piece, it helps to refer to this miniature version so you don't get caught up in fine details.

Figure 2.6 *Navigator panel*

Figure 2.7 Adjustments panel

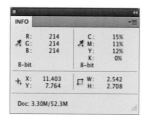

Figure 2.8 Info panel

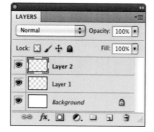

Figure 2.9 Layers panel

Figure 2.10 Channels panel

Figure 2.11 Paths panel

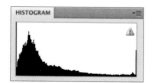

Figure 2.12 Histogram panel

4. Adjustments Panel   This panel opens automatically when you apply an adjustment layer for color correction, allowing you to apply color corrections to your image nondestructively (Figure 2.7).

5. Info Panel   This panel gives you information about your open document, including color values, height and width of selections, document size, and the location of your cursor in the interface (Figure 2.8).

6. Layers Panel   You can have many layers in a project. This panel displays the opacity, transfer mode, fill percentage, and location of each layer in relationship to the others (Figure 2.9).

7. Channels Panel   This panel shows you the individual channels that make up your RGB image. Additionally, this is where you access alpha channels (Figure 2.10).

8. Paths Panel   This panel contains the vector-based lines and shapes that you create using the Pen and Shape drawing tools. You'll use the Paths panel in Chapter 4, "Perspective Basics" (Figure 2.11).

9. Histogram panel   This panel gives you information about the spread of tones in your project. It's useful to monitor what parts of the tonal range your image is using (Figure 2.12).

10. History Panel   This panel lets you go back through many levels of undo if you make a mistake (Figure 2.13). Use the simple keystroke Command+Z/Ctrl+Z to undo the current step. However, if the problem is further back, history can be a lifesaver. You can choose how many levels of undo you want. Go to the top menu, choose Photoshop → Preferences → Performance on the Mac or Edit → Preferences on the PC, and specify up to 1,000 history states. What you did most recently is at the bottom of the scrollable history stack, whereas earlier actions appear higher up.

11. Actions Panel   This panel allows you to automate many operations in Photoshop by assigning keyboard shortcuts (Figure 2.14). A set of useful shortcuts is included in the Chapter 2 section of the DVD, entitled CustomActions.atn. Try these out to see how to use the function keys for common operations and get inspired to create your own.

12. Brush Panel   This is the most important panel for matte painting (Figure 2.15). In-depth instructions on using this panel follow.

Figure 2.13 *History panel*

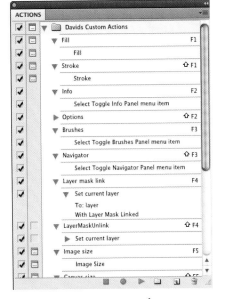

Figure 2.14 *Actions panel*

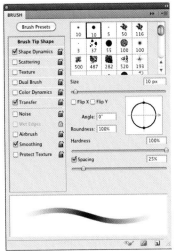

Figure 2.15 *Brush panel*

Using Custom Brushes

As you work on the projects in this book, you'll build your own custom brushes. What are custom brushes? They're brushes with special characteristics turned on, including opacity, jitter, scatter, size, and color variation. The first brush that appears in the default Photoshop CS5 brush set, called Soft Round, has no custom brush characteristics. Start with this basic brush to examine the different parameters, one by one.

With the Brush tool selected, go to the upper-left corner of your workspace and click the Brush Preset Picker. Click the arrow in a circle at the upper-right of the Brush Preset Picker pop-up menu. Doing so opens the Brush Preset menu. Choose Reset Brushes, and a dialog comes up asking if it's OK to replace the current brushes or if you want to Append or Cancel. Click OK to load Photoshop's default brush set. Return to the Brush Preset menu, and make sure Small List is checked to show the name of each brush. Soft Round is the first brush at the top of the scrollable brush menu (Figure 2.16). If you're using an earlier version of Photoshop, select a Soft Round brush from the Brush Preset Picker.

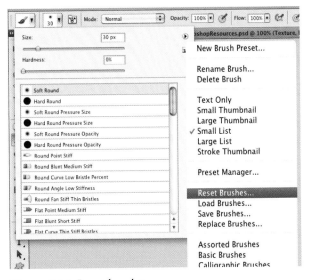

Figure 2.16 *Reset brushes*

To give this default brush more character, you need to open the Brush panel containing the adjustable brush characteristics. Open the Brush panel in your customized workspace. To do so, click the icon in the dock 🖌 or select the icon in the upper-left corner of the workspace 🖌, alongside the Brush Preset Picker.

Brush Tip Shape

With the Brush panel open, notice that none of the controls are checked. If any of the boxes are checked, or if you're using an earlier version of Photoshop, manually deselect all the checked boxes in the Brush panel.

Click Brush Tip Shape, enlarge your brush to 78 pixels, and make sure Hardness is set to zero. Paint a squiggly line to view the brush. It will produce a soft, airbrushy mark without much character (Figure 2.17). Let's click the various brush controls and turn your brush into a more interactive tool.

Each of the brush parameters opens a different interface when clicked. Let's start with Shape Dynamics.

Figure 2.17 Soft Round brush with no brush settings selected

Shape Dynamics

Click Shape Dynamics to turn it on. The name turns blue to show that you've selected it, and a check appears next to it. Select Control in the Size Jitter parameter, and then choose Pen Pressure from the drop-down menu. If you try to select Pen Pressure using a mouse, a triangle containing an exclamation mark appears next to Control ⚠ Control: [Pen Pressure ⇕] . This warning indicates that Pen Pressure doesn't work with a mouse. Many of these parameters only work with a pressure-sensitive digitizing tablet. Thus if you have no tablet, you can't do custom brushes in this manner.

Shape Dynamics maps the thickness of the line to the pressure of the digitizing pen. When you press down lightly with the pen, you get a thin line. Press down harder, and you get a thicker line. The thickest the line can be is the maximum diameter of the brush set in Brush Tip Shape. You get a preview of what the brush now looks like at the bottom of the Brush panel, which updates as you change the parameters. For instance, with these settings, the preview shows the line thin at the beginning, fat in the middle, and thin at the end (Figure 2.18).

Figure 2.18 Size Jitter in Shape Dynamics set to Pen Pressure

Transfer

Next, select Transfer in the Brush panel. Under Opacity Jitter, select Pen Pressure from the Control drop-down menu. Doing so maps Pen Pressure to the opacity of the brush. This controls how much paint is applied when you press down with your pen. Press down lightly, and you get a faint mark; press down harder, and you get a more opaque mark. With this variation, you have both size and opacity mapped to the pen pressure (Figure 2.19).

Figure 2.19 Opacity Jitter turned on

Return to the Brush Tip Shape parameters, and experiment with the Spacing parameter. Reduce Size to 25, and increase Spacing to 80%. This produces an intermittent brush stroke that's no longer a continuous flow of paint, but rather identical dots at regular intervals (Figure 2.20).

Figure 2.20 Spacing set to 80% to create an intermittent line

Scattering

Now, select Scattering. Select the Both Axes check box, and set Scatter to 200%. Reduce Spacing in Brush Tip Shape to 25%. This gives you a much more randomized stroke, like a flow of individual particles (Figure 2.21).

Figure 2.21 Scatter set to 200% on both axes

Color Dynamics

Next, click the Color Dynamics parameter. Set Hue Jitter, Saturation Jitter, and Brightness Jitter each to 60. Color Dynamics adds random variation to the color of the stroke. This example dramatically shows the feature with extreme changes in color within a brush stroke. More practically, adding a small number (from three to five) produces slight variations in color to achieve more photographic realism per brush stroke (Figure 2.22).

If you zoom in close on any photo, you'll notice there are no flat colors. All color is a broken, mottled tone, with subtle variations throughout the picture (Figure 2.23). Adding Color Dynamics makes your brush mimic this natural color variation.

Figure 2.22 Color Dynamics turned on

Image Credit: Corel Stock Photo Library

Figure 2.23 *Natural color variation in photos*

Dual Brush

Turn off Scattering and Color Dynamics, and increase the brush size to 70. Now, click Dual Brush. This parameter combines two tips to create a textured brush mark. With Dual Brush selected, pick a second brush from the menu of brushes on screen. The second brush's texture is applied within the brush stroke of your primary brush; only the areas where the brushstrokes intersect are painted. If you have a smooth brush to start with and run it through a heavily textured brush, you get a much rougher stroke combining elements of both brushes (Figure 2.24).

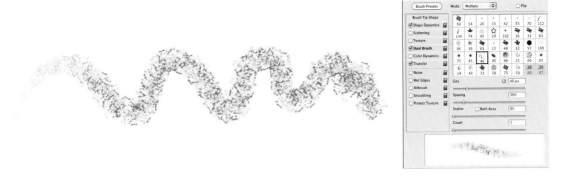

Figure 2.24 *Dual Brush setting to produce a textured stroke*

Working with Image-Based Brushes

You can create more interesting and variable brushes by exploring the singular and combined properties of the brush parameters. At this juncture, you'll learn to use one of the most powerful aspects of Photoshop custom brushes: the ability to use images as the basis of your brush.

Creating a Cloud Brush

To demonstrate this versatile tool, let's create a production-ready brush for painting clouds. Although you can use a photographic reference of a cloud as the basis of your cloud brush, it's easy to create the brush from scratch. Go to the Brush Preset Picker, select the Soft Round brush in the default brush set, and customize it by mapping Opacity Jitter, in Transfer, to Pen Pressure. You can follow along with these steps in Figure 2.25:

1. Create a new document sized at 800 pixels wide × 500 pixels high. With the Soft Round brush, paint a puffy cloud top.
2. Paint some more of the cloud, making it softer at the bottom than at the top.
3. Soften the cloud using the Blur tool.
4. Try some of the other tools in the toolbar as you go along. Select the Smudge tool and, in the Brush Preset Picker, set it to the Chalk 36 Pixels brush, included in the Photoshop default brush set. Use this to roughen up the edges of the cloud.
5. Paint in more detail at the bottom of the cloud. When it's looking good, you can define it for use as a brush.

   Draw a box around the cloud using the Rectangular Marquee tool. You'll create a large image brush, around 500 pixels square; doing so gives you a very high-resolution image brush that can be scaled down for detailed work. Choose Edit → Define Brush Preset, and name the brush **New Cloud**.

   You may want to save the file in which you've painted this cloud for later use. Make a new file, sized at 1,600 × 1,200 pixels, and save it. You'll use it to experiment with the brush dynamics and to draw a cloudscape.

6. The brush you created is too large for this project, so scale it down by reducing Size to 300. Draw a stroke with the brush. The stroke resembles a dark cloud. In the next section, you'll add more dynamics to the brush to randomize the strokes and vary the tonality.

When you define an image brush, Photoshop records the brush in black and white. If you use color when creating custom image brushes, only the tonal information is saved. You assign color using the Color Picker.

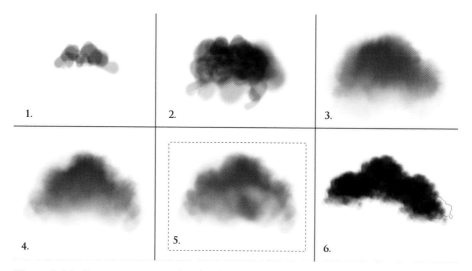

Figure 2.25 Creating an image for the cloud brush

Painting a Cloudscape

In your new file, you'll paint a fast cloudscape to get this brush set up properly. With the Gradient tool selected, choose dark blue for the foreground color and white for the background color. Drag the Gradient tool from the top of the screen downward, and it will create a dark blue-to-white gradient for the basis of your sky (Figure 2.26).

With a gradient added as a background, create a new layer for painting the clouds. Now, you'll add dynamics to the image-based cloud brush. Make sure your cloud brush is still selected and sized to 300. Select Shape Dynamics in the Brush panel, and change Angle Jitter to 2 and Roundness Jitter to 20, both with Control set to Off. Angle Jitter makes each cloud stroke at a different angle, and Roundness Jitter makers each stroke somewhat more squashed or stretched than the one before. By setting Control to Off, Pen Pressure doesn't control these two parameters, which randomizes their use.

In the Minimum Roundness section, check Flip X Jitter. This makes the stroke flip horizontally so there will be additional variation from left to right in each cloud stroke. Next, click Transfer, and set Opacity Jitter to Pen Pressure.

Using the Eyedropper tool, select a medium sky tone from your gradient sky. Open the Color Picker by clicking the Set Foreground Color box, and make the color you selected with the eyedropper darker and less saturated. Dab in a few strokes to see how the cloud looks. Let's start by adding the dark clouds.

In order to get the sky looking naturally random, you must vary your brush size constantly. In Photoshop CS5, you don't have to go to the brush menu to change the brush size. Instead, you can Control+Option+drag left or right/Alt+right-click+drag left or right to resize the brush interactively. Setting Spacing to a high number, such as 200, will add more randomness and distance between dabs of cloud paint. Don't be afraid to set your brush size as high as 700 while painting broad areas of your cloudscape. You won't get only huge clouds, because Size Jitter is set to Pen Pressure. Therefore, when you press hard, you get a big cloud stroke; when you press softly, you get a small cloud stroke. The hardest thing to do is to paint something truly random, so allow Photoshop to add unpredictable natural variation (Figure 2.27).

Figure 2.26 Add a gradient sky.

Figure 2.27 Paint the dark side of the clouds.

When you have a picturesque dark-cloud pattern, select white in the Color Picker to add lighter clouds on top. Keep your hand on the undo keys (Command+Z/Ctrl+Z) so you can try and reject different attempts until you get something that works. Because you're depending on Photoshop to add randomness to the clouds, it may take you many tries to get a result you like. Press Command+Option+Z/Ctrl+Alt+Z several times to undo multiple levels without having to go to the History panel.

As you work, you must keep in mind the direction of the light. In this example, light is coming from the left. If you don't pay attention to the light source, your clouds will never look well formed (Figure 2.28).

You can again use the Smudge tool set to Chalk 36 pixels to roughen the edges of the clouds and harden some of the soft areas. The default Soft Round Brush, with Opacity Jitter set to Pen Pressure, lets you lightly paint over and unify the cloud masses. With experimentation, you can create a realistic cloudscape (Figure 2.29).

You can see my Photoshop file of the cloudscape, `CustomBrushCloudPainting.psd`, and watch a time-lapse version of the painting in progress, `Chapter_2_CustomBrushCloudscape.mov`, in the DVD's Chapter 2 materials.

One final piece of advice concerning custom brushes using images: simpler is better. When I do this cloud demo in the classroom, many students initially paint an entire cloudbank rather than a single cloud, thinking a more complex image will paint even more dramatic clouds. In fact, a less elaborate image—one that can be randomized, squashed, and stretched to create naturally irregular clouds—is significantly more useable and versatile.

Figure 2.28 Paint in the light side of the clouds.

Figure 2.29 Add the finishing touches with the Smudge tool and a Soft Round brush.

Save Your Brushes

Now that you've created a custom brush that is ideal for a specific task, it's important to save it for future use. Remember: the brush you saved as New Cloud has none of the dynamics you've added. Save the new souped-up version as **New Cloud Dynamic**. It will be invaluable to your work to build a library of custom brushes. I've fallen victim to neglecting to save many times. For instance, if you select another brush before saving your new brush, you'll lose all your work and have to re-create it to use it again. Assign descriptive names so that you'll know at a glance what a custom brush does.

Experiment with custom brushes, and you'll find them to be powerful tools for painting natural objects like clouds, trees, and rocks, as well as for manmade objects like windows in office buildings. In the Chapter 2 section of the DVD, you'll find a set of custom brushes that I've collected over the years, called `Custom Brush Examples.abr`. I built some of the brushes from scratch, and others were created by fellow artists. I want to mention a great brush set called Blur's Good Brush, created by Yang Xueguo. That brush set is available for free through the CG Society at `http://features.cgsociety.org/story_custom.php?story_id=5152&page=2`.

Keep your eyes out for brushes that artists offer to share on their websites. This is a ready source of inspiration for enlarging your brush library.

Now that we've thoroughly explored the panels and tools essential to creating a matte painting and looked at how to use and create custom brushes, you're ready to put this knowledge into practice.

three

CHAPTER

Composition and Concept

With the basics of Photoshop *under your*

belt, it's time to begin your first matte painting project. You don't want to launch into a 2,000-pixel-wide matte shot without first experimenting with different solutions, so you must produce some concept sketches. These quick, roughed-in idea sketches can be the most challenging and exciting phase of any project. Here you work out the main compositional issues: the atmospheric mood, the overall color, and where elements are placed. To aid you in this process, you will learn the basic rules of composition. In addition, this chapter will help you to set up your workspace to optimize your creative time. After a brief discussion of the special color space you will work in as a matte artist, it's time to challenge yourself to see how many different ideas you can come up for a castle on a bluff.

Creating a Castle on a Hill

For your first matte painting, you'll paint over a photo I took of a hill in Scotland. Because it's the photographic source for your matte painting, it's referred to as a *plate*. You can consider this matte painting your training-wheels project, because you don't need to create the background. This image will be used as the basis for learning about perspective, delineating light and dark sides, and applying textures to achieve a photorealistic effect. Concentrate on coming up with a visually compelling concept that you'll use to complete the next several chapters.

Let's first take a closer look at the plate you'll be painting over (see Figure 3.1). This scene is relatively neutral, so you'll be able to set different moods through the application of color overlays or color corrections.

Understanding 16-bit Color

There is something special about this plate. Open `CastlePlate16Bit.psd` (included in the Chapter 3 materials on the DVD) in Photoshop, and take a moment to examine it before you proceed.

Most photos taken with an inexpensive camera, or those pulled off the Internet, are in 8-bit color. An 8-bit image is 2 to the eighth power, or 256 levels of information for each channel. An 8-bit RGB (red, green, and blue) image in Photoshop uses numbers from 0 to 255 to represent each constituent color, or *channel*, in the image. Thus 0 is the absence of a color, and 255 is the maximum amount possible of that color. (Photoshop shows the top level as 255 because it begins counting with 0 instead of 1.)

Digital pictures are made up of combinations of red, green, and blue pixels, so in an 8-bit RGB image, the maximum possible red is listed as (255, 0, 0), whereas the maximum possible green is listed as (0, 255, 0). An 8-bit plate has 16.8 million (256 × 256 × 256) possible colors.

That may sound like a lot; but for feature film work, everything is done with 16-bit color, which has vastly more color information. A16-bit image is 2 to the sixteenth power, or 65,536 levels of information for each channel. Multiplying the three channels (65,536 × 65,536 × 65,536) gives you an astounding 281 trillion possible colors with which to work. Because of the additional precision it offers, most of what you do as a matte artist will be in 16-bit color.

You can find out the bit depth of an image by going to Photoshop's top menu and choosing Image → Mode → 8, 16, or 32 Bits/Channel. A checkmark appears next to the bit depth of the current image (see Figure 3.2).

You need to know the bit depth in this case because many of the filters are turned off in Photoshop when you work in 16-bit color. Return to the top menu and choose Filter (see Figure 3.3).

Notice how many of the filters are grayed out and unavailable for use, such as Distort, Pixelate, and Sketch. With each new release of Photoshop, Adobe rewrites more of the filters to work in 16-bit. The filters available in version CS5 are the most useful ones, like Blur, Noise, and Sharpen.

Figure 3.1 *Plate*

You need to keep in mind two things about 16-bit plates:

- A 16-bit plate is twice as large as an 8-bit plate. Therefore, if your 8-bit plate is 9 MB, and you change it to 16-bit, the document size will be 18 MB. The current document size is listed after Doc in the lower-left corner of your document window (see Figure 3.4).

- When you change a 16-bit plate to an 8-bit plate and save it, you permanently lose half of the plate's information. This can come as a nasty surprise if you planned to use all the data in the 16-bit plate. There are, however, practical reasons for switching between the depths. During the concept phase, when you want to capture your ideas quickly, you'll find that your brushwork is faster in 8-bit. When you switch back to 16-bit, I recommend you cut the painted elements in the 8-bit plate and paste them into the original 16-bit plate. This trick allows you to make the transfer from one bit depth to another without a loss of data. For this reason, when you get a 16-bit plate from a client, make sure you save a copy!

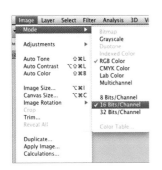

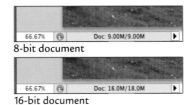

Figure 3.2 Finding the bit depth of your document

Figure 3.3 Filters turned off in 16-bit color

Figure 3.4 8-bit vs. 16-bit document size

Rules of Composition

As you begin work on your concept sketch, you need to follow some basic rules of composition. Here are five compositional rules that I use in my work: four are common-sense rules any artist should know, and one is an advanced compositional ratio used by artists for hundreds of years:

- Avoid symmetry.
- Don't paint objects flat-on to the viewer.
- Follow the principle of balance.
- Obey the rule of thirds.
- Understand the golden mean.

Avoid Symmetry

When composing your matte shot, you should generally avoid setting up a symmetrical composition. *Symmetry* means the right and left sides of your shot are roughly the same. Why avoid symmetry? To put it bluntly, symmetrical compositions are boring.

This side equals → | ← This side

Figure 3.5 Symmetrical composition

In the hands of a master, symmetrical shots can be powerful. Film director Stanley Kubrick used symmetrical shots at the climax of his films because of their iconic power. Symmetry can be used to excellent advantage in certain situations: to achieve a sense of dominance, majesty, or conformity. However, when a beginner uses symmetry, it's a sign they lack knowledge of composition. For this castle painting, don't set up your shot symmetrically (see Figure 3.5).

Don't Paint Objects Flat-on to the Viewer

As a matte painter, you should avoid painting objects, especially buildings, flat-on to the camera. The flat view of a building tends to be the most uninteresting. Setting it at an angle gives you a better silhouette and view of the subject (see Figure 3.6).

Figure 3.6 Object at an angle

The Principle of Balance

This principle, also known as *the fulcrum-lever rule*, is a quick and easy way to balance multiple objects in your composition. Think of your composition as a heavy-set man on a teeter-totter with a baby. If the heavy man is too far out on the teeter-totter, the baby can't balance him (see Figure 3.7).

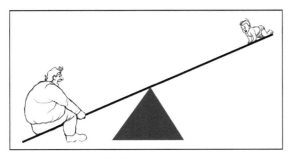

Figure 3.7 Out of balance

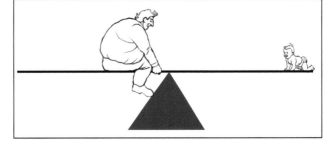

Figure 3.8 In balance

In order to correct the imbalance, the man needs to move nearer to the middle—the fulcrum—of the teeter-totter. This same principle works with objects in a composition. A larger object situated near the center of the composition can be balanced by a smaller object on the outside edge. Returning to the teeter-totter scene, if the heavy-set man moves toward the fulcrum, he can balance the baby (see Figure 3.8).

The Rule of Thirds

The rule of thirds states that, whenever possible, you should place the focus of your picture one-third of the way from the edge of your frame. This discourages you from placing your subject smack in the middle of the picture or from having your horizon divide your picture in half (see Figure 3.09).

For vertical elements in your composition, you can use the division lines making up the rule of thirds as alignment guides. Note how the doorway to the castle has been placed in the lower-left focus point (see Figure 3.10).

The Golden Mean

The golden mean, also known as the *golden measure* and the *divine proportion*, is a uniquely pleasing spatial division that has been used by artists as far back as the Renaissance. It involves a mathematical relationship between the long and short sides of a rectangle, where the length of the long side equals 1.61803… times the length of the short side. Like pi, the number is irrational and never resolves itself, though mathematicians have factored it out to a million places. Don't be afraid if, like me, math isn't your forté. I'm about to show you how easy it is to set up a rectangle with the golden mean without any math.

The Rule of Thirds

Equal	Equal	Equal
Equal		
Equal	Place your focus at these points.	
Equal		

Figure 3.9 The rule of thirds

Figure 3.10 Using the division lines as guides

Here are the steps to draw the golden mean:

1. Start a new file in Photoshop measuring 1,500 pixels wide by 1,000 pixels high. On the left side of the picture, draw a square with all 4 sides of equal length, as shown in red in Figure 3.11. You can constrain the Rectangular Marquee tool to a square by holding down the Shift key.

2. Draw an X from corner to corner, as shown in the figure in light blue. If you're using the custom brush set included in Chapter 2, the Hard Round Solid 5 brush works great for drawing straight lines if you click, hold down the Shift key, and click again.

3. Draw a vertical line through the center of the X to find the middle of the bottom side, as shown in dark blue.

4. Draw a line from the center of the bottom of the square to the top-right corner, as shown by the purple line with the arrowhead.

5. Using the base of the pointed purple line as the center point, draw an arc, as shown by the dashed green line.

6. Draw a line extending from the bottom-right corner of the original red square, as indicated by the black line. Where it meets the arc is the far edge of the golden rectangle.

7. Draw a line up from where the arc meets the extended bottom line and from the top-right corner of the original red square to close the rectangle shown in dark red.

You can now construct another golden rectangle inside of the part of the rectangle you just created. If you continue to do this for several iterations, you get a series of nested golden mean shapes. Using these shapes as guides, you can draw a spiral as shown in gold (see Figure 3.11). You now have your own golden mean template in a file, so you can easily cut it out and paste it into a new project to use as reference while composing.

Amazingly enough, this complex mathematical ratio describes a phenomenon in the natural world: the perfect spiral. One of the finest examples is the nautilus shell (see Figure 3.12).

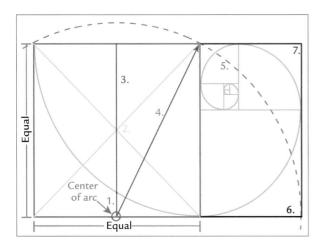

Figure 3.11 Constructing the golden mean

Figure 3.12 Nautilus shell showing the golden mean

Image Credit: Wikipedia

When you become familiar with the golden mean, you'll recognize its use in countless works of art. Artists as diverse as Leonardo Da Vinci, Maxfield Parrish, Piet Mondrian, and Georges Seurat have used the golden mean as the basis of their artwork. One of my favorites is Jacques Louis David's *The Death of Socrates*, which is displayed in the Metropolitan Museum of Art. With apologies to David for defacing his masterpiece, I have overlaid the golden mean on his painting to demonstrate how closely he adhered to it (see Figure 3.13).

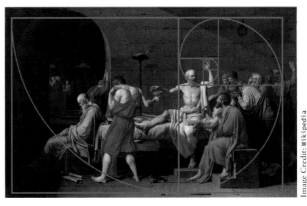

Image Credit: Wikipedia

Figure 3.13 Jacques Louis David's The Death of Socrates

Creating a Concept Sketch

It's time to start your first matte painting. Your project will be to create a castle on top of the Scottish bluff overlooking the sea. As you sit down at your computer with a plate on your screen, the question invariably arises, "What am I going to paint?" If you were working on a movie, you would be given direction as to the look and feel of the piece. You have the hardest and most creative task of all—you can do whatever you want. I encourage you to do several concepts with distinctly different moods, and then pick the best of the group to work on in subsequent chapters. As you continue, let me share some ideas on how to unleash your imagination.

Coming Up with Ideas

My students often try to short-change the concept phase in order to start on the "real painting." They're only cheating themselves. This is the most creative part of the project. If, after reading this chapter, you shut the book and spend the next 10 hours creating castles of all descriptions and types, your final project will be better for the time you spent doing so. The temptation is to go with your first idea, but I find that, if you discipline yourself to do several concepts, you'll discover new approaches and broaden your artistic vision. Remember that a bad idea, no matter how meticulously rendered, is still a bad idea.

In coming up with concepts, avoid the temptation to jump into research on the Internet. If you immediately go to Google and download a bunch of castles for inspiration, you'll short-circuit your own creative process. Give yourself an hour or more with no reference, and see what you can come up with, no matter how rough. Otherwise, you're bound to be influenced by existing imagery that will block any original ideas you might have.

Getting In the Zone

Artists talk about the *zone*: a unique mental state where time stands still and nothing exists but your artwork. While working on a project, you slip into the zone, and awareness of the outside world recedes. This is the most productive part of the workday, because your concentration is given undividedly to the work at hand. Unfortunately, the contemporary world offers increasingly more distractions that make it harder to get into that mental space.

Here are some tried-and-true suggestions on how to prepare your workspace and tune out the noise:

1. Turn off email on your computer. I think email is the single greatest distraction to concentrated work known to humankind. I used to keep the email icon at the bottom of my computer screen. Every time an email alert appeared, I had to check it. You'll never get into the zone if you're interrupted every 15 minutes by an incoming email. Take the program out of your computer dock, and force yourself to open it manually.

2. The same goes for cell phones and texting. Turn off your cell phone, and forbid yourself to send or receive texts, tweets, or any other distraction while you're concentrating.

3. Clear your computer workspace of outside distractions. Perhaps it's generational, but I'm puzzled by students who work at their computer while simultaneously watching an onscreen episode of their favorite TV show. The chances of getting into the zone under these circumstances are next to zero. Make sure the only thing you can see while working on your project is your project.

4. Darken your room. My studio has blackout curtains and is illuminated with just a little ambient light so the monitor doesn't burn into my eyes. This also lets me focus entirely on my project.

5. Set aside a block of time where you won't be interrupted. I know this is easier said than done. Everyone deals with competing demands on their time. Yet, as an artist, you must carve out a discrete block of time to think and come up with ideas. The time of day will vary for each individual. Early risers have the house to themselves in the morning, when others are still sleeping. Night owls wait to put the kids to bed and say goodnight to their significant other before getting down to work. Whatever your lifestyle and circadian rhythms, find a time to claim as your own.

6. Set up mood playlists on iTunes. My students laugh when I assign this musical exercise, but many have become believers. I have found that music is a direct pathway to the emotional centers of your mind. Music can put you in a place instantly to produce artwork with a specific emotional quality. When I feel I'm in a rut or at an impasse, I turn to set musical selections for inspiration. For this current project, I suggest setting up playlists to evoke different feelings: upbeat music to inspire a sunlit fairytale castle, or somber dirges for a medieval castle on a gloomy day. For this demonstration, I listened to Bach's *Toccata & Fugue in D minor*, the second movement from Beethoven's *Symphony No. 7*, and Albinoni's *Adagio in G Minor*. Now you have a soundtrack as I lead you through the steps I took for this 30-minute concept sketch.

30-Minute Concept Sketch, Step By Step

While doing your concept sketch, refrain from directly using any photography. Force yourself to paint the concept. You'll use photography later to add photographic textural detail to the castle. However, at this point in the process, it's painting only!

In doing the exercise, advanced users of Photoshop should read through the chapter, then do the Assignment section at the end. If you are a less experienced Photoshop user, I recommend that you use the CastlePlate16Bit.psd file to follow along. Learn the material by doing the steps as they are shown. . Having done the project once along with the demonstration, you should be able to put the principles into action and create concept sketches of your own at the end of the chapter.

Figure 3.14 shows the raw plate on top of which you'll be painting. During the course of this lesson, you'll use several basic Photoshop tools, including the Brush, Eyedropper, Gradient, Eraser, and Lasso.

Figure 3.14 *The raw 16-bit plate*

Extracting an Element Using Channels

The first step is to extract the hill from the sky so they're separated. With matte paintings, it's a good idea to break out the major elements onto different layers. That way, you can preserve the sky while developing the foreground.

I'm going to show you how to extract an element in your plate onto a separate layer using the color channels. This is a task you'll find yourself doing over and over as a matte artist. You can always use the Lasso tool to make a manual marquee around an item, and you'll sometimes have to do that. But before you do any manual work, it makes sense to look through your color channels to see if you can manipulate them to give you a clean selection. As a plus, a selection you get from a modified color channel is generally more accurate than one you do manually.

Here are the steps:

1. In the right panel, choose the Channels tab and look through the color channels to find one you can use to extract the hill cleanly.

   Take a moment to examine the three channels in Figure 3.15. You can view them individually by clicking Red, Green, or Blue in the Channels panel. To view the full-color RGB image again, click RGB in the panel. Which one of the panels—Red, Green, or Blue—do you think offers the most contrast between the foreground and background hills? The Blue channel has the most contrast, with the hill mostly black and the sky mostly white.

2. Having made your choice, duplicate the Blue channel. Select the Blue channel, and drag it

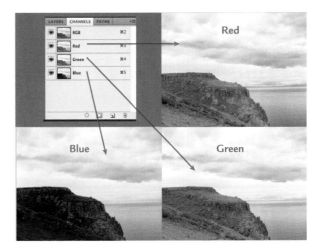

Figure 3.15 *Examine the Red, Green, and Blue channels.*

to the third icon on the bottom of the Channels palette that looks like a square with the lower-left corner turned up ⬑. This is the Create New Layer icon, but if you drag an existing channel to it, that channel is duplicated. You don't want to work over the original Blue channel, because doing so would affect the color of the entire composition (see Figure 3.16).

3. Select the duplicated Blue channel, and choose Image → Adjustments → Curves (keyboard shortcut: Command+M on the Mac, Ctrl+M on the PC). This opens the Curves palette (see Figure 3.17).

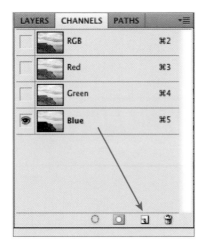

Figure 3.16 *Duplicate the Blue channel.*

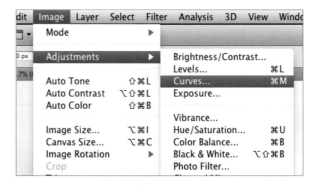

Figure 3.17 *Open the Curves palette.*

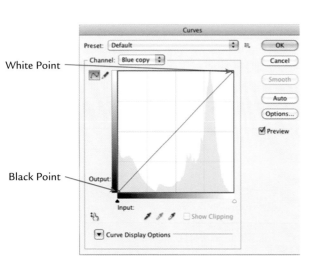

Figure 3.18 *The white and black points in the Curves palette*

You need to wipe out any grays in the hill to turn it solid black. You also need to wipe out any grays in the sky to turn it all white. For this task, use the Eyedropper tool 🖋.

Notice that the Curves palette is open and will work along with the Eyedropper tool. You need to understand the location of *black point* and *white point* on the Curves palette graph. The Curves palette maps all the tones—from solid black on the left to solid white on the right—and all the grays in between. The black point at bottom left represents the darkest possible black, and the white point at upper right represents the brightest white possible (see Figure 3.18).

Place the Eyedropper on the lightest gray in the hill. On the Curves palette, a round indicator comes up, showing the location of that gray tone on the curve (see Figure 3.19).

Take note of where that tone is on the curve, and, using your cursor, click and drag the black point horizontally along the bottom of the graph to a position directly below the light point you picked with the eyedropper. By doing so, you'll black out the entire hill shape (see Figure 3.20). Don't worry if there are a few white dots, as long as most of the hill is black. You'll manually clean up those remaining white bits.

Now you need to use the same process to white out the sky. In this instance, place the eyedropper on the darkest point that you find in either the sky or water. That dark gray tone appears as a circle on the Curves palette (see Figure 3.21).

Using your cursor, click the white point, and drag it horizontally to the left across the top of the palette to a position directly above the gray point. The sky goes white, and the water nearly so except for some tones in the right corner (see Figure 3.22). Accept the changes you made in the Curves panel by clicking OK.

Black point   Position of the light part of the hill on the curve

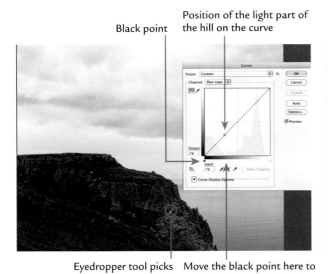

Eyedropper tool picks   Move the black point here to
a light tone on the hill   make the hill entirely black

Figure 3.19 *Find the black point.*

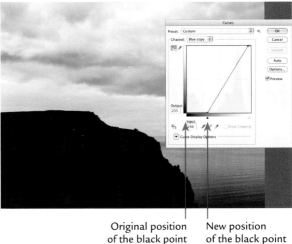

Original position   New position
of the black point   of the black point

Figure 3.20 *Move the black point directly below the lightest point on the hill, and the hill will turn completely black.*

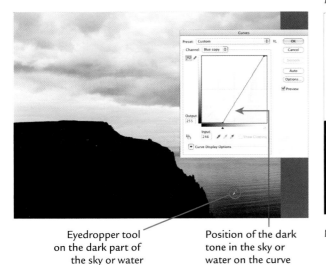

Eyedropper tool   Position of the dark
on the dark part of   tone in the sky or
the sky or water   water on the curve

Figure 3.21 *Find the white point.*

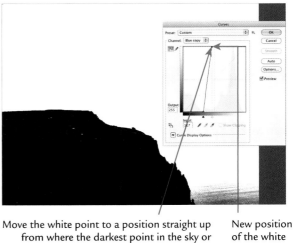

Move the white point to a position straight up   New position
from where the darkest point in the sky or   of the white
water was indicated   point

Figure 3.22 *Move the white point.*

There are still some dark tones in the lower-right corner and some white specks in the hill that you need to clean up with the Lasso and Paint tools. Make the area of the hill pure black and the sky and water pure white. With a modest amount of work, you'll have a clean channel to extract the hill from the plate (see Figure 3.23). Because this isn't a color channel used to create your RGB image, it's an alpha channel. You can have as many alpha channels as you want, stored in the Channels panel. They're used for masking and for saving selections you may want to use again in your project.

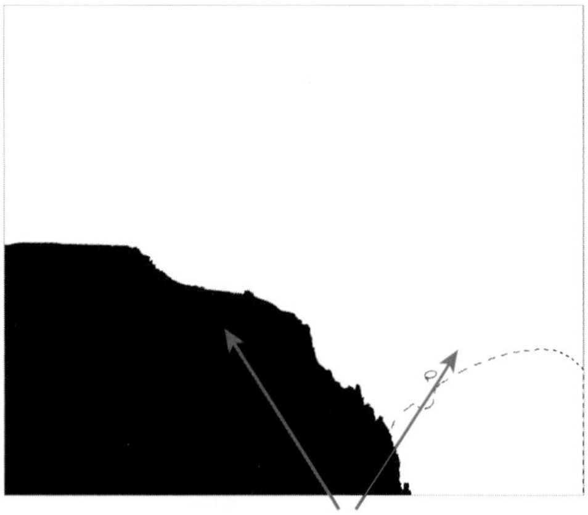

Next, you need to extract the hill using this alpha channel. There is a problem, however. In Photoshop, when you select an area, that is the only area you can work on. With the current alpha channel, the white sky and water are the only areas selected. If you load the selection by Command+clicking/Ctrl+clicking the duplicated Blue channel in the Channels palette, the sky and water are selected instead of the hill. Because you need to extract the hill, this is the reverse of what you need. The problem is easily corrected by taking one more step.

Use the Lasso and Paint tools to clean up problem areas in the water and the hill

Figure 3.23 Cleaned-up extraction channel

You need to invert the alpha channel. Start by selecting the entire channel (Command+A/Ctrl+A), and then choose Image → Adjustments → Invert (Command+I/Ctrl+I) so the hill is completely white and the sky is completely black. In this case, you've inverted the pixels rather than the selection (see Figure 3.24).

Now you can Command+click/Ctrl+click the modified, duplicated Blue channel to get a selection for the hill. With the selection loaded, your work area will be defined by a rapidly moving dashed line, or *marching ants*, that surrounds the selection. That is the area of action in Photoshop that you'll work on (see Figure 3.25).

In the Channels panel, click RGB to return to your full-color plate. In the same tabbed group as the Channels panel, select the Layers panel to open it. Select the layer with the original plate, and press Command+J/Ctrl+J to create a new layer with only the hill on it. Rename this new layer Hill by double-clicking the layer name and typing in the new name.

Figure 3.24 Inverted alpha channel

In the Layers panel, click the eyeball next to the original plate labeled Background . The eyeball will disappear, indicating that you've turned off visibility on the original plate. The area with a gray and white checkerboard indicates no pixels or transparency (see Figure 3.26).

Marching ants

Figure 3.25 *Selection loaded*

Figure 3.26 *New layer with the separated hill*

Tinting the Sky

It's time to start painting. (Listening to the eerie strains of Bach's *Toccata & Fugue in D minor* I imagine a forbidding castle against an ominous, moonlit sky.)

Obviously, the light clouds won't do, so you must tint the sky darker. Add a new layer by clicking the New Layer icon. Set this layer to Multiply by going to the top of the Layers panel and clicking the drop-down menu set to Normal ⬜ . From the different transfer modes that appear—Normal, Darken, Multiply, Color Burn, Linear Burn, Darker Color, and so on—select Multiply (see Figure 3.27). (Transfer modes will be discussed in depth in Chapter 7, "Texturing and Color Correction.")

What is Multiply? The technical definition is that Multiply uses the color information in each channel to multiply the base color by the blend color. The resulting color is always darker. Multiplying any color with black produces black. Multiplying any color with white leaves the color unchanged. I like to think of Multiply as applying a wash of watercolor paint. It always goes darker, because watercolor is a glaze of color, but it still reveals the detail from the underlying layer. Because this layer set to Multiply is higher up in the Layers panel than Hill or Background, it will affect those two channels below it. (see Figure 3.28)

You'll use the Gradient tool to lay down a dark blue color using a ramp from the foreground color to transparency. Select the Gradient tool (shortcut: G). An icon of gradient color appears at the top-left corner ⬛ . Click this bar of gradient color, and the Gradient Editor appears on the screen. Select the second preset named Foreground to Transparent. I use this particular gradient all the time, because

Figure 3.27 *Layer transfer modes*

Figure 3.28 *Set Layer 2 to Multiply.*

it starts out at 100 percent opacity and then gently blends to 0 percent opacity. It's a great tool for laying down smooth washes of color that fade out (see Figure 3.29). Make sure your foreground color is set to a dark blue. Because this gradient fades to transparency, the background color doesn't matter.

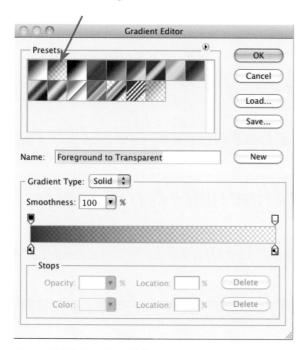

Figure 3.29 *Gradient Editor*

In the layer set to Multiply, use the Gradient tool twice: once from the top down to darken the top of the sky, and a second time from the bottom up to darken the water and hill. If it comes in too dark, you can lighten the gradient by lowering the percentage of the opacity (currently at 100 percent) by using the opacity slider in the Gradient tool's control panel.

This process tints your sky and hill darker and bluer but doesn't wipe out the detail in the plate (see Figure 3.30). Change the name of the Multiply layer you just worked on to **Sky**.

Before you finish tinting the sky using transfer modes, let me show you the difference between the sky set to Normal and to Multiply.

On Multiply, the detail from the clouds shows through, and the color is overall darker, like a glaze. Note that the opacity is set to 100 percent in both examples (see Figure 3.31).

Drag the Gradient tool down from the top to darken the clouds

Drag the Gradient tool up from the bottom to darken the water.

Figure 3.30 *Using the Gradient tool to darken the sky and water*

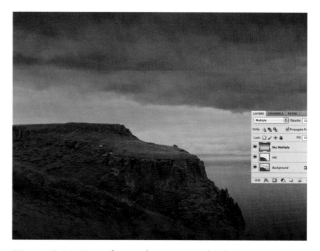

Figure 3.31 *Transfer mode set to Multiply*

If you set the same layer to Normal, the layer now behaves like opaque paint and blocks out the original cloud detail on the layer. It also obscures much of the detail on the hill (see Figure 3.32).

You can see that using the Multiply mode on this project gives you much better results.

To paint additional low-hanging clouds, add a new layer on top of the Multiply layer and rename it **Clouds**. Any new layer is in the default Normal transfer mode, which is fine for painting. This is a perfect time to use the New Cloud Dynamic custom brush you created in the previous chapter. Load in a color darker than your sky to paint in a couple of new, low cloud banks. The scene looks more somber with the dark sky and thickening clouds (see Figure 3.33).

Figure 3.32 Transfer mode set to Normal

Figure 3.33 Paint clouds on the new Normal layer.

Now you need to add some background mountains. Switch to ChalkVarOpacity, a block-in brush included in `Custom Brush Examples.abr`, the brush presets from the previous chapter. It has an irregular shape, like a piece of chalk, and the opacity is variable: the harder you press, the darker the mark. That way, you can get a variety of tones from the brush, from very dark to very light, using your digitizing tablet (see Figure 3.34).

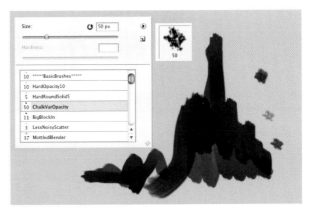

Figure 3.34 Block-in brush with variable opacity

Add yet another layer on top to paint in some background mountains on the right, and rename it **Mountains**. Doing so makes the distant coastline more interesting (see Figure 3.35). Before this concept is through, you'll have worked on six different layers. By creating a new layer for each new element, you protect the work you've already done. If you make a mistake, you can always delete the layer and start over.

Painting the Castle

Create one more layer, and rename it **Castle**. This is the last new layer you'll create, because you don't want to have too many layers in a quick-concept sketch.

Begin painting just the silhouette of the castle. If you have a strong silhouette, you're halfway to having an interesting castle. For this scary castle, you want the shape to be dark and foreboding, with lots of spiky towers (see Figure 3.36).

Figure 3.35 Add background mountains.

Figure 3.36 Castle silhouette

There should be a road down from the castle to the base of the hill and some rocks leading to the shore across the bay (see Figure 3.37).

Look at the rocks in the water. Maybe it would be interesting to experiment with a long bridge to the other shore. After you draw that in, it seems logical that the bridge should lead to another castle on the far shore (see Figure 3.38).

When you're satisfied with the basic silhouette of the castle, you're ready to start painting details. Select the areas into which you've painted—the castle, the bridge, and the path down the bluff—on this single layer. Go to the Layers palette, and click the preview of the layer (Command+click/Ctrl+click); you now have a selection of the castle and the bridge, both delineated by marching ants. Another term for these outlined areas is a *selection mask*. Just as when you extracted the hill using a selection, only the area within the selection will be acted on by Photoshop. In this case, when you paint, only the interior of the selection will accept brush strokes.

Using selection masks is one of the most powerful techniques for painting in Photoshop. Think of a stencil. When you paint over a stencil, only the cut-out areas let the paint through. The same thing happens with selection masks. If you loosely apply color across a larger area, the paint will show up only in the selection mask's interior. In other words, you stay within the lines.

Figure 3.37 Road down from the castle, and rocks in the water

Marching ants can be a distraction, so you may want to hide them when you're working on the selected area (see Figure 3.39). To do so, choose View → Extras (Command+H/Ctrl+H). The ants will disappear. You can get the selection-indication back by pressing the same keyboard combination again.

Figure 3.38 Add a bridge.

Figure 3.39 Marching ants indicate the selection area.

Figure 3.40 Castle dark side

Figure 3.41 Add lights.

Figure 3.42 More lights

Start defining the dark side of the castle, where the entrance is, and adding some detail to the towers. Even at this sketch stage, you'll want to keep the light and dark sides distinct to give your castle form (see Figure 3.40).

Now that you have the castle basically formed, add some warm lights to show that it's inhabited, and paint some light glow climbing up the walls of the castle keep (see Figure 3.41).

Continue to dot in lights in the castle. Torches on the bridge would be a nice touch, so go ahead and add them. Add a large flame and some tiny lights on the distant castle (see Figure 3.42).

Zooming In and Out

All this time, you've stayed zoomed out so you can see all of the painting as you work. You never want to zoom in closer while you're blocking in the composition, because you're creating the overall look of the scene. Getting involved with tiny detail too early isn't economical. Now that everything is blocked in, allow yourself to zoom in on the castle to scribble in some more detail.

Press Z on your keyboard to select the Zoom tool. Then, if you have Photoshop CS4 or 5, press down with the pen or mouse. Drag right and left, and the image will zoom in and out interactively (see Figure 3.43). If you have an older version of Photoshop, the Zoom tool works in set increments. Don't zoom in too close; this first pass at a concept should remain rough. If you add fussy details, you're wasting your time.

Pan down and to the right using the Hand tool. You can either hold down the spacebar to get the Hand tool or press H (for *hand*) on your keyboard. Add more detail showing how the flames cast warm light on the bridge and the rocks that support it (see Figure 3.44).

Next, zoom all the way out to make sure nothing has gotten too busy while you were working close up. With this full view, also touch up and darken some of the details (see Figure 3.45).

Figure 3.43 Zoom in to add detail to the castle.

Figure 3.44 Pan over to add detail to the bridge.

Figure 3.45 Zoom out, and darken the details.

You're finished painting inside the castle, so press Command+D/Ctrl+D to deselect everything. This allows you to paint outside the boundaries of your castle again. Stay on the Castle layer, and add a moon. You could switch to the Cloud layer, but you're going to add a dramatic new effect to the sky. If you worked on the Cloud layer and erased something you didn't like, you'd remove the underlying clouds. By staying on the Castle layer and painting into an area that doesn't have any previous painting on it, you have more flexibility. Any spooky castle requires a full moon, so paint the moon with an atmospheric glow and highlights on the clouds (see Figure 3.46).

This looks like too much moon glow, so remove some of it using the Eraser tool. Because you're painting on the Castle layers, the clouds behind the moon are undisturbed. While you're at it, paint reflections from the moon in the water.

That's it for the 30-minute sketch (see Figure 3.47). It has a distinct mood and gives a sense of castle's architecture. Could you spend more time on it and make it better? Sure, but your time will be better spent by doing another concept sketch, to see if you can come up with something better. Limit yourself to 30 minutes, and stop there.

Figure 3.46 Add a moon and cloud highlights.

Figure 3.47 *Finished 30-minute sketch*

You can look at the finished Photoshop file of this castle concept painting in the Chapter 3 materials on the DVD. It's called `CastleConcept_Horror.psd`.

Figure 3.48, Figure 3.49, and Figure 3.50 are three more sketches, completed in less than 30 minutes, each with a different look. Notice how tinting the background can make a huge difference in the mood of the scene.

Assignment: Create Your Own Castle Concepts

Create your own concept sketches based on the principles you learned in this chapter.

- Turn off your critical brain, and let yourself jump in and have fun, no matter how messy the sketch is. The important thing is to get a mood and feel going.
- Think carefully about the silhouette of your castle. A "happy" castle will have soft, rounded shape, whereas a forbidding castle will have threatening spikes and angular forms.
- You should do at least three different sketches, and save each as a separate file. Feel free to do more if you like.
- When you have done several sketches, review your production and pick your favorite concept. You will use it in Chapter 5: Perspective Drawing.

Figure 3.48 *Oriental castle*

Figure 3.49 *Happy castle*

Figure 3.50 *Classical castle*

four

Perspective Basics

No matter how *carefully rendered, if your painting doesn't follow the rules of perspective, it will never look "right," even if your viewers can't put their finger on what is wrong with it. Now that artists can sandwich photos together to make a painting, perspective problems have gotten even worse. Also, because many art students today work in 3D, they never really learn the rules of linear perspective. Even if you'll be incorporating 3D into your work, knowing the rules of perspective will give you far more control over your picture creation.*

The rules of perspective are an artist's greatest tools for giving a picture depth. Because matte shots tend to be establishing, or beauty shots, you'll want to make your shots as majestic and deep as possible. Even films with fantastic worlds and landscapes, such as the Lord of the Rings *trilogy and* Avatar, *evidence the rules of perspective.*

A Brief History of Linear Perspective

Before the invention of linear perspective, and without a working knowledge of vanishing points or the horizon, artists had a number of ways to create depth in a painting. One early technique was to place objects closer to the viewer lower in the composition, and to place those farther away higher up. Another was to overlap figures, because any figure that cuts off another from view was in front of that figure. Linear perspective didn't formally appear until the early 1400s.

The invention of linear perspective is generally attributed to the architect Filippo Brunelleschi (1377–1446), designer of the dome of the Duomo in Florence. He suggested a system that explained how objects shrink in size according to their position and distance from the eye.

Figure 4.1 Early perspective painting by Pietro Perugino

Image credit www.wikipedia.org

Figure 4.2 Giovanni Battista Piranesi's phantasmagorical perspective masterpiece

The first book about linear perspective—*On Painting*, by Leon Battista Alberti (1404–1472)—appeared in 1435. Alberti's formalized system of measurement in paintings revolutionized how artists composed pictures. Alberti put forward the concept that an artist created a ground or stage for each painting. The artist then drew a receding grid to act as a guide to scale figures and objects in the picture. One superb example is the Pietro Perugino fresco on the side of the Sistine Chapel, titled *Christ Handing the Keys to Saint Peter.* You can clearly see the grid on the piazza, just as Alberti suggested in his book (Figure 4.1).

Knowledge of perspective developed rapidly after that, with artists tackling more and more complex perspective subjects. Perhaps the summit of artistic exploration of perspective was the work of Giovanni Battista Piranesi. His series *The Prisons* (1745) took perspective to surreal heights (Figure 4.2).

The Three Types of Perspective

The three types of perspective—linear, color, and atmospheric—can be used alone or in combination to establish depth in a picture. Linear perspective requires the most study. The other two are easily learned, and can add enormous depth to any picture, so let's start with them.

Atmospheric Perspective

Atmospheric perspective, also known as *value perspective*, is based on the variation of dark and light values from the foreground to the background. The darkest and brightest values are almost always closest to the viewer. As objects move away from you toward the horizon, the difference between dark and light values decreases. Objects farthest away from you have the least detail and are often just silhouettes.

Why does this happen? The farther away you are from an object, the more atmosphere is between you and that object. Air has density, so as the distance grows between you and an object, you see more air and less of the object. Even the sky shows the effect of atmospheric perspective. The sky overhead, where you're looking through less air, is usually a deep blue; the sky at the horizon, where you're looking through hundreds of miles of air, is much paler. If air were completely transparent, when you looked up you would see the black of outer space.

Moist air evidences this atmospheric effect more than dry air. Dry air is more transparent. Think of how far you can see in a desert as opposed to a rain forest. In most situations, the air has some moisture, and you can see atmospheric perspective at work. You'll often exaggerate atmospheric perspective in matte paintings to achieve additional depth.

Try this experiment. In Photoshop, do a sketch of a cityscape to try out the power of atmospheric perspective. Start with a canvas 2,000 by 1,500 pixels. Create a hard-edged brush, 20 pixels square, with opacity and size jitter turned off. Then, follow these steps:

1. Add a gradient sky, medium blue at the top and pale blue at the bottom. Choose a light gray from the Color Picker. On a new layer, paint a line of small buildings all the way across your canvas. Draw a second line of slightly darker buildings immediately in front of the first set (Figure 4.3).

2. Create another new layer, and pick a slightly darker gray color. Increase the size of your brush, so the square shape will paint larger buildings. Paint another line of buildings all the way across the canvas, varying the size of your brush as you work. Fill this layer all the way to the bottom of the canvas with medium gray so no white peeks out between the foreground buildings as you paint them. These layers will be silhouettes, because you'll save the detail for the foreground.

3. Continue to paint lines of buildings on new layers until you have five or six layers, making each layer darker than the one before it. Add some foreground roadways and smaller buildings to give life to your city without tying it up with fine detail.

4. On the final two layers that are closest to you, choose slightly darker and lighter tones to add blocky detail to the buildings, such as structural indications or highlights at the top of buildings. With the cloud brush you created in Chapter 2, "Photoshop Workspace, Tools, and Custom Brushes," add some clouds to the sky and some mist in the foreground to add more depth and separation between the closest buildings. In a few minutes, you've created the impression of a multilayered cityscape, with the distant buildings fading into the sky. This is the power of atmospheric perspective.

Figure 4.3 *Atmospheric perspective exercise*

Figure 4.4 *Color perspective usually works from warm in the foreground to cool in the background.*

Figure 4.5 *Sunsets show reverse color perspective, with the foreground cooler than the background.*

Color Perspective

As objects recede into the background, they pick up more of the sky color. Generally, that color is blue, so in most cases the foreground is warmer than the background (Figure 4.4).

In the case of a sunset, this is reversed. Because the sunset sky is warm, and the light coming from the back is cool, objects in the background are warmer than those in the foreground (Figure 4.5). Color perspective almost always works together with atmospheric perspective.

The Hudson River School

If you want to study good examples of color and atmospheric perspective, you need look no farther than the Hudson River School artists. These mid-19th century artists—most notably Thomas Cole, Albert Bierstadt, Frederick Church, and Thomas Moran—created pictures of awe-inspiring depth and grandeur. Their paintings are quintessential examples of the mastery of atmospheric and color perspective. A fine example is Bierstadt's *The Rocky Mountains* in the Metropolitan Museum of Art (Figure 4.6). Notice how the mountains in the background progressively fade out and take on the sky's blue coloration. Two other notable examples of this school are Bierstadt's *Storm in the Rockies* and Church's *Cotopaxi*.

Linear Perspective

Linear perspective is used for buildings, mechanical objects, and virtually all features of the manmade world. To use linear perspective, you must find the scene's horizon line and then construct a perspective grid as a guide for painting objects.

Perspective Terms

Here is a glossary of terms you'll use while studying perspective.

Icons are used to identify the important perspective elements in the illustrations.

Horizon and Eye Level

The horizon line ⬡ always occurs at your eye level. If you're sunbathing at the seashore and staring out at the water, the horizon line is where the ocean meets the sky and occurs

Figure 4.6 *Color and atmospheric perspective demonstrated in Bierstadt's* The Rocky Mountains

at your eye level. When you glance out of an airplane window at 3,000 feet, the horizon line is where the land meets the sky and occurs at your eye level. The horizon is an invisible plane that cuts through everything. It isn't a fixed line in space; it's always at your eye level. This can be confusing, because the horizon is based on your changing vantage point. If two people are looking at the same scene, but one person is standing at a higher elevation than the other, each will have a different view of where the horizon occurs, because their eye levels are at different heights.

You may be thinking, "What if I'm looking down? Is the horizon now on the floor?" The answer is no. Where you're looking isn't the same as your eye level. You can lower or raise your gaze, but your eye level stays the same. Your eye level is at the height of your eyes, not where you're looking.

The horizon is where the earth meets the sky if there are no obstructions. The horizon often isn't visible, because it's blocked by mountains, buildings, or anything else in the natural world, so you'll often need to draw a *virtual* horizon.

Vanishing Points
A *vanishing point* (VP) ✷ is a spot on the horizon where all lines that are parallel to each other converge. You can have many vanishing points in your picture, because objects that are set at different angles have different vanishing points. Only objects that are parallel to each other vanish to the same points.

Lines of Convergence
Lines of convergence ◬ are lines that converge, or vanish, to the vanishing point. All lines that vanish to the same VP are parallel to each other. You can set up lines of convergence in your painting as an aid to getting objects to line up properly to the VP.

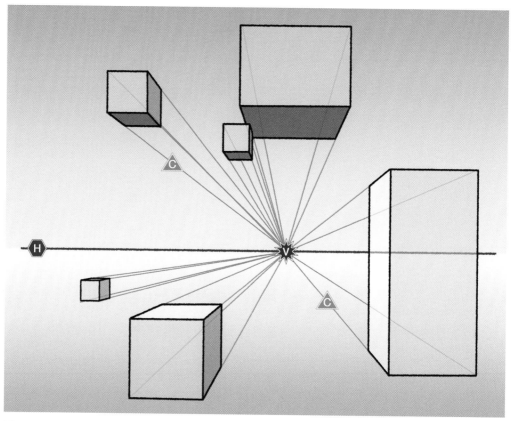

Figure 4.7 *One-point perspective*

Figure 4.8 *Railroad tracks offer a classic example of one set of lines converging to the horizon.*

Photo credit Environmental-Textures.com

Three Types of Linear Perspective

There are three different flavors of linear perspective, each with unique uses and setups. Most of the time, you'll use a variation on two-point perspective, but it's good to know about all three.

One-Point Perspective

One-point perspective is the simplest form of perspective, using a single VP. It's associated with power, solidity, and symmetry. Any time you face the VP of a set of parallel lines, you have one-point perspective (Figure 4.7). In one-point perspective, there is another set of lines of convergence, but all of those lines run parallel to the horizon. That side is flat-on to the viewer. You could almost say that the second VP doesn't vanish, because all the lines for that side are horizontal.

The most obvious example of one-point perspective is looking down railroad tracks (Figure 4.8). If you have a flat enough stretch of track, the rails seem to come to a point on the horizon.

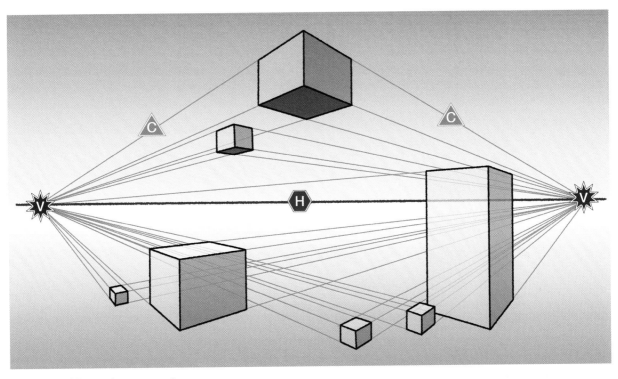

Figure 4.9 Two-point perspective

Two-Point Perspective

Two-point perspective is the most common form of perspective and uses two VPs (Figure 4.9). As a matte artist, this is the perspective you'll use the most.

Examples of two-point perspective are all around you. As you walk down a street looking straight ahead, you have a classic two-point perspective view of houses and shops. The Roman temple in Figure 4.10 has long sides and an open roof that clearly show the two points of convergence.

Figure 4.10 This Roman ruin clearly shows two lines of convergence.

Three-Point Perspective

Any time you walk through a city and look up at tall buildings, you witness dramatic three-point perspective vistas (Figure 4.11). Looking up or down on an extreme angle, involves three VPs (Figure 4.12). Notice the crop box: you normally don't see the horizon line in a picture with three-point perspective. Only one of the three VPs for this example is visible. As a general rule, you won't have more than one VP for an object inside your picture area, and often you won't have any.

Figure 4.11 Times Square in New York City shows three-point perspective.

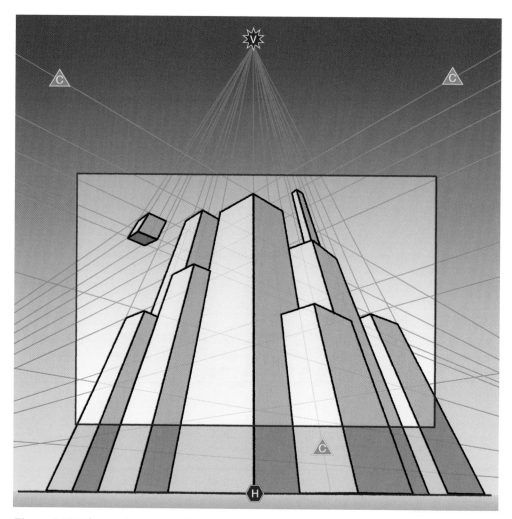

Figure 4.12 Three-point perspective

Setting Up Vanishing Points and Lines of Convergence

After you determine whether your scene will use one-point, two-point, or three-point perspective, you need to place your VPs and make a grid of your lines of convergence.

Photoshop provides an easy way to find the position of VPs and set up lines of convergence by using the Pen tool. Select the Pen tool 🖋 and, in the Control panel at upper left, select the Paths icon ▣. Open the Paths panel, and click the Create New Path icon at the bottom of the panel 🔲. Name the new path **VanishingPointLeft**. Now, follow these steps:

1. Click the Pen tool to the left of your canvas, hold down the Shift key, and click to the right of the canvas. This forces the new path to be a horizontal line.
2. Pick the Direct Selection tool ▸ in the toolbar, or press A for the shortcut.

You want the white arrow for the Direction Selection tool, not the black arrow for the Path Selection tool. You may need to press Shift+A to cycle through the two tools.

---

3. Click the small outlined square at the right end of your path. If no square is visible, click the path so that the control squares appear on both ends. Click only the right-end control point. When it's selected, the small square turns from an outline to a solid color. Make sure your VanishingPointLeft path layer is still selected, and copy the path. Paste it into the same Path layer, on top of the first path. Don't make a new Path layer; you want these path lines right on top of each other.

4. Click the right-end square again, and move it up slightly. If the entire line moves, you've clicked the line rather than the end square; you want to move the right side of the line, not the entire line. The path's left-end square should remain on top of the first end square you created, so the two paths converge onto each other. Do this 15 or so times, moving the paths above and below the horizon until the path lines cover most of your canvas. When you're finished, your paths should look like Figure 4.13.

Lines of convergence drawn with the Pen tool can be seen outside the active area of your document. By zooming out on the document, you can put your VPs as far to each side as you want.

---

5. Duplicate the path containing the left lines of convergence by dragging the layer to the bottom of the Paths panel onto the Create New Path icon ▣ . You want a new path layer this time, to separate the right VP from the left. Double-click, and rename the new path layer **VanishingPointRight**.

6. Click the new path layer and, with the Direct Selection tool, select all the points on the right side; then, Shift+drag them to the left side. Don't drag these points to the exact same area where all the lines converge—you still need to be able to select the left VP. Deselect the points by clicking anywhere there aren't any paths.

7. Marquee-select the points that are on your VP. You can't click-select in this case because you want to select all the points that are on top of each other at the VP. To keep this VP at the same height as the left VP, Shift+drag the VP to the right.

Now you have moveable lines of convergence for your left and right VPs. Only the path layer that is selected will be visible in the canvas area. You can have many path layers, but only one layer can be selected, visible, and edited at a time.

Your right and left VP path setup should look like Figure 4.14. For the sake of illustration, the figure shows both the right and left sets of paths at the same time.

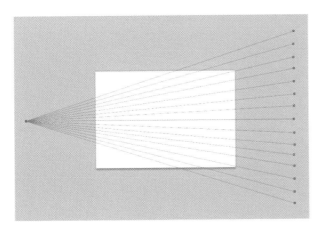

Figure 4.13 *A single set of converging lines set up in the path layer panel*

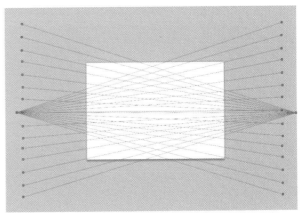

Figure 4.14 *Right and left lines of convergence in separate path layers*

You only have to go through this procedure once. The next time you set up VPs, you can open this document, select the paths for the left and right VPs, and drag them into your new document.

Now that you have the paths for your VPs set up, you need to position the VPs. One of the most common mistakes is to place the points too close together. Except in unusual situations, VPs should be far apart to avoid creating a distorted view. If your VPs are in close proximity, you get a warped perspective, as if the scene were photographed using an extreme wide-angle lens (Figure 4.15).

With the lines of convergence in a path layer, it's easy to set up more distant VPs by marquee-selecting all the points on the VP with the Direct Selection tool and moving them farther out. With the VPs set apart, you get a more natural, relaxed perspective (Figure 4.16).

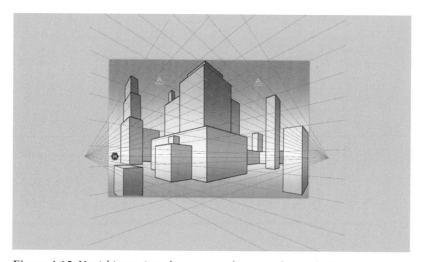

Figure 4.15 *Vanishing points that are too close together and give a distorted view*

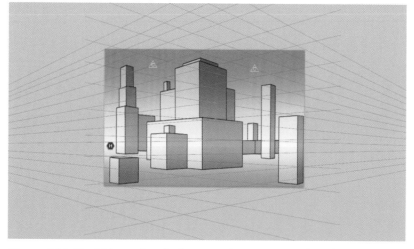

Figure 4.16 *Vanishing points farther out, giving a more relaxed, natural perspective*

If your composition looks strange or distorted, you probably need to put more distance between your VPs.

When you're satisfied with the location of your VPs, you should paint their outlines onto two separate layers. Stroking paths lets you paint the paths as outlines so they're visible while you work. To do this, select a very thin brush, one or two pixels thick, and drag the path layer you want stroked to the Stroke Path icon ◎ at the bottom of the Paths panel. Keep the lines thin so they won't distract you while you work. Stroke the right and left lines of convergence on separate paint layers and in different colors so they work independently of each other. This way, you can turn one, the other, or both off when needed.

Perspective Techniques

Perspective techniques fall into the 90/10 rule: 90 percent of the time, you'll use just 10 percent of what you know about perspective. For our purposes, you'll learn the critical 10 percent you need for these exercises, and you can pursue the rest on your own. There is a list of excellent reference books on this topic at the end of this chapter to fill in the other 90 percent.

The following are some of the perspective techniques you'll use most often. First, you'll see how these tasks were traditionally accomplished in linear perspective. Then, you'll learn to perform the same tasks more quickly and easily using Photoshop's digital-perspective tools.

Equal Divisions in Perspective

Often, you'll need to break up an object or landscape into equal divisions in perspective: for instance, windows on a building, square tiles on a floor, or regularly spaced fence posts.

If you divide the space equally using a ruler and attempt to use those measurements in perspective, the spacing will look wrong. When you're using lines of convergence, the space between each division must get smaller as the divisions recede into space. Using equal spacing, you get the opposite effect, as though the distance is becoming greater between each division (Figure 4.17). Your measurements must be brought into perspective in order to work with lines of convergence.

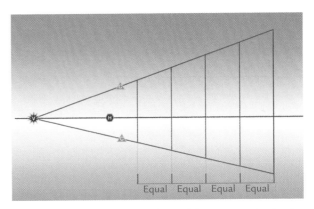

Figure 4.17 *Incorrect use of equal divisions going back in space*

Open the file `Equal_Divisions.jpg` in the Chapter 4 DVD materials. Subdivide the purple line on the right into four equal vertical sections. These divisions aren't in perspective, but you'll use them to construct the proper divisions:

1. Draw lines of convergence to the left VP from the four equal divisions. Draw another line in purple halfway back to show the section you intend to divide into four (Figure 4.18).

2. Draw a diagonal (shown in yellow) from the bottom of the right purple line to the top of the left purple line. Where that diagonal touches the lines of convergence is where the equal divisions will occur in perspective.
3. Draw blue vertical lines through the intersection of the yellow diagonal and the green lines of convergence to complete the division (Figure 4.19).

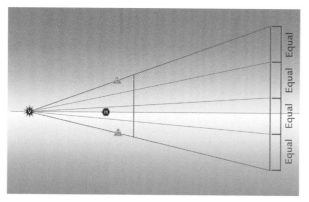

Figure 4.18 *Break the vertical line into four equal divisions, and draw lines of convergence to the VP.*

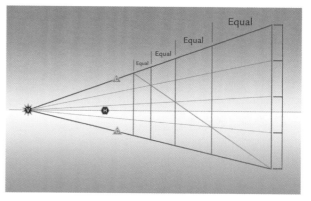

Figure 4.19 *Draw a diagonal. Where it touches the lines of convergence is an equal division in perspective.*

Another important concept is how to find the center of a rectangle in perspective. From the Chapter 4 DVD materials, open the file Division_Rectangles.jpg to try this yourself:

1. Draw an X (shown in red) from corner to corner in the blue rectangles (Figure 4.20). The center of the X will be the exact center of each rectangle in perspective.

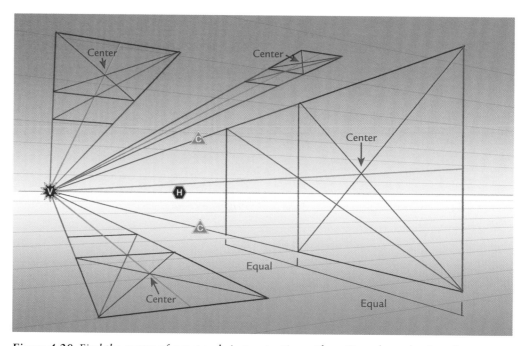

Figure 4.20 *Find the center of a rectangle in perspective with an X, and use that location to create equal divisions.*

2. Draw a line of convergence (shown in yellow) back to the VP through the center of the red X. Where that yellow line intersects the right and left sides of the rectangles is the exact midpoint of those sides.
3. Draw another diagonal (shown in purple) from one of the front corners of the rectangle through the midpoint of the rectangle's opposite side. Where that new diagonal meets the opposite line of convergence forms a new rectangle that is identical in size to the original one.

Repeatedly using this technique for finding equal divisions going back in perspective, you can extend divisions back as far as you want. Open the file Fence_Posts.jpg. The first three posts are drawn in for you: extend the line of posts back another 12 steps to try this technique. When you've drawn your long line of fence posts, you can reuse the divisions you drew to create equal horizontal divisions on the ground.

Draw lines of convergence from the base of each fence post to the opposite VP (Figure 4.21). You'll need to use the path VP technique to place the VP far off to the right. The horizontal divisions on the ground are precisely equal to the vertical divisions for the fence posts.

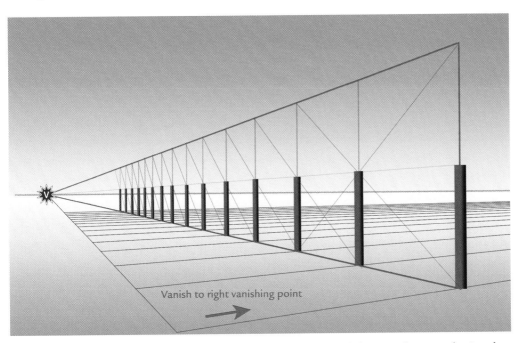

Figure 4.21 *Using the divisions from the vertical uprights, extend them on the ground using the right VP.*

That traditional approach works, but it takes a lot of steps to get your fence posts back 15 steps. Let me show you an easier way, using the Photoshop Distort tool:

1. Open the same file you used to create manual divisions, Equal_Divisions.jpg. If it's already open, and you want to keep the file for future reference, save it under another name.

2. Turn on the rulers, if they aren't already showing, by pressing Command/Ctrl+R. (You can turn the rulers on and off using this keyboard shortcut.) Click the Info panel at upper right; in the upper-right corner is a drop-down menu. From that, choose Panel Options. In the Info Panel Options dialog, under Mouse Coordinates, chose inches

Mouse Coordinates
Ruler Units: [Inches   ↕]
.

You can switch back to any ruler units you want after this exercise. This is just to make sure our measurements match.

3. Create a new layer in Equal_Divisions.jpg. In the Tools panel, choose Brushes; select the HardRoundSolid5 brush from the set of brush presets on the DVD. This is a drawing brush with no opacity or size jitter; it functions like a pen.

4. Looking at the ruler at the top of your canvas, you see that this canvas is 7.75 inches wide. Find the 0.5 inch mark on the left side, and hold down the Shift key to constrain your brush vertically. Starting at exactly the 0.5 inch measurement, draw a straight line down that covers half the canvas. It's important that your measurements are precise, so your spatial divisions will be accurate. Move to the 1 inch mark, and make another vertical stroke about the same size. Move 0.5 inches to the right each time until you reach the 7.5-inch measurement and have 15 vertical strokes.

5. You want all the marks exactly the same size; so, using the Rectangular Marquee tool, draw a marquee around the bottom of the marks and press Delete to trim the bottoms at the same place. Do the same at the top. Don't trim off too much—you need the lines to be about half the height of the canvas for this to work properly, but the lines must all be same size.

6. It's time to transform these marks into perspective. Select all the marks with the Rectangular Marquee tool, and press Command/Ctrl+T to activate the Transform tool. A box with eight small square handles appears, delineating the area you're distorting. By default, you're free-transforming rather than distorting. To access the Distort tool, Control+click/Right click, and choose Distort from the pop-up menu (Figure 4.22).

7. Move the middle-side control boxes on the distortion area horizontally so the lines cover roughly the same area as the 15 fence posts from the previous exercise. Holding down the Shift key, move the corner handles of the distortion box to line up with the top and bottom edges of the lines of convergence.
The Shift key keeps the sides of the box vertical. If either vertical side of the distorted area is at an angle, it won't give you accurate results. Only the top and bottom of the distortion box are allowed to angle to follow the lines of convergence.

8. Press Return/Enter to accept the results, and you'll find that your divisions are in perspective (Figure 4.23). The nearest line on the right is thick and uneven from the distortion, and the farthest left line may be semi-transparent, so both will need to be cleaned up. Nevertheless, Photoshop did most of the work for you in creating equal divisions in perspective.

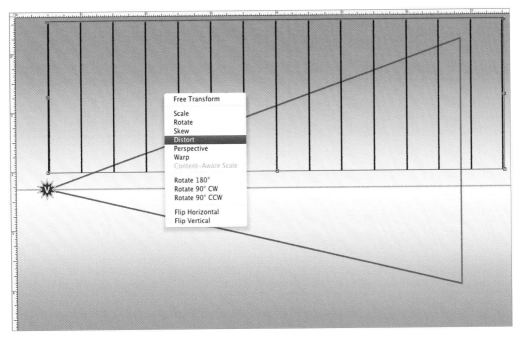

Figure 4.22 *Activate the Transform tool, then Control+click/Right click to access the Distort tool from the pop-up menu*

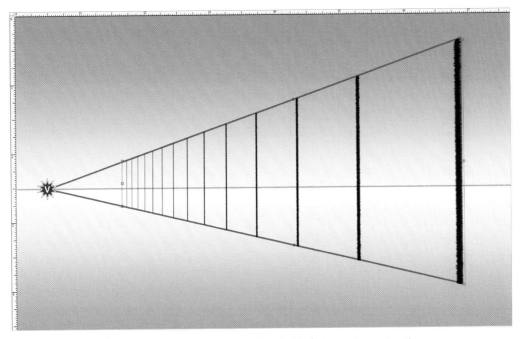

Figure 4.23 *Use the Distort tool to create equally-divided spaces in perspective*

Ellipses in Perspective

An *ellipse* is a circle in perspective. A circle viewed at anything but a flat angle looks like an ellipse. You need to know about several bits of ellipse anatomy concerning the long and short axes, also known as the *major* and *minor* axes. The long axis is a line running across the long side of the ellipse, and the short axis is a line across the short side of the ellipse. These two lines always cross at a 90-degree angle on a properly drawn ellipse (Figure 4.24).

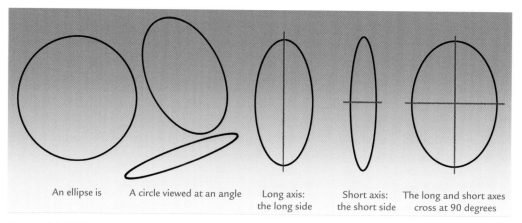

| An ellipse is | A circle viewed at an angle | Long axis: the long side | Short axis: the short side | The long and short axes cross at 90 degrees |

Figure 4.24 The anatomy of an ellipse

Five Rules of Drawing Ellipses in Perspective

Drawing ellipses can be very confusing, so here are five rules that can help. If you have any question whether an ellipse is properly constructed, double-check this list:

- An ellipse can only be drawn inside a perfect square in perspective. No matter what angle your square is to the viewer, the ellipse will touch the midpoint of each side of the square (Figure 4.25).
- If you think of an ellipse as a wheel, the short axis follows the axle of the wheel. If you draw a box around the wheel, this axis will align with the box's second VP (Figure 4.26). The most common mistake in constructing ellipses is to align the short axis to the center-line of convergence for the square that contains the ellipse.
- If an ellipse is horizontally oriented, or flat to the horizon as in a castle tower, the long axis is always parallel to the horizon. The short axis is always perpendicular to the horizon (Figure 4.27).
- The long and short axes form a 90-degree angle. When you draw a cylinder, the long axis of the ellipse forms a T with the centerline of the cylinder. The short axis occurs along this centerline and becomes the centerline of the cylinder (Figure 4.28).
- A properly constructed ellipse, when folded across the short axis, folds exactly over itself. This is the final check to see whether you've constructed an ellipse correctly (Figure 4.28).

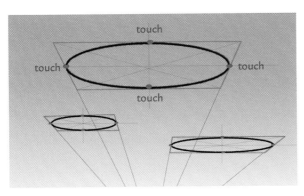

Figure 4.25 *A properly drawn ellipse touches the midpoint of the sides of the square that contains it.*

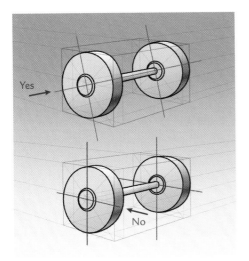

Figure 4.26 *If you view your ellipse as a wheel, the short axis aligns with the axle of the wheel.*

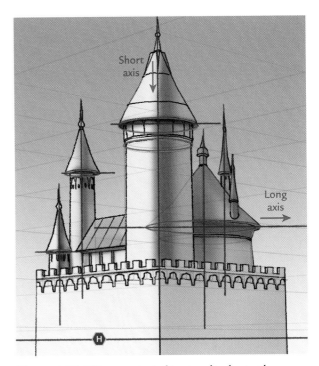

Figure 4.27 *Ellipses oriented perpendicular to the horizon*

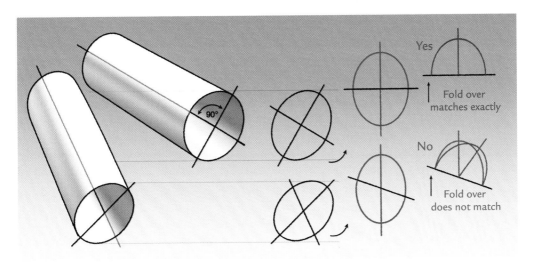

Figure 4.28 *When you fold an ellipse over the short axis, the two sides must perfectly coincide.*

Ellipses the Photoshop Way

Whew! That's a lot to remember when drawing ellipses! Luckily, Photoshop simplifies the process when you use the Paths panel and draw vector-based ellipses.

Open the `Allign_Ellipse.jpg` file in the Chapter 4 materials. Your mission is to line up ellipses on each side of this cube. First, you need to prepare the face so you can position the ellipse. Start with the upper-left face of the cube:

1. On a new regular layer, draw an X from corner to corner on the upper-right face of the cube to find the center.
2. Draw the axis for the ellipse that will sit on that face by drawing a line through the face center and back toward the cube's left VP. You can use the three sides of the cube that already vanish to the left as references.
3. Using the center of the face again, draw lines to find the midpoint of each side of the face. Remember that your ellipse will touch the center point of each side when it's properly positioned (Figure 4.29).

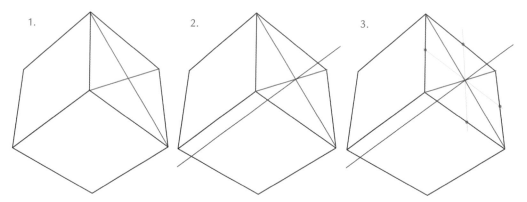

Figure 4.29   Preparing a cube face for positioning an ellipse

You should do this preparatory work for each face when you're learning how to position ellipses. After you understand the process, you can skip these steps and visualize the position of the axis.

4. From the toolbar, select the Ellipse tool ⬭, by pressing U. You may need to cycle through the shape tools by pressing Shift+U repeatedly until you get that tool.

   One more detail about the shape tools, including the Ellipse tool, is that they have several different functions accessible through the top Control panel. You want the Paths function; so, in the top Ellipse tool Control panel, make sure that the Paths icon is selected ▢⬭▢ . If you draw a shape and discover that it's creating a masked shape in a regular layer, the wrong icon is selected.
5. Create a new path layer in the Paths panel, and call it **Ellipses**. With that layer selected, use the Ellipse tool to draw an ellipse about the size of the cube.
6. You're ready to orient the ellipse to be in perspective. Press A on the keyboard to access the selection tools. In this instance, you want the Path Selection tool ▶ so you can select the entire path rather than individual points as you did before. You may need to press Shift+A to cycle through the other tool. When you select the ellipse, notice that four control handles appear exactly on the long and short axes of the ellipse (Figure 4.30).

7. You don't want to move any of the control handles individually, because doing so would throw off the long and short axes that are set up for you automatically. Instead, press Command/Ctrl+T to free-transform the ellipse path. If you limit yourself to free transforming the ellipse, the ellipse will always keep the axes properly aligned at 90 degrees. The angle will change if you distort, skew, or warp the ellipse.

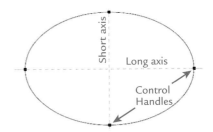

When you use the Free Transform tool, the selection boxes on the long and short axes remain visible. Using the axis you drew to prepare the face of the cube as a guide, align the short axis to it by scaling, rotating, and moving the ellipse into position. Also pay attention to the edges of the ellipse: they must touch the center of the sides of the cube face. When the ellipse is lined up, click Return to accept the transform (Figure 4.31).

8. Position ellipses on the other faces of the cube for practice.

Figure 4.30 Selected ellipses' control handles appear at the long and short axes.

> Ellipses created this way remain shapes in your Paths panel until you stroke, fill, or make selections out of them to use in your composition.

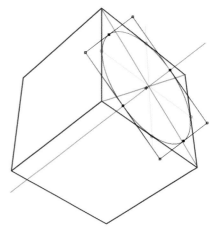

Figure 4.31 Align the ellipse to the face of a cube using the control handles and the short axis.

The Vanishing Point Tool

The Vanishing Point tool automates linear perspective in Photoshop. It allows you to set up two planes going to your VPs, adjust and extend those planes, and then copy, clone, and paint in perspective.

From the Chapter 4 DVD materials, open `Castle_VP_Tool.jpg`. This is a photo of the Scottish castle used in the movie *Monty Python and the Holy Grail*. The castle is partially ruined and under restoration. Let's imagine that a producer wants the castle wall reconstructed with additional windows on all sides and some Python-style graffiti added.

Make a new blank layer on top of the Background layer. It's better to have the Vanishing Point tool work on a new layer instead of on top of the original image so you can easily edit what you add.

Choose Filter ➢ Vanishing Point from the top menu. The Vanishing Point tool opens in its own interface. The first step is to set up two planes that align to the image:

1. Choose the Create Plane tool 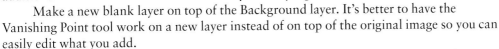 at left in the interface. With this tool, you'll create planes that coincide with the two perpendicular walls in this picture. Start on the right wall: click the upper-left corner, and then click the lower-left corner. Move the cursor to the right side, and click the lower-right and upper-right corners. The Vanishing Point tool creates a grid that covers the wall.

2. If you're unhappy with the number of subdivisions on the grid, adjust the Grid Size value at upper-left in the interface. A larger number gives you a larger grid with fewer squares, and a smaller number gives you a smaller grid with more squares. A value of 90 works well for this document Grid Size: 90.

3. Using the Edit Plane tool , you can adjust the grid by pulling the eight small white squares spaced around the perimeter of the grid. The grid must remain blue for the perspective solution to work: if the grid turns red or yellow, it means there is no possible perspective solution for that grid position. The exact configuration of your grid may vary depending on the grid size and the exact angle at which you place the grid, so it may look slightly different from the illustration (Figure 4.32). Take a moment to line up the edges of the grid with the perspective of the wall.

Figure 4.32 Align the grid to the right wall of the castle.

4. When you're happy with the alignment, Command/Ctrl+click the left-center white square on the grid, and pull a new grid at a right angle to the one you just set up. Depending on how you set up the first grid, the new one may not come out at the correct angle and may need adjustment. Pull on the new grid's corner squares to adjust it to fit the second wall. The lower-left corner of this wall isn't visible in the picture, but you can use both the base of the wall and the far-left projecting wall to guide the alignment. Consequently, you'll have to keep readjusting the grid's angle.

While you're working on this second grid, it's important that the grid remain blue: if it turns red or yellow, it needs additional adjustment. If you overwork the grid and push and pull the corners to extremes, the tool may become unresponsive. If, after many attempts, the grid refuses to turn blue, or it jumps in uncontrollable ways, it's best to cancel out and start over again.

You can only adjust the corners of your grids when you have one or two grids. When you add a third grid, a circle with a line through it appears when you try to adjust the corners. When you create two grids, the Vanishing Point tool considers the perspective solution resolved, and you can only add additional grids to the setup. You can still pull out the center squares of the grids to extend them or reposition them, but the corners are no longer adjustable.

Notice that as you align the left grid, the right grid adjusts itself to remain in perspective. Always keep an eye on both grids: you'll need to work back and forth between the two to get an acceptable solution. When the two grids are aligned, they should look like Figure 4.33.

Figure 4.33 Grids aligned to two perpendicular walls

5. Now the fun begins! Using the Vanishing Point Marquee tool ▦ in the Vanishing Point toolbox at left, draw a square marquee around the window on the wall facing you. Notice how the shape of the marquee is constrained to follow the perspective grid. Soften the edge of the marquee by adjusting Feather to 5 `Feather: 5` in the Options bar at the top of the Vanishing Point interface. Holding down the Shift key to keep the duplicated window at the same height horizontally, Option/Alt+click and drag the marquee to the right.

Holding down the Shift key keeps the new window in perfect alignment with the original window.

The window is duplicated in perfect perspective. With the new window still selected, Shift+Option/Alt+click and drag the window to the left and onto the grid for the left wall. Notice how the window flips onto the wall in perspective. However, there is one problem: the window should be reversed to sit on the wall properly. Press Command/Ctrl+T to transform the duplicated window. You could grab one of the transform handles and flip the window, but the Flip check box does it automatically  .

Now your flipped window is in perfect perspective. Duplicate the window one more time so you end up with two windows on each wall. Your project should look like Figure 4.34. Click OK to accept your work and return to the regular Photoshop interface.

Figure 4.34 Copy the window from the right wall to the left wall, and flip it.

6. The windows on the left don't blend into the wall as well as they can. Because they were created on a new layer, it's easy to fix the blending with the Eraser tool. Using a soft eraser, remove the edges that don't match until the window sits in perfectly.

7. Now you need to tackle the broken top of the walls, and remove the modern surveyor and his tool. Open the `Castle_Top.psd` file in the Chapter 4 materials. This is a section of castle *crenellation*: the blocky ramparts at the top of a wall with open spaces for firing weapons at attacking enemies. This section of crenellation isn't in perspective but is flat-on to the viewer. This is how you want to prepare material for use with the Vanishing Point tool, because the tool will place it in perspective for you. Copy the castle piece, and return to the `CastleVanishingPointTool.jpg` file.

This would be a good time to save, because the Vanishing Point tool is known to be one of the more unstable tools in Photoshop.

8. Create a new layer, and re-open the Vanishing Point tool. Notice that your grids appear again. Photoshop saves grids that are set up in the Vanishing Point tool, allowing you to reuse them instead of starting from scratch each time.

   To add the top to the wall, you need to set up four more planes. Click the left grid to make it live with the Edit Plane tool . Command/Ctrl+click the top-center square of the grid, and drag to the left to create another plane that follows the pathway on top of the wall. Make this plane fairly shallow; it shouldn't be more than a few feet wide. On the new pathway grid, Command/Ctrl+click the top-center square, and drag up to create another grid for the back of the wall.

   If you Option/Alt+drag the edge of a grid, it will rotate. That isn't what you want to do here.

   Select the right wall, and repeat the procedure to create a pathway and a back wall on the right side. When you're finished, you should have three grids for each wall: the original wall, the narrow walkway, and the upper wall that you'll restore (Figure 4.35).

Figure 4.35 Three grids each for the right and left walls

9. Press Command/Ctrl+V to paste the castle crenellation from the clipboard into the Vanishing Point tool interface. (You'll often get a Paste Profile Mismatch warning when you paste in photo sections. This is all right; click OK to dismiss it.) The pasted material appears in the upper-left corner. Click the wall top, and drag it to the upper-left grid.

This is at a higher resolution than needed, so press Command/Ctrl+T to scale it down. Hold the Shift key to scale uniformly. When you have a size you like, press Return/Enter. Without deselecting, Shift+Option/Alt+click and drag the material to the right to duplicate it multiple times and fill the top of the wall. If you had deselected the wall top, made a new marquee, and duplicated it, everything in the marquee—including the underlying bricks and sky—would have been copied. By not deselecting, you can duplicate the wall top as many times as needed without copying the background pixels.

Make sure each time you make a duplicate that you line up the edges so you have a regular pattern of crenellations. Depending on how large you made the wall top, you may end up with a gap between the crenellations and the lower section of the wall. This too, is fixable: draw a marquee around the original wall, and duplicate a bit of the stone in perspective up to fill in the gaps. Click OK to accept your work and exit the Vanishing Point tool (Figure 4.36).

Figure 4.36 Adding wall-top detail that's pasted in from another file

10. The wall crenellations on the left wall look suspiciously 2D, almost as though they're made out of cardboard. You need to add a dimensional backside. Because all of the Vanishing Point tool's work was done on a separate layer, add a new layer behind the crenellations, and paint in the darker, left-facing side (Figure 4.37). Feel free to fix any other details such as lightening the top walkway, painting out the fence at the bottom, and finalizing the blending of the duplicated windows into the wall.

Figure 4.37 Left: no depth to the wall top. Right: the back side has been added.

11. One last touch—or, as Monty Python's knight would say, *pièce d'résistance*! Let's deface the castle you've so carefully reconstructed. Open the file Python_Rules.psd, and copy this bit of graffiti to the clipboard.

Back in the castle file, make a new layer, and choose the Vanishing Point tool. You'll use the brush tool in Vanishing Point, but let's start with the image file. Paste it in, and move it onto the right-side wall. It immediately jumps into perspective. Scale and transform it to your satisfaction.

Click the left grid, and experiment with the Brush tool 🖌. You'll find this brush much less sensitive than the native Photoshop brush, but it works fine for simple tasks. Add some graffiti of your choice on the left wall. Notice how the Vanishing Point tool forces whatever you paint to follow the perspective grid. Click OK to exit.

One more detail—the graffiti looks too garish. Dial down the transparency on the layer to 40 percent so the writing sits on the wall better, and your masterpiece is finished (Figure 4.38)!

Figure 4.38
Paste in some writing for the wall, and then write in perspective using the Brush tool.

In the next chapter, you'll put this all into practice when you do a perspective drawing over the castle concept painting.

Where to Learn More

Perspective: A Guide for Artists, Architects and Designers by Gwen White is a terrific in-depth overview of the topic. I love the funky cartoon diagrams that are used throughout the book.

Perspective Drawing Handbook by Joseph D'Amelio is simply written but gives a full overview of linear perspective.

Perspective Made Easy by Ernest R. Norling reads like it was written a long time ago, because it was originally published in 1939. But although the style can seem extremely dated, the information is timeless.

Some of these books may be out of print, but you can often find them secondhand on Amazon.com.

five

CHAPTER

Perspective Drawing

The entire last chapter was *devoted to the principles of perspective for a reason. It forms a primary foundation of what you'll do as a matte painter. This chapter will put those principles into practice. You'll do a perspective drawing over the top of the castle concept painting. This will involve finding the horizon in the plate, setting up the vanishing points, and delineating the large forms. Then, you'll use the technique for subdividing a surface in perspective to work out the fine details. Using a new technique, you'll delineate all of the ellipses in the round parts of your structure. Finally, you'll create a clean perspective drawing as the basis for lighting and texturing your castle.*

Setting Up Your Vanishing Points

In this chapter, you will do a perspective drawing over the concept painting you created in Chapter 3. If you are new to perspective drawing, I recommend that you work along with the demonstration using the same file. More advanced readers should study this chapter, then do the assignment at the end.

If you are working along with me, open the demonstration concept painting from Chapter 3, `CastleConcept_Horror.psd`, on the Chapter 3 DVD materials. You don't need multiple layers for your perspective drawing. Merge all of the background layers into one, keeping only the Castle layer separate. You will now have two layers, Castle and Background. Save it as a new file called `Castle_Perspective_Drawing.psd`.

Figure 5.1 The horizon line

Your first task when starting a perspective drawing is to figure out the location of the horizon line. If you get this wrong, your drawing will never look right, and your structure won't align properly with the landscape. Create a new layer for the horizon, and visualize where it would be if there were no mountains, trees, structures, or obstructions in the way. When you've located the horizon, draw it in using a bright green color (Figure 5.1).

Using the Pen Tool to Set Up Lines of Convergence

Use the technique you learned in the last chapter to set up your right and left vanishing points (VPs) with the Pen tool in separate path layers. With your concept painting as a reference, and remembering that your VPs must be located on the horizon line, explore some different locations for the VPs. You can grab the VP where all of your paths converge and move it around while holding down the Shift key to constrain the movement horizontally to follow the horizon line. Find locations for your two VPs that match the painting and are placed far enough apart to avoid distorting the structure. The closer the VP is to the center of the picture, the less you'll see of the side of the structure that vanishes toward it. In this example, the right VP is placed closer to the center so the entryway of the castle is angled away from the viewer and illuminated by the moon. The castle walls that vanish to the left VP face more toward the viewer because that VP is twice as far from the center of the picture (Figure 5.2).

When you're satisfied with the position of the VPs, click the Layers panel tab and create two new layers named **VP left** and **VP right**. Select the VP left layer. Pick a 2-pixel brush with opacity and size jitter turned off so there will be no variation in the mark, and choose a bright blue color. Return to the Paths panel, and drag the VP left path down to the Stroke Path With Brush icon at the bottom of the panel to stroke the lines of convergence with blue.

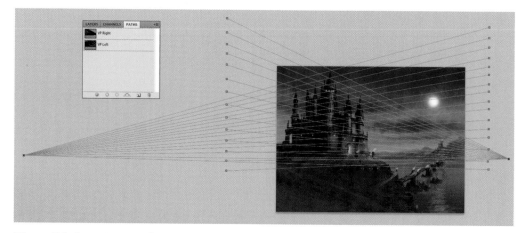

Figure 5.2 Locating vanishing points using paths

Select the VP right layer in the Layers panel, and pick a bright red color. Repeat the stroke process in the Paths panel with the VP right path to make the right lines of convergence visible (Figure 5.3).

Select these layers along with the layer with the horizon line and, while holding down the Shift key, click the Create A New Group folder icon 📁 at the bottom of the Layers panel. Doing so creates a group containing all of your perspective lines. Rename the group **Perspective**. You can turn the opacity of the entire group down to 20 or 30 percent so the lines don't overwhelm your workspace.

Figure 5.3 Stoked paths visible in work area

Drawing the Basic Shapes

Create a new layer called **Drawing**, and position it below the perspective lines in the Layers panel. With those lines visible, start to draw your structure as a series of boxes and cylinders. The largest forms must be delineated before you get involved with detail. If the basic forms are incorrectly drawn, no amount of detail will disguise the fact that your castle isn't in perspective. Draw in white for a dark scene, or black for a light scene, so the lines show up. You can also turn the opacity of your brush down to 30 percent so you can sketch in some trial lines and get a feel for the proper position. Make sure these basic forms line up with the VPs.

The Main Structure

Start by drawing a box for the largest outer walls of the castle. You'll base your drawing on this first form, so take the time to get it right (Figure 5.4).

> The drawing can become difficult to read with the multiple guidelines, so the area being actively delineated appears in red in each illustration.

Useful Brush Controls For Perspective Drawing

To quickly change the opacity of your brush, press the keyboard's top or side number keys: 0 makes your brush 100 percent opaque, 7 makes it 70 percent, 3 makes it 30 percent, and so on. To draw straight lines, turn off the size and opacity jitter on the brush by unchecking Shape Dynamics and Transfer in the Brush panel. Then, when you click, hold down the Shift key, and click again, you'll get a straight line with no variation in size or opacity between the two clicks. To vary the size of your brush slightly in one-pixel increments, use the bracket keys to the right of P on the keyboard.

Figure 5.4 The first box defines the outer castle walls.

When you've delineated the main box for the castle, start drawing some of the other large boxy structures, such as the bastions, which are the large rectangular solids on the corners of the walls (Figure 5.5). In places where the drawing falls between the lines of convergence, lightly draw in guides with your brush set to 30 percent opacity to help you keep everything lined up.

The Front Entrance

This castle's entrance is in the center of the front wall, so use the X technique to position it (Figure 5.6):

1. Draw an X from corner to corner to find the center of the front wall.
2. Draw a vertical line through the center of the X to mark the center of the wall.
3. Draw a rectangle centered on that line to locate the entrance.
4. Using the lines of convergence as a reference, create a projecting box to serve as the entryway.

Figure 5.5 *Boxes for the castle bastions*

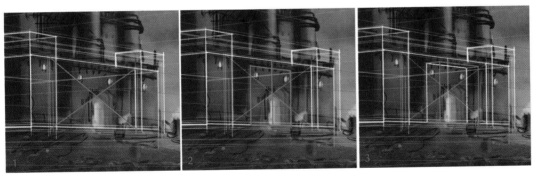

Figure 5.6 *Using the X technique to center the castle entrance*

Now, begin drawing the inner walls. First, you should reposition the two front towers that extend too far out in the concept sketch. These towers typically would be symmetrical with the entrance, but they're drawn to the right of the entrance. Select the layer that has the castle painting on it, draw a marquee around the towers, and move them to the left (Figure 5.7). While working on this perspective drawing, you'll notice that portions of the concept sketch aren't in proper perspective. Feel free to marquee-select and reposition any element that doesn't look right when you start drawing.

Figure 5.7 *Drawing the inner walls, and correcting the concept sketch*

Return to the Drawing layer to draw tall cylinders for the towers. To make sure the towers aren't listing to one side, draw a line down the center of each tower while pressing the Shift key to constrain your mark vertically. This center line will also serve as the short axis of the ellipses you'll add later for the towers.

Most towers are thicker at the bottom than the top, so draw a faint guideline that runs straight up and down on each side of the tower. Then, darken the opacity of your brush, and draw the two sides of the tower angling slightly in toward the guidelines. You'll figure out the shapes of the ellipses later. For now, draw horizontal lines across the tops of the tower cylinders. Add cones for the tops of the cylinders to finish roughing in the towers (Figure 5.8).

Figure 5.8 *Drawing the castle towers using cylinders*

Adding Detail to the Castle

By first blocking in the basic shapes of the castle, you won't get overwhelmed by the little details. Now that you have the big forms blocked in, you can add embellishments.

Equal Divisions in the Castle Walls

Let's start by adding detail to the top of the castle walls. You'll create equally spaced lines and then use the Distort tool to divide the space. You could draw equal divisions using the rulers as reference, as you did in the previous chapter, but here is a quick way to draw precisely equal divisions:

1. Start a new layer, and call it Divisions. At the top of your workspace, away from the main drawing, add a short vertical line by dragging downward while holding the Shift key.
2. Draw a marquee around that line, and then Command+Option-drag/Ctrl+Alt-drag while holding the Shift key to constrain the copy horizontally to create a new line to the right. The distance should be approximately the width of one crenellation.
3. Draw a new marquee around both lines. While holding down the Shift key to constrain the move horizontally, copy+drag the two lines to the right. Overlay the first copied line over the second original line in order to maintain the same spacing. Now you have three equally spaced vertical lines.
4. Select the three lines, and copy+drag them the same way you did in step 3. To continue to maintain the spacing, overlay the first of the duplicated lines over the last of the original lines. You now have five lines. Repeat the process two more times until you end up with 17 equally spaced lines.

Figure 5.9
Duplicating lines for equally spaced divisions

The lines accumulate at an astonishing rate. If you did that trick 10 more times, you'll have 16,385 equally spaced lines. Luckily, you only need 17 lines (Figure 5.9).

Although the 17 lines are equally spaced, they aren't in perspective. To place them in perspective, select them and Command/Ctrl+J to copy them into a new layer. Rename the layer **Divisions Distort**. Keep the original lines to reuse when dividing other areas (unless you enjoy duplicating lines). Marquee-select and drag the lines on the Divisions Distort layer to the left wall of the castle, where you'll add the crenellations.

Now you can distort the divisions into proper perspective. Choose Edit → Transform → Distort. You need to line up the top and bottom guidelines of the Distort tool with the lines of convergence for the top of the wall. The sides of the distortion box must be vertical for this to work. If either end of the distortion box is at an angle, you'll get inaccurate results.

Carefully manipulate the Distort tool box to follow the lines of convergence of your castle wall. Double-check that the sides are vertical before you press Return/Enter (Figure 5.10).

You don't have to restrict yourself to lines for the divisions. You can design a fancier shape to add a lot of detail quickly. Open the file Fancy_Crenellation.psd on the Chapter 5 DVD materials, and try this design on the castle (Figure 5.11).

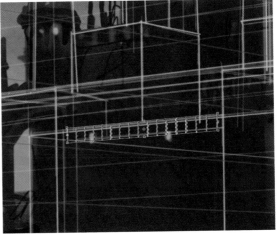

Figure 5.10 Using the Distort tool to place divisions in perspective

Using the opposite VP, sketch in the sides of the forms to give the wall depth (Figure 5.12). Use the same technique to add crenellations to as many of the walls as you want. Reusing a single distinct design throughout the castle will unify the look of the structure (Figure 5.13).

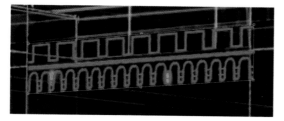

Figure 5.11 *Distorting more complex shapes into perspective*

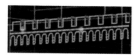

Figure 5.12 *Adding sides to the crenellations*

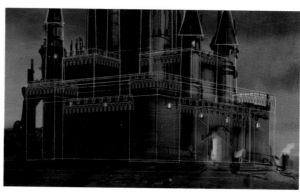

Figure 5.13 *Distorting the same shape throughout the castle*

Mechanical Perspective vs. Eyeballing

You can use a technique known as *mechanical perspective* to determine exactly how an ellipse looks from a particular view of a structure. Using mechanical perspective, you can use top, side, and front schematic layouts of a room or structure and render it in perspective. This is also known as *orthographic projection*. You'll need to know how to use this form of perspective if you're ever involved with set design or architectural drawing. However, in most instances with matte painting, you don't need your drawing to be mechanically accurate—it just has to "look right."

Ted Youngkin and Eyeballing

When I was a student at Art Center College of Design, I had an extraordinary perspective teacher named Ted Youngkin. His class was hard—one of the most demanding I took in art school. My love for perspective grew out of this class. In preparation for a final assignment, he took us on location to sketch. He was drawing along with the students, and I was surprised to observe that he didn't formally work out the perspective. I asked him why he wasn't drawing lines of convergence, or mechanically constructing ellipses, and he responded, "I don't need to do that. I'm just eyeballing it."

By *eyeballing*, he meant making an educated guess as to what would look good to the viewer rather than plotting the solution mechanically. I don't recommend you give up working out your VPs and lines of convergence; but when working with ellipses, eyeballing avoids a load of complex plotting. If you make an educated guess as to the shape of your first ellipse and then carefully match all the other ellipses in your composition to that first one, your drawing will be in perspective.

The Ellipse Bank

Start by eyeballing one ellipse for the tallest tower in your painting. Because an ellipse near the horizon is very flat, it's best to draw the first ellipse toward the top of the painting. This way, you can work with a relatively wide ellipse.

Using the Ellipse tool will allow you to try several different ellipse sizes. Let's start with a circle to learn about ellipse percentages. Using the Ellipse tool, hold down the Shift key to constrain your drawing to a circle. If you watch the Info panel while drawing, you'll see that the circle has identical Width and Height dimensions. Draw a circle the size of the horizontal dimension of the tallest castle tower.

With the ellipse still selected, press Command/Ctrl+T to activate the Transform tool. Look in the Options bar at the top of the interface at the H, or Height, readout, to see the percentage of the ellipse. Because you start at a height of 100 percent, whatever the H readout in the Options bar says is the current percentage of the ellipse. Transform the height of the ellipse, and experiment with different percentages. Make sure the W, or Width, percentage stays at 100 percent, and change only the Height percentage. As you try various ellipse sizes, you'll get a feeling for what looks natural in the scene by comparing it to the concept painting. For example, if you choose a 50 percent ellipse (not recommended), the VPs will have to be very close in, and the scene will be distorted. If you choose a 10 percent ellipse, the VPs must be very far out. The scene will look flat, but it won't suffer from distortion. You'll find that around 25 percent works for this plate (Figure 5.14). Press Return/Enter to accept the transform.

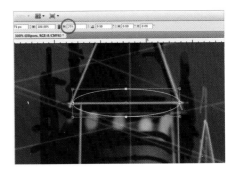

Figure 5.14 *Using the Options bar to find the proper ellipse percentage*

Degrees versus percentages can be confusing if you're used to referring to ellipses by degrees. In the context of the viewing angle, a 90-degree ellipse is viewed straight on, and hence is seen as a circle. A 0-degree ellipse is sideways to the viewer with no dimension, and is viewed as a line. In Photoshop, there is no read-out for degrees, only percentages. So, while you're working digitally, a 100 percent ellipse is the same as a 90-degree ellipse, and both are circles.

After you find a satisfying first ellipse, base the rest of the ellipses in the project on it. You can make a series of ellipses for different heights above the horizon, and then marquee and duplicate ellipses on the side whenever you need to use one in the composition. I call this an *ellipse bank*. Here's how you set it up.

Think of the reference ellipse as a huge hoop that you can slide down the tower to the point where the tower meets the horizon line. At the top of the tower, the ellipse is at 25 percent. If you slide it down halfway to the horizon, it will be at half of that, or 12.5 percent. When it meets the horizon, it will be at 0 percent. You can use those measurements to prepare a series of ellipses on the edge of the composition:

1. Using a 3-pixel brush with opacity and size jitter turned off, draw a rectangle the height of the tallest tower with the base at the horizon. Using the X trick, divide the rectangle first in half, then in quarters, and then in eighths. Hold down the Shift key, and drag horizontally with the brush to mark each point dividing the rectangle into eighths (Figure 5.15).

   Place the 25 percent ellipse you made with the Ellipse tool at the top of the box. With the layer selected in the Paths panel, duplicate the ellipse shape, and slide it to the middle division of the box. Scale this ellipse shape so it's 50 percent of the top ellipse, because it's halfway to the horizon.

2. Copy and paste the top ellipse shape again. This time, place it at the ¾ mark on the box, and scale it to 75 percent of the top ellipse. Do that for the other five divisions, so you have eight premade ellipse shapes at 100 percent, 87 percent, 75 percent, 62 percent, 50 percent, 37 percent, 25 percent, and 12 percent. You can add a 0 percent ellipse if you want, but it's a flat line.

   If you have any ellipses below the horizon, select all of the ellipse shapes in the Paths panel and duplicate them. With the copies still selected, press Command/Ctrl+T to scale them -100 in the H (Height) box in the top Option bar [W: 100.00% H: -100.00%]. Move the copied paths so they mirror the top paths vertically below the horizon.

3. The ellipses are still paths, so stroke them with a 2- or 3-pixel brush on a new layer in the Layers panel for use in your composition.

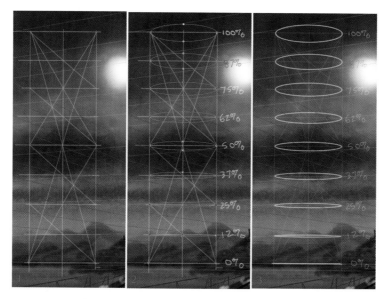

Figure 5.15 *The ellipse bank*

Now, whenever you need an ellipse for one of your towers, look to the side where you have the ellipse bank, draw a marquee around the ellipse that is closest to the horizontal level of your tower, and Command+Option+drag/Ctrl+Alt+drag the ellipse into place. If you hold the Shift key while dragging, you'll constrain the position horizontally so it doesn't move up or down while you drag. You can scale your ellipses larger or smaller to fit the specifics of a tower, but make sure you hold the Shift key while scaling to constrain the dimensions horizontally and vertically.

Don't be confused because your 25 percent ellipse is now labeled 100 percent. Because you're basing the rest of the ellipses in the composition on this first one, it becomes 100 percent, and the ellipses below are between 100 and 0. In the context of the ellipse bank, the top ellipse is always 100 percent in relation to those underneath.

You'll often require an ellipse that is between one of the preset ones: for instance, a 69 percent ellipse, between the 75 percent and 62 percent presets. In that case, choose the preset ellipse closest to what you need and enlarge or reduce it a smidgen to match the proper percentage.

Generally, you won't use the backside of the ellipses, so you need to delete them or use the eraser to lighten them for use as guides.

Go ahead and add ellipses to all of your towers (Figure 5.16).

Figure 5.16 *Adding ellipses to the towers using the ellipse bank*

Dividing a Round Tower

Your next task is to add crenellations to the widest round tower in the center of the castle keep. To accomplish this, you'll draw equal spacings on an ellipse in perspective (Figure 5.17):

1. Start a new layer in the Layers panel, and call it Circle. Draw a circle the same size horizontally as the tower top you want to subdivide, and place it directly above the tower. While holding down the Shift key to constrain the brush vertically and horizontally, draw a square around the circle.

2. Start another new layer, and call it **Eighths**. Draw an X, corner to corner, inside the square. Draw vertical and horizontal lines through the center of the X. The points where each of the lines meets the edge of the circle are equal subdivisions of the circle, dividing it into eighths.

3. Duplicate the layer with the division lines, rename the duplicate **Sixteenths**, and rotate the lines from the center point where they all meet by 22.5 degrees to divide the circle eight more times.

4. Merge the sets of lines from step 2 and step 3, and then duplicate that combined layer. Name the duplicate **Thirty-Second**. Rotate the new layer 11.2 degrees to get a total of 32 subdivisions.

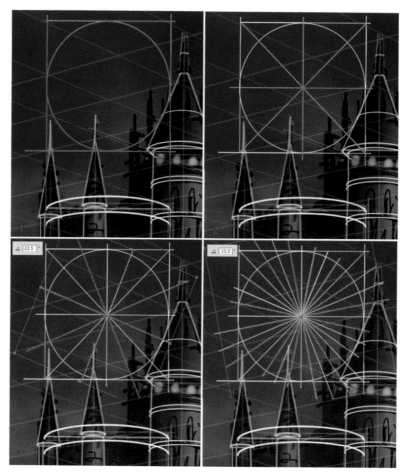

Figure 5.17 *Dividing a circle into 32 sections*

With the circle broken into 32 slices, you need to project these divisions onto the ellipse for the top of the large tower.

Holding down the Shift key, draw vertical lines from the divisions on the flat circle straight down to the ellipse. Where the lines meet the ellipse is the proper breakup of the circle in perspective. You're taking a flat-top view of the circle and projecting it downward onto the same circle in perspective: the ellipse (Figure 5.18).

Figure 5.18 *Projecting divisions onto an ellipse*

When you have the divisions of the ellipse, draw the crenellations and then their sides to give them dimension. You can define the back edge of the crenellations by drawing another ellipse just inside the tower edge. Use the X method to find the center of that ellipse to vanish the sides of the crenellations (Figure 5.19).

You can reuse this subdivided circle to divide other ellipses in the composition, even if the ellipse isn't the same size. Scale the divided circle to the size of the new ellipse, and use the projections to measure the divisions (Figure 5.20).

Figure 5.19 *Adding sides to crenellations around a tower*

Figure 5.20 *Subdividing a smaller tower*

Adding Fine Detail

So far, you haven't used a photo reference while making the perspective drawing because you've been blocking in the large forms. Now that you have the shapes, you can refer to other castles for distinctive details.

One reference used in this painting is a photo of St. Vitus Cathedral, a beautiful gothic structure in Prague (Figure 5.21). The imposing edifice has the sort of spiky towers that will add some spice to the project. You can find the photo on the Chapter 5 DVD materials, in the file St_Vitus.jpg. Display this photo to one side on your monitor as reference, but don't use it directly by copying it into the composition at this point.

Drawing Symmetrical Towers

Figure 5.21 *Saint Vitus Cathedral*

Using the St. Vitus photo as inspiration, sketch a bristling top on the left-front tower. Because most towers are symmetrical, you really only need to draw one side (Figure 5.22):

1. Draw one half of a complex tower top, and marquee-select it.
2. Command/Ctrl+J to copy the tower top to a new layer, and then Command/Ctrl+T and horizontally transform it negative 100 percent.
3. Line up the two sides with each other. An added benefit of working this way is that the tower will always be straight and not lean to one side because the sides are mirrors of each other.
4. Connect the two sides using the ellipse bank, and add the finishing details.

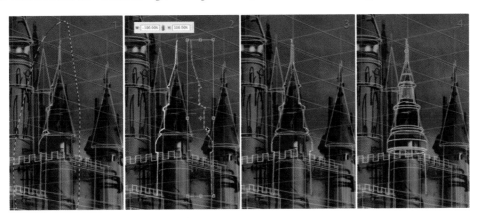

Figure 5.22 *Duplicating tower sides*

Duplicating Identical Towers

There are two identical towers at the front of the castle, but the right one is further away from the viewer and consequently smaller in perspective. Select the finished left-front tower at the castle entrance, and Command+Option+drag/Control+Alt+drag to duplicate it. Move it into the position of the right tower. Check to see that key features, such as the tops and bases, are in alignment. You can add guidelines on another layer if you're having trouble visualizing the lineup. Command/Ctrl+T to scale down the duplicated tower and move it into position to match the lines of convergence (Figure 5.23). Press Return to complete the new tower.

Figure 5.23 *Duplicating and scaling identical towers*

This trick works best when two similar towers are in close proximity. However, if you reuse a tower that is separated from the original by a wide margin, the perspective will be different, and you'll have to adjust it accordingly. Also, be attentive to changes in the percentage of the ellipses. For instance, if a tower is placed high in the composition, and you move it lower, you'll have to redraw all the ellipses because they will need to be flatter.

As the perspective drawing takes shape, you may want to revise the concept sketch so it continues to function as a guide. Feel free to transform walls on the sketch to match the drawing, and reposition walls and towers to be in proper perspective.

So far, you've only worked on the castle. Before you proceed to a final clean drawing, delineate all the background items, such as the hill, sky, background castle, and bridge. Make sure you indicate the location of every element in the composition. When you're happy with your work, save the file.

I gave myself more room at the top of the composition to show the guides by extending the sky. The final dimensions of the drawing are 2,048 × 1,800 pixels. Your final rough drawing should look something like Figure 5.24. You can check the final rough demonstration file with all the different layers on the DVD, in the file `Castle_Rough_Drawing.psd`.

I know what you must be thinking: "That's pretty messy!" As you'll discover, all your hard work will pay off as you prepare the final clean drawing.

Save the file under a new name, `Castle_Perspective_Drawing_Final.psd`.

The Final Drawing

In the old, predigital days, when I was working on a perspective drawing, I would make several versions, each on a new piece of tracing paper. The tracing paper obscured the underlying drawing just enough that I could clearly see the new drawing. This allowed me to be fairly loose with the first drawing and then clean it up on a new piece of paper.

You will do the digital equivalent of this tracing paper process. Add a new layer, fill it with white, and turn down the transparency so you can see the drawing underneath. Rename the new layer **TracingPaper.** Now, merge all of the drawing layers into one or two layers. If you have any guides that you want to keep for later use, such as the ellipse bank or circle divisions, put them on one layer. Rename the layer with the drawing so far **RoughDrawing.**

Figure 5.24 *Rough castle drawing*

Each layer of tracing paper obscures the underlying layers slightly more. You want to see the concept sketch the least, so it will be under two layers of Trace Paper. You want to see the rough drawing more clearly, so it will be under one layer of Trace Paper. You need to see the clean drawing best of all, so it's on top, with no Trace Paper layer. Here's how to stack them (Figure 5.25):

1. Move the RoughDrawing layer above the TracingPaper layer. Since the drawing for this demo was in white, you won't be able to see the lines very well, so open Levels. Under Output Levels at the bottom of the dialog box, move the white arrow all the way to the left, to cover the black arrow ![Output Levels dialog showing values 0 and 2]. Doing so turns the line work black. Press OK to close Levels.

2. Duplicate the TracingPaper layer, and move this copy above the RoughDrawing layer. Name it **TracePaperTop**.

3. Start a new layer on top of the stack, and call it **DrawingFinal.**

4. Adjust the transparency of the lowest Trace Paper layer to 50 percent so you can still see the concept painting somewhat.

5. Set the top TracingPaperTop layer to 40 percent opacity so you can see the RoughDrawing layer more clearly than the concept sketch.

If you've followed this process correctly, you should be able to see clearly a mark made on the DrawingFinal layer.

Figure 5.25 *Tracing paper setup*

A copy of the file prepared to do the final drawing is on the DVD as `Castle_Clean_Drawing.psd`, with the DrawingFinal layer left blank. You'll create the final clean drawing on top of this stack. Use the rough drawing as the primary guide to produce the clean perspective drawing. Depending on how rough your first version is, you may need to go through a couple of iterations to arrive at the final clean drawing. When you have the final clean drawing, place a new layer behind it, and fill that layer with 100 percent white to block out all the older versions.

Keep all the guides on a separate layer in case you ever need to come back and rework the project. Save the final perspective drawing (Figure 5.26). You can check out the final flattened demonstration drawing in the Chapter 5 DVD materials: `Castle_Final_Drawing.jpg`

Assignment

Working over the concept painting you chose at the end of Chapter 3, create a clean perspective drawing of the castle. To get ready to do the perspective drawing, do the following:

- Reduce the concept painting to only two layers: the background, and the castle. This will allow you to adjust the perspective on the castle as you work.
- Find the location of the horizon line.
- Set up the right and left VPs.
- Add a new layer to do the perspective drawing on.

The final drawing should include:

- Walls, turrets, doors, windows, and crenellations drawn in proper perspective.
- All ellipses that encircle round towers must be in drawn in proper perspective. Remember the trick of setting up an "ellipse bank" for your project, and space them at regular intervals down to the horizon.
- Don't worry about texturing or detailing. Don't draw in the stones or roof tiles, just the major features.

The finished file should consist of a clean black line drawing against a white background. You will use this perspective drawing in Chapter 6, "Tone."

Figure 5.26 *Final perspective drawing*

Matte Artist Profile: Eric Chauvin

Eric Chauvin is a rarity in the world of matte painting—a true independent. While most matte artists work for studios and hand off tasks like 3D modeling and compositing to other artists, Eric does it all himself. Living in Washington State, he runs his own production house, Blackpool Studios. His list of credits is impressive. The highlights of his film work include all three *Star Wars Special Edition* releases, *Starship Troopers*, *Blade Trinity*, *Vertical Limit*, *The American President*, and *Elf*. Some of his best work has been done for television, including all of the contemporary *Star Trek* series, *Babylon 5*, *The Young Indiana Jones Chronicles*, *Alias*, *Pushing Daisies*, and *Lost*. His web site, http://www.blackpoolstudios.com, contains an impressive compilation of his many shots, and is a valuable resource for aspiring matte painters.

Figure 5.27 Eric Chauvin

David Mattingly First, tell me a little bit about your background, your parents, where you grew up, and how you became interested in art.

Eric Chauvin I was born in Santa Ana California and raised in Santa Ana and Orange California. I was raised by a single mom my whole pre-adult life. My parents divorced before I was born and I am an only child. My mom worked mostly as a secretary when I was growing up. My father was a pilot and salesman, living and working in South Louisiana.

I'm not sure when I became interested in art. I think finding a vocation is based on what you are naturally drawn to (pardon the pun). I guess I was always doing creative things as a kid. Including making a mural on the living room wall with crayons one Saturday morning before my mom got out of bed. That was probably my first large scale piece.

When I was in the 4th grade, my teacher told my mom that if I pursued it, I could make a living as an artist. I think that may have indirectly steered me down that path later in life.

DM Who are your most important artistic influences?

EC Well, that has changed over the years but I have always been more attracted to representational art. Growing up I was always enthralled with Norman Rockwell (still am) but also Maxfield Parish and other early 20th century illustrators. My taste in fine art early on was the time period of the baroque artists such as Ingres, David, and the Flemish and Dutch painters of that time. I know this is heresy to say, but I never got much from the impressionist painters.

Figure 5.28 Portland Rose Festival promotional painting

Later on, and to this day I can say my favorite artists are Sargent, Waterhouse, Bouguereau, and Gerome. Right now, I'm absolutely in love with the Orientalist painters of the late 19th century.

DM Where did you go to school? Also, how important do you think going to art school is for a matte artist?

EC I went to school at California State University in Fullerton. I spent A LOT of time there and ended up getting a BFA and an MA. I only went back to graduate school because when I graduated the first time, I couldn't find a job anywhere that even remotely utilized skills in art. I ended up working in the Human Resources department for a very large mortgage company. I had my own desk piled with paperwork. I had to wear a suit and tie. And one of my duties was filling out the paperwork for employees who were about to be fired. I hated that job and that environment. One day I came home to my recently married wife and told her my job was killing me and that I wanted to go to graduate school. She agreed and that's where I went for the next two years. It was in graduate school that I focused on matte painting as my course of study. They didn't teach that there, most of the faculty didn't know what that even was, but I was able to tailor my curriculum to focus on that kind of painting.

So to answer your question about the importance of art school for matte painters, for me it was essential. However, everyone will find their own way if they are passionate enough about doing the work. Is art school necessary? Probably not, but for most, it would be a really good start.

DM How did you become interested in matte painting, and how did you get your first job as a matte artist?

EC I was always interested in film. As a kid, I wanted to be a movie director like every other kid in America. I always made short films growing up using a regular 8 then Super 8 camera. When I was 14, I got a subscription to *American Cinematographer* magazine. That was the year they did a feature on *Close Encounters of the Third Kind*. They showed the miniature work and some of the matte shots in that article and I was hooked. Within a few years, I was making my own special effects epic with my Super 8 camera. I never finished it but I did experiment around with making miniatures and even glass painting. That was when I was in high school.

It wasn't until college and more specifically graduate school when I really wanted to pursue matte painting as a career. Since I had a love for art as well as a love for film, matte painting seemed like the perfect intersection between the two worlds.

My first job as a professional matte artist was in 1991 when I was hired at ILM as a matte painting assistant. I had literally graduated graduate school the week before I started. I got the job strictly through serendipity and amazing luck. I was hired to assist the actual matte painters who were there working principally on Spielberg's *Hook*. My job was really non-glamorous but I loved every minute of it. I like to tell people I learned more about painting in the six months I was at ILM the first time than I learned in the five years I was taking art classes. Being there and seeing guys who have done that work for a while and picking up their techniques for creating really believable images quickly was really something. To me, it was like being an apprentice to a magician!

DM You have worked both traditionally and digitally. Speed and economic realities aside, which do you prefer?

EC Ah. This a tough question to answer. When I started at ILM, I fully expected that that would be the beginning of a long career working traditionally. I only worked traditionally for about a year and a half before it went digital overnight. Since I don't have a long history working the older way, I've always lamented not having a chance to work that way longer and really have a chance to hone my painting skills. That said, working digitally really is a miraculous way to create imagery. Working as a traditional matte artist, you would most likely do only the painting while someone else shot it. If it needed any kind of FX animation work, that would be done by the camera guy in conjunction with an animator or someone in optical printing. Since going digital, I get to do all those things and so much more.

Figure 5.28 *Matte painting for* War of the Worlds *(2005 direct to DVD edition)*

Over the years, I have come to realize that what I enjoy even more than the artistry of what I do, is the conjury of what I do. I love the fact that a good matte painting is completely invisible to the audience.

DM When working digitally, what software to you use? How much 3D do you use in your work? Do you do your own compositing?

EC I principally use these apps in the work I do:

- Photoshop
- After Effects
- Modo
- ElectricImage
- Boujou

I generally use 3D in every shot I do that has architectural elements in it. Otherwise I utilizing photo reference and do Photoshop work.

I usually do everything in the shot but shoot the plate; matte painting, compositing, match moving, model building, animation, keying. The one thing I don't do myself is roto. I can do it, but it's such a tedious job, I just don't have the patience for it. Fortunately I work with someone who does the roto work for me when the need arises.

DM For aspiring matte artists, what advice would you give them?

EC The one thing that is more important than worrying about what art school you should go to, is having an absolute passion for the work. That can probably be said for any career one would want to spend the rest of their life doing. But especially for this job and here's why; It is a very stressful job, you often work with people who are jerks, and it's an extremely competitive field. When I got into the biz, Visual Effects work was still photo-chemically based and the people doing the work were a handful of very experienced, very talented people. Now, with the explosion of digital tools and content, everyone wants to get into doing visual effects work. Including facilities operating in countries where the wages are impossibly low compared to American standards. VFX work is getting outsourced like many other jobs in America. But—if you are passionate about the work, you will succeed. Some film makers will always want to hire the cheapest but most will want the best. If your passionate about the job, you will be the best. I have always lived by the understanding that one day I will be replaced by someone younger, smarter, and more talented than myself. I don't think that's pessimistic; I think that's a wonderful thing because it pushes me to always do MY best work.

DM You have been an independent for a long time. Could you talk about the pluses and minuses of working alone?

EC I have the kind of personality where working alone really suits me. When I get angry, I can shout and swear and beat my fist on my desk without having to apologize to anyone afterwards for my unprofessional behavior. Also, I've been working this way so long, that I would feel really out of place if I had to work in a facility with other people on a daily basis. I feel I'm more pro-ductive working alone and I can work all day without interruptions (most of the time). However, most of the time, I DO work all day, every day. Working for yourself means working many more hours than if you worked for a facility.

The other down sides to working alone are obvious; no camaraderie with colleagues and no immediate exchange of ideas and techniques. However, you also don't have to go to dailies every morning, no meetings, no distractions from the paging system constantly paging for someone to dial extension xxx.

DM Tell us about a favorite shot that you worked on, what problems it presented, and how you solved it.

EC I've thought a lot about this question and can't really answer it satisfactorily. I've been work-ing as an independent artist for 15 years and have worked on thousands of shots so it's hard to even remember most of them let alone a favorite one. On the splash page of my website I have a slide show of shots I've done that work well as a static image. I'm rather partial to those, I sup-pose. Nearly every shot poses some kind of problem, whether it's compositional or simply has to get done in a shorter time frame than I would prefer, requiring compromises in order to finish it on time. I guess the shots I like the most are the ones that are the most successful in the context of the show they are ultimately seen in. I did a shot for the miniseries *The Mists of Avalon* that I was really proud of at the time, but once they put it in the show and color corrected it, it looked awful! So ultimately that was an unsuccessful shot. Same thing happened to a really complex shot I did for the movie *Blade:Trinity*. What I delivered I really liked but what is seen in the movie looks ter-rible because of the color "correction" they did before making the final prints of the film. Both of these shots can be seen as I delivered them, on my website.

CHAPTER

six

Form

Now that your perspective drawing

is complete, it's time to give form to your castle. As a matte artist, you want to give your paintings as much form as possible to achieve a lifelike appearance. This chapter will teach you how to use light and dark to reveal the full dimensionality of your composition.

To do this, you need to determine the direction of light and then brighten the illuminated surfaces. Next you'll add cores, which are the dark areas that occur between the light and dark sides. Finally, you'll paint cast shadows and darken surfaces that receive less reflected light. When you have completed this process, you'll have a fully formed castle, ready for texture and color correction.

Finding the Light and Dark Sides

At the end of this chapter, you will add form to your own perspective drawing that you completed at the conclusion of Chapter 5. If you are unfamiliar with the process of adding form to a drawing, I recommend that you work along with this demonstration using the same file as is shown in the figures. More advanced readers should review the material, then complete the assignment at the end using your own perspective drawing.

If you are following along step-by-step with the demonstration, open `Castle_Final_Drawing.jpg`, on the Chapter 5 DVD materials. Re-save it to your hard drive as `Castle_Form_Painting.psd`. This drawing will be the basis for the form study. Rename the background layer with the perspective drawing on it **Drawing**.

Isolating the Silhouette

You first must define the silhouette of the castle as a solid mass. You don't want to select any of the background, just the castle. Choose the Magnetic Lasso tool by pressing Shift+L repeatedly until the icon of a lasso with a magnet appears in the Tools panel. In the options bar, set Feather to 0 px, Width to 10 px, Edge Contrast to 10%, and Frequency to 50. The Magnetic Lasso tool sticks to any edge you move it close to. Click the left outside edge of the castle with the Magnetic Lasso tool, and trace around the contour of the castle. To capture fine detail that the Magnetic Lasso tool may omit, you can manually set a point by clicking the mouse button or digitizing pen while drawing. The path of the Magnetic Lasso tool is shown in red for emphasis (Figure 6.1).

You can temporarily turn the Magnetic Lasso tool into the regular Lasso tool by holding down the Option/Alt key. As long as this shortcut is depressed, you can draw free-hand with the Lasso tool. When you release Option/Alt, the tool once again becomes the Magnetic Lasso. The Magnetic Lasso tool remains active until you click the starting point a second time or press Return/Enter. When you've drawn all the way around the edge of the castle, including the front steps and torches near the entrance, click the starting point to create a selection. You use the Magnetic Lasso tool to get a rough contour, so don't be concerned if you missed some areas. The final selection is again shown in red for emphasis (Figure 6.2).

Figure 6.1 *Use the Magnetic Lasso tool to draw a rough silhouette of the castle.*

Figure 6.2 *Completed Magnetic Lasso tool selection for the castle*

Using the Lasso Tool to Add, Subtract, and Intersect Selections

You probably didn't get a perfect selection, so you'll need to do some additions and subtractions. Return to the regular Lasso tool by pressing Shift+L until it appears. The Lasso tool will change appearance and function according to the mode (Figure 6.3). Here are the four things you can do with this tool:

Create a new selection. Draw a new selection ℘.

Add to an existing selection. Hold down the Shift key while drawing with the Lasso tool to add to the selection ℘₊.

Subtract from an existing selection. Hold down the Option/Alt key while drawing with the Lasso tool to subtract from the selection ℘₋.

Intersect with an existing selection. Hold down Shift+Option/Shift+Alt, and whatever you draw that overlaps with the selection becomes the new selection ℘ₓ.

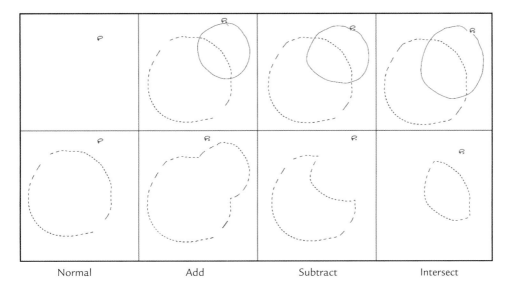

| Normal | Add | Subtract | Intersect |

Figure 6.3 *Using the Lasso tool to alter a selection*

You can access these four modes through the options bar for the Lasso tool, but using the keyboard shortcuts is much faster. Find an area of the drawing where the Magnetic Lasso tool didn't completely cover the castle. Hold down the Shift key, and draw in the area with the Lasso tool to add to the selection. Find an area where the selection went beyond the edge of the castle; then, while holding down the Option/Alt key, draw with the Lasso tool to subtract from the selection. You probably won't need to do any Shift+Option/Shift+Alt intersecting to select the castle, but it's a nifty shortcut to keep in mind, and one you'll use later in this chapter.

Drawing Straight Selections

You'll frequently want to draw straight lines while creating a selection with the Lasso tool. You can turn the regular Lasso tool temporarily into the Polygonal Lasso tool ⋈ by holding down the Option/Alt key while drawing with it.

Begin creating a freehand selection with the Lasso tool. When you want to add a straight line to the selection, press the Option/Alt key to turn it into the Polygonal Lasso tool. Lift the pen or release the mouse button, and move to the end of the straight selection. Click again, and a straight line will be drawn between the two points. As long as you continue to hold down Option/Alt, you'll create a straight selection each time you click.

Often, when you've completed a selection, you'll need to add more straight selections to it. You can accomplish this by holding down the Shift key to enter Add mode and then drawing. While still working on the selection, you can also press Option/Alt, release, and click to create as many straight lines as you need.

Operating the Lasso tool with the Option/Alt key can be confusing. Remember:

- If you press and hold the Option/Alt key first and then draw with the pen, you'll subtract from an existing selection.
- If you click, begin to draw, and then press and hold the Option/Alt key, when you release and click again you'll get a straight line (Figure 6.4).

In the figure, the Polygonal Lasso tool selection is shown in red for clarity.

Figure 6.4 *Press the Option/Alt key after you begin drawing, to get straight selections.*

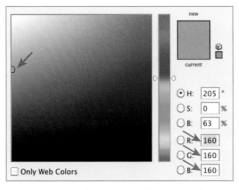

Figure 6.5 *Medium neutral gray resulting from RGB values of 160, 160, 160*

When the castle structure is fully selected, make a new layer called **Silhouette** above the Drawing layer. In the Color Picker, choose a neutral gray for the foreground color by setting the RGB readout to 160, 160, 160 (Figure 6.5). Fill the selection by choosing Edit → Fill.

Set the opacity of the layer to 70% at the top of the Layers panel so you can still see your perspective drawing. This is the basis for the tone drawing (Figure 6.6).

Defining the Light Side

Not having a defined light direction is a surefire way to end up with a formless structure, so your next task is to define the light and dark sides clearly. A full moon is visible in this composition, so it's the primary light source. Deselect the castle, and, on a new layer called **LightDirection**, draw an arrow from the moon to show the direction and angle of the light source (Figure 6.7).

Figure 6.6 Silhouette filled with gray on the left, and the layer's opacity set to 70% on the right

Next, you'll tone the light side of the castle. You'll define the walls of the castle and then the towers. Select all the walls on the side facing the moon. Using the lasso techniques discussed earlier, select all the faces of the walls that the moon would light if there were no obstructions. Light that is obstructed by objects in its path creates cast shadows, which you'll deal with on a separate layer. When all the moonlit walls are selected, create a new layer called **LightSide** above the Silhouette layer. Fill in the selection with the same neutral gray as before. Set the blending mode on the LightSide layer to Screen.

The Screen blending mode lightens the value of the *base*, or underlying layer, by the value of the *blend*, or upper layer. The result is always lighter, so all the light-side walls will be brighter than the rest of the castle (Figure 6.7).

Figure 6.7 Light-side walls

Defining the Dark Side

Now, define the walls facing away from the light source. Make sure you include the back side of the crenellations on the light-side walls. After you marquee off all the dark-side walls, create a new layer above the LightSide layer, and name it **DarkSide**. Fill this layer with a medium neutral gray, and set the blending mode to Multiply. Multiply is the opposite of Screen: it darkens the value of the base layer by the value of the blend layer. The result is always darker. Consequently, the dark-side walls will be darker than the rest of the castle.

Figure 6.8 shows what the dark-side walls should look like with the LightSide layer turned off to add clarity.

Figure 6.8 Dark-side walls

Select the Silhouette, LightSide, and DarkSide layers, and Shift+click the Make New Group icon at the bottom of the Layers panel ▢. Doing so creates a new group with the selected layers in it. Name this group **Form** (Figure 6.9).

Figure 6.9 Form group

Adding Form to the Towers

Now that you've worked out the walls' light and dark sides, it's time to do the same thing for the towers. To do that, you'll learn how to use pixel information on layers to alter selections.

Using Layers to Add, Subtract, and Intersect Selections

Earlier, you learned how to add, subtract, and intersect selections with the Lasso tool. You can use layers to perform the same operations, and the layers can be saved for reuse.

You can use each layer's pixels to create a new selection. You can also use them to add, subtract, or intersect with an existing selection. You load the selection from a layer by clicking the small preview of the layer's contents located at left, called a *layer thumbnail*. When you click the layer thumbnail, any part of the layer that has pixels on it will be included in the selection you load from the layer. You can create a new selection or interact with the existing selection in the following ways:

- Command/Ctrl+clicking the layer thumbnail creates a selection based on the pixels on the layer.
- Shift+Command+clicking/Shift+Ctrl+clicking the layer thumbnail adds the selection of the pixels on the layer to an existing selection.
- Option+Command+clicking/Alt+Ctrl+clicking the layer thumbnail subtracts the selection of the pixels on the layer from an existing selection.
- Shift+Option+Command+clicking/Shift+Alt+Ctrl+clicking the layer thumbnail intersects the selection of pixels on the layer with an existing selection.

The keyboard shortcuts for making selections from pixels on a layer are the same as those used for the Lasso tool, except for intersection. Intersection using the Lasso tool is Shift+Option/Shift+Alt, but for layer pixel information it's Shift+Option+Command/ Shift+Alt+Ctrl.

Using Layers as Reusable Masks

Marquee around a selection of towers that don't touch each other. The selection should include the following:

- The two front towers
- The middle, highest tower
- The middle and back buttresses supporting the largest round tower
- The far-left buttress

For illustration purposes, the towers to be included in this selection are highlighted in red (Figure 6.10). Although you need to be precise in defining the edges of the towers within the castle, you can be sloppy in the areas outside the borders of the castle and base of the towers. You'll fix these areas in the next step.

Shift+Option+Command/Shift+Alt+Ctrl and click the layer thumbnail for the Silhouette layer in the Form group. Doing so causes the Silhouette layer to intersect with the existing selection and removes any part of the selection that is outside the silhouette of the castle.

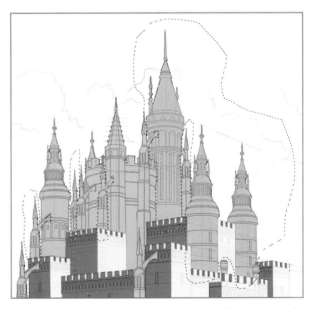

Figure 6.10 *Loosely select the towers highlighted in red.*

To clean up the bottom of the tower selection, Option+Command/Alt+Ctrl and click the layer thumbnail for both the LightSide and DarkSide layers. Doing so deselects any pixels that were selected in those areas. Manually subtract the small side points on the two front towers and the tallest tower. You'll need to do a modest amount of manual cleanup to isolate the towers (Figure 6.11).

Figure 6.11 *Castle towers cleanly selected*

Figure 6.12 *Towers1 filled with bright green.*

Create a new layer above the Form group, call it **Towers1**, and fill it with bright green by choosing Edit → Fill (Figure 6.12).

With the Towers1 layer still selected, Shift+click the Create New Group icon ▭ at the bottom of the Layers panel. Doing so creates a new group with the Towers1 layer inside it; rename the group **Masks**. If the Masks group has accidently been created inside the Form group, select and drag it outside and above the Forms group (Figure 6.13). I call these *mask-loading layers* because you use them to hold reusable masks, but the information on them isn't meant to be part of the final image.

Now, lasso-select the two towers beside the tallest tower, the two round details above the entrance, the middle back tower, the middle buttress around the wide tower, and the tall back tower.

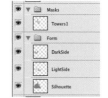

Figure 6.13
Masks group placed above the Form group

You don't have to be precise, because you'll use the masks you've already created to refine this selection. Here's how you do it:

1. Intersect the Silhouette layer in the Form group.
2. Subtract the DarkSide and LightSide layers in Form.
3. Subtract the Towers1 layer in the Masks group.

You may see stray bits of selection outside the towers. Delete them manually. When you have clean selections on all these towers, create a new layer called **Towers2** inside the Masks group, and fill it with a bright blue color (Figure 6.14).

Figure 6.14 Towers2 filled with bright blue

Next, select the widest round tower and the flame holders flanking the entrance. Use the existing masks to isolate these three. Create a new layer inside the Masks group, and call it **TowerWide+FlameHolders**. Fill this layer with a dark blue (Figure 6.15).

Create a new layer in the Masks group, and call it **Buttresses+Detail**. Roughly select the two buttresses nearest the viewer and all the pointy side spikes on the tower tops. You should be able to use the existing layers to add, subtract, and intersect to get a clean selection without doing any hand cleanup. Fill the layer with violet (Figure 6.16).

Figure 6.15 Widest tower and flame holders filled with dark blue

This process has given you clean mattes for each tower. It's important that no tower touches another tower within the same matte. The distance is necessary when you begin creating the light and dark sides on the towers.

You need four more mattes to have a complete set of selections for all the structures in the castle. The Form group contains selections for the walls in the LightSide and DarkSide layers. You'll take the upper walls and lower walls on each layer and turn them into separate masks. Let's begin the process:

1. Command+click/Ctrl+click the LightSide layer thumbnail in the Form group to load the layer selection.
2. Create a new layer in the Masks group, and name it **LowerWallLight**.
3. Fill the selection in LowerWallLight with a red-purple color.

Figure 6.15 Two front buttresses and top tower details filled with violet

Figure 6.17 Selection of upper light-side walls

4. Select the upper wall on this layer. In making this selection, you only need to be precise where the inner and outer walls meet—the rest will be handled by intersecting with the layer selection. Double-check that you include the back side of the upper wall crenellations in the selection (Figure 6.17).

5. Command+Shift+J/Ctrl+Shift+J to cut the pixels in the selection and place them on a new layer. Make sure the new layer is inside the Masks group, and name the layer **UpperWallLight**.

6. Command+click/Ctrl+click the UpperWallLight layer thumbnail to make a selection, and fill it with red (Figure 6.18).

Follow the identical process to create two new layers in the Masks group for the dark-side walls; call the layers **LowerWallDark** and **UpperWallDark**. Fill the LowerWallDark selection with orange and the UpperWallDark selection with yellow (Figure 6.19).

This is a lot to take in; if you've gotten lost or want to double-check the file setup at this point, open `Castle_Form_Masks.psd` on the DVD. When you turn on all the layers in the Masks group, the file should look like Figure 6.20.

Holy mackerel! This is the worst party-colored paint job ever. Let's make this psychedelic color scheme invisible. Select the folder for the Masks group, and set the opacity to 0%.

Figure 6.18 Light side upper and lower walls broken into two mask loading layers

Figure 6.19 Dark-side upper and lower walls broken into two mask-loading layers

Figure 6.20 *Mask-loading layers filled with bright colors*

With the mask-loading layers set up in the Masks group, let's look at a quick way to find, select, and use any layer without a trip to the Layers panel. When you Command+right-click/Ctrl+right-click a spot in the composition, a pop-up menu lists all the layers visible under the cursor at that point. This is extremely valuable when you add many layers and can't figure out which particular layer has a section of texturing or painting on which you want to work. You can do this no matter what tool you're using. Try it—Command+right-click/Ctrl+right-click, and hold the cursor over the lower light-side wall. The pop-up menu shows not only all the layers under the cursor but also all the groups. Try it in other spots—the menu will change depending on the layers beneath the cursor (Figure 6.21). If you select a layer in the pop-up menu, it becomes selected in the Layers panel.

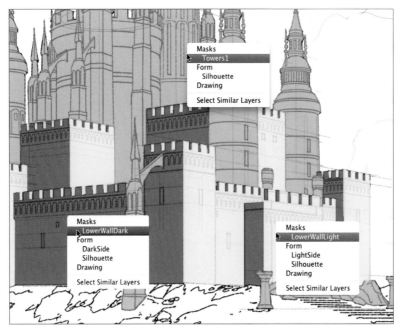

Figure 6.21 *The pop-up menu reveals what layers are beneath the cursor at any point in the composition.*

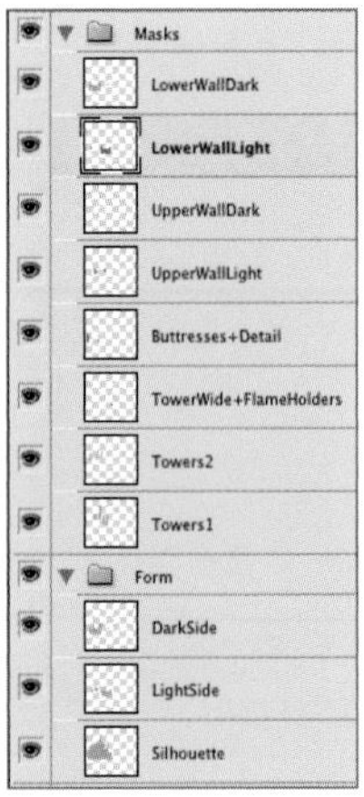

Figure 6.22
Masking and Form layer thumbnails in the Layers panel

You set the opacity of the Masks group to 0%, rather than turning off the group's visibility, because layers that aren't visible don't appear in the pop-up menu.

Since you filled the mask-loading layers in the Masks group with bright colors, you can glance at the layer thumbnails to pick out the mask you need quickly while you're using the Layers panel (Figure 6.22).

Using the Gradient Tool to Create Rounded Surfaces

You'll use the masks to add form to the towers with the Gradient tool. Load a middle neutral gray into the foreground color. Then, press Shift+G until the Gradient tool becomes active. The top control panel contains several options for the Gradient tool. From left to right, they are Linear, Radial, Angle, Reflected, and Diamond. Choose Reflected (Figure 6.23).

Still in the gradient options bar, open the Gradient Editor by clicking the preview gradient to the left of the gradient types (Figure 6.23). Load the default gradient set if it isn't already there, and choose Foreground to Transparent, the second choice ▨. Click OK to exit the Gradient Editor.

Figure 6.23 *Reflected Gradient tool in the center and a preview gradient on the left*

When you experiment with the Reflected Gradient tool, you'll find it creates a mirror image of the gradient on the opposite side with maximum opacity in the middle, fading to transparent on each flank. If you hold the Shift key while clicking and dragging the Gradient tool horizontally, it will draw a constrained vertical bar of mirrored gradient tone.

You can check back to Chapter 3, "Composition and Concept," for a more detailed look at the Gradient Editor.

With the Masks group set to 0% opacity, you should be seeing only the layers in the Form group, not the brightly colored Masks group. Here is the procedure for adding a smooth gradient light side to the tower (Figure 6.24):

1. Command+click/Ctrl+click the Towers1 layer thumbnail icon  to load the selection for the first set of towers. Select the LightSide layer in the Form group.

2. With the selection from the Towers1 mask-loading layer visible, use the Gradient tool on the selection for the left-front tower. Create a reflected gradient starting from the middle of the front side of the tower facing the moon. Hold down the Shift key, and drag horizontally to the right until the gradient indicator reaches slightly beyond the right edge of the tower.

3. Release the mouse button, and you get a nicely rounded tone on the light side of the tower.

Because the selections in the mask-loading layers are spaced apart, no tower in a selection touches another. As a result, the gradient doesn't spill over onto the other towers. The Gradient tool finishes most of the tower light side in one swipe. However, you still need to do some hand painting in the selection with a soft round brush to follow the tapering tower top. If the gradient bleeds over onto the dark side, or your hand painting doesn't quite match the pointed top, use a soft eraser to clean up the edges.

With the LightSide layer's blending mode set to Screen, the neutral gray makes the layer lighter. Finish adding all the light-side gradients to the towers in the Towers1 selection (Figure 6.25).

Figure 6.24 *Using the Gradient tool to add the light side to rounded towers*

Load the other mask-loading layers in the Masks group—Towers2, Buttresses+Detail, and WideTower+FlameHolders—one by one, and paint the light side of each tower and the details the same way. Some manual cleanup will be required, but when you're finished, the completed light side of the castle should look like Figure 6.26.

Select the DarkSide layer in the Form group. Make sure the middle neutral gray is still loaded into the foreground color, and follow the same procedure you used for the light side using the Gradient tool. Because the DarkSide layer's blending mode is set to Multiply, the middle gray makes the layer darker. When you're finished, the castle should look like Figure 6.27.

Figure 6.25 *Towers1 selection light side finished*

Figure 6.26 *Adding the light side to all the towers using the Gradient tool*

Figure 6.27 *Adding the dark side to all the towers using the Gradient tool*

A Final Note about Lighting

I can't emphasize enough how important it is to set up consistent light and dark sides on objects in your scene. When you paint landscapes, you must have one main light source, which is usually the sun or moon. Everything in the scene must be lit from the same direction. In an interior scene, you can have multiple sources of light that illuminate people and objects in the room differently. However, for landscapes, consistent lighting is a must.

Also keep the light and dark sides separated tonally. Make sure that when you look at your structure, there is no question which is the light or dark side. If the light side is a middle gray and the dark side is only marginally darker, your structure will look mushy and lack solidity.

Cast Shadows

The castle now has light and dark sides, but it still doesn't look realistic. What is missing are the *cast shadows*. Cast shadows occur when one surface blocks light that would otherwise illuminate another surface. Cast shadows are generally darker than other shadows on an object, because they receive less fill light. *Fill light* comes from the sky, the atmosphere, and other objects in the environment that reflect light onto the dark side. Without fill light, objects would be black on the dark side—a lighting situation almost never seen except in outer space. Fill light should never be brighter than the main source of illumination.

Create a new layer at the top of the Form group, name it **CastShadows**, and set the blending mode to Multiply. The castle entrance is blocking the light that would fall on the wall behind it, so begin by drawing the cast shadow from the main entrance. You'll eyeball the length of the cast shadows as opposed to plotting them, so use your judgment as to what looks realistic.

Select the Lasso tool, and add softness by setting Feather to 3 px in the options bar. You'll occasionally see razor-sharp cast shadows on a clear sunlit day, but it's more natural looking to take the edge off shadows. To draw the shape of the entranceway's cast shadow, do the following (Figure 6.28):

1. Using the position of the main light source as a reference, begin drawing from the top edge of the entrance where it meets the wall. Press the Option/Alt key to turn the Lasso tool temporarily into the Polygonal Lasso tool. The top edge of the shadow matches the direction of the light. Draw the shadow extending out on the wall to a reasonable distance. Click, and then draw a straight line to the ground; click again, and draw the edge of the shadow back to the base of the entrance.
2. Release the Option/Alt key, and lift the cursor. The selection appears.
3. Command+Option+click/Ctrl+Alt+click in the LowerWallDark layer thumbnail to trim the shadow to align with the edge of the entrance. Using the Gradient tool, click the corner where the structures meet, and drag out beyond the edge of the shadow.
4. Cast shadows tend to be darkest at the source of the shadow. By starting the gradient in the corner and dragging out, you make the shadow lighter away from the wall casting it.

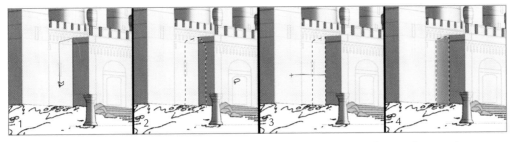

Figure 6.28 Draw the shadow for the castle entrance, and fill it using the Gradient tool.

Next, you'll create the shadow for the right-front bastion. Select the Rectangular Marquee tool, and feather it 3 pixels. Follow this procedure (Figure 6.29):

1. Command+click/Ctrl+click the layer thumbnail for the LowerWallLight layer to load that selection.
2. With the Rectangular Marquee tool, Shift+Option/Shift+Alt and drag over the area of the selection to the left of the right bastion. Doing so selects only the area that the marquee intersects. This shadow isn't as long as the one for the entranceway because the bastion doesn't project out from the wall as far as the entrance.
3. Use the Gradient tool to create the shadow.

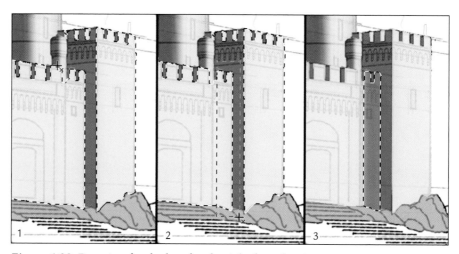

Figure 6.29 *Drawing the shadow for the right front bastion*

Using Selections to Cast Shaped Shadows

You should look for opportunities to use the forms in the structure to cast shaped shadows. For instance, the upper-left inner wall is mostly in shadow from the wall to the right of it, whereas the topmost section is illuminated. Because the wall casting the shadow has crenellations, the blocky forms should be evident in the shadow. You can add a shaped shadow to the opposite wall by following these steps (Figure 6.30):

1. Load the UpperWallDark layer selection, and marquee Shift+Option/Shift+Alt around the right dark wall to isolate it. Choose Select → Transform Selection. Control+right-click/right-click, and select Distort from the pop-up menu.
2. Distort the shape into position on the left light wall by clicking the control points of the Distort tool and moving them as shown. Press Return/Enter to accept the distortion.
3. Choose Select → Modify → Feather, and feather the selection 3 pixels to soften the edge. Manually add to the bottom of the selection to cover the lower part of the wall that isn't selected.
4. Shift+Option+Command+click/Shift+Alt+Ctrl+click the layer thumbnail for UpperWallLight to intersect with the existing selection and confine it to that wall. Use the Gradient tool to create the cast shadow.

Continue creating the rest of the cast shadows on your own. When you're finished, the cast shadows should look like Figure 6.31.

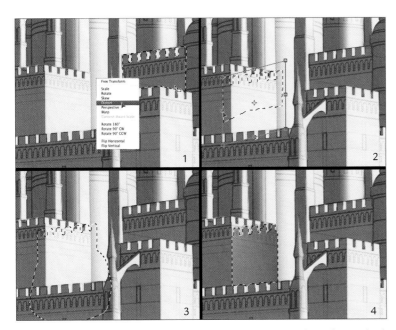

Figure 6.30 *Using the forms in the structure to create shaped cast shadows*

Figure 6.31 *Cast shadows completed*

Layer Masks

One problem remains with the cast shadows: they aren't dark enough. Why? Because the illumination from the LightSide layer is still on, and this lightens the cast shadows. You need to turn off the illumination in the shadowed areas to achieve the correct tonal density. Doing so requires a technique called *layer masks* that you haven't used before. You'll use a layer mask on the LightSide layer to block it wherever cast shadows occur.

Layer Masks vs. Mask-loading Layers

Layer masks and mask-loading layers are two different beasts, and they're easy to confuse. *Layer masks* is an official Photoshop term referring to a special mask attached to a layer that stops part of that layer from showing through, much like a stencil.

Mask-loading layers is a term I coined to refer to layers where I park masks for reuse. In the past, I kept masks in the alpha channels. Whenever I wanted to use this stockpile of masks, I had to go to the Channels tab, Command+click/Ctrl+click the channel to load a selection, and then go back to the Layers panel to use it. Having masks accessible in the Layers panel is much easier, and you can find them on the fly by Command+right-clicking/Ctrl+right-clicking in the composition.

To apply the layer mask, follow this process:

1. Command+click/Ctrl+click the thumbnail for the CastShadows layer to load the selection.
2. Anything not selected is masked off, so you need to choose Select → Inverse or Shift+Command+I/Shift+Ctrl+I to invert the selection.
3. Select the LightSide layer, and, at the bottom of the Layers panel, click the Add Layer Mask icon ▣.

Voilà! The cast shadows are instantly darker because the layer mask prevents the LightSide layer from showing through. Notice how the LightSide layer now has a second thumbnail of the layer mask to the right of it ▣⊠ LightSide. The linked chain between the two icons signifies that you can move the layer, and the mask will move with it. If you need to move either of them independently, you can click the chain to unlink the layer and the layer mask. If you rework the cast shadows, you should delete the layer mask and redo it so that the cast shadows and layer mask always match.

The cast shadows should be even darker. Select all, and then press Command+M/Ctrl+M to open the Curves dialog box. Click and pull down the middle of the curve to make the cast shadows the darkest tone on the castle. The final cast shadows should resemble Figure 6.32.

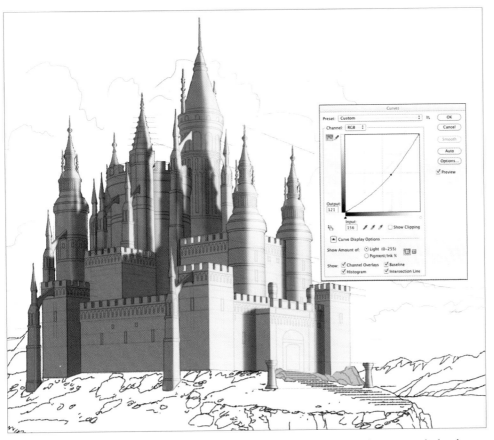

Figure 6.32 *Apply a layer mask, and darken the cast shadows using the Curves dialog box.*

Cores

Cores are the dark areas that occur where the light side
meets the dark side on rounded surfaces. These areas get
the least reflected light. They're a great way to give your
surfaces added definition. For that reason, cores are often
exaggerated in life drawings. The example in Figure 6.33,
by Michelangelo (no slouch in the life drawing department),
shows an exquisite use of cores. Done as a study for the
Libyan Sybil in the Sistine Chapel, it has a clear core running
all the way down the figure's back and another on the left
forearm.

With the mask-loading layers completed, adding cores
will be a snap. Follow these steps:

1. Command+click/Ctrl+click the layer thumbnail for
   Towers1 to load the selection. Make a new layer at the
   top of the Form group, rename it **Cores**, and set the
   blending mode to Multiply.

Figure 6.33 *Michelangelo's drawing demonstrates
the use of cores.*

2. Use the Gradient tool, set to Reflected Gradient, and choose Foreground to Transparent in the Gradient Editor. Choose the same neutral gray you used before as the foreground color. Set the opacity of the gradient to 40% so you can use the tool a couple of times to build up the core.

3. Hold down the Shift key to constrain the gradient to where the light and dark sides meet. Add a vertical core down the center of the far-right tower. Because the tower comes to a pointy top, you'll need to use the Eraser tool to remove the excess core as the diameter tapers. Cores on a round surface should be smooth, so work in big strokes at low opacity to add the core to the cone tops. When you're finished with the first tower, the core should look like Figure 6.34.

4. Go ahead and add cores to the rest of the towers. A core can occur on ttowers that are in shadow, such as the lowest left-side buttress. Although it isn't receiving illumination from the main light source, the buttress will have more definition if you add a subtle core.

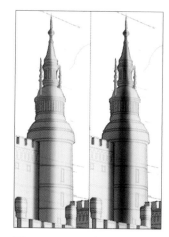

Figure 6.34 *Add a core the first tower.*

When you're finished with the cores, the castle should look like Figure 6.35.

Figure 6.35 *Cores on all the towers*

Final Form Layer

You need to paint one more layer to give the castle full form. To add more definition to the structure, look for areas where the forms intersect, downward-facing surfaces, and regions that receive less reflected light.

Darkening Where Two Surfaces Intersect

Create a new layer called **FinalDarks** at the top of the Form group. Set the blending mode to Multiply. With a brush sized to 10 pixels, 0% hardness, and 40% opacity, darken spots where two surfaces intersect on an inside corner. This resembles the natural world, because wherever two objects meet to form an inside corner, there is more opportunity for dirt to get trapped and less open area for light to illuminate the surface. Where two walls abut as described, or two towers intersect, add a soft dark line (Figure 6.36).

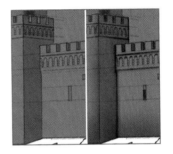

*Figure 6.36
Darken any area
where two surfaces
intersect.*

Darkening Downward-Facing Surfaces

Still on the FinalDarks layer, darken any surfaces facing downward. Surfaces facing the ground get less reflected light, as well as show darkening from the elements—rain, pollution, and grime. Darken the under surfaces on both the light and dark sides (Figure 6.37).

*Figure 6.37
Darken any
surfaces that face
downward.*

Darkening Areas Below Projections

Wherever a surface projects from another surface, the area below the projection is also darkened by the effects of the elements. For example, where the arm of a buttress meets the wall, you should add dark streaks to show this discoloration (Figure 6.38). Do this throughout the structure to show the wear-and-tear beneath projecting surfaces.

*Figure 6.38
Dark streaks under
projecting surfaces*

Darkening Areas That Receive Less Reflected Light

You also need to darken interior walls that receive less reflected light. To darken these walls and add shading, do the following (Figure 6.39):

1. Command+click/Ctrl+click the layer thumbnail for the UpperWallDark mask-loading layer to load that selection. Add to the selection by Shift+Command+clicking/Shift+Ctrl+clicking the mask-loading layers for, respectively, UpperWallLight, Towers2, and TowerWide+FlameHolders. Doing so isolates the center of the castle, which should be darker.
2. Use the Gradient Tool set at 30% opacity to build up the darks above the lower walls. Experiment with the Radial Gradient option ■ to get a more localized round gradient.

3. Command+Option+click/Ctrl+Alt+click the layer thumbnail for UpperWallDark and UpperWallLight to subtract them from the selection and isolate the area behind and above the upper walls.

4. Use the Gradient tool to darken the area behind the upper walls, which gets even less reflected light. The effect, although subtle, is important to giving the castle full form.

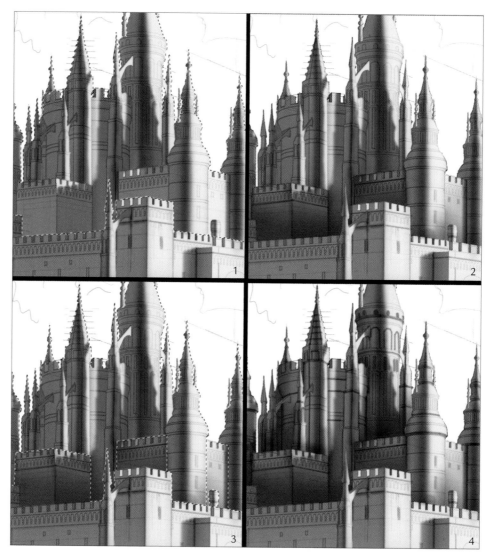

Figure 6.39 *Darken the area behind the lower walls and intersections of two surfaces.*

When you're finished, the castle should look something like Figure 6.40.

Figure 6.40 Castle with final dark areas added

Adding the Line Drawing

It would be nice if you could see the line work clearly over the top of the form painting. There is a problem, however: if you move the drawing to the top layer and set it to Multiply, it obscures the tone work. Use the Curves dialog box to thin out and lighten the lines so the form painting shows through. Here's how you do this:

1. Duplicate the Background layer, rename it DrawingLighter, and move it above the Form group.
2. Set the blending mode to Multiply.
3. Open the Curves dialog box. Move the white point in halfway to the left to erode the black lines and make them thinner.

4. Raise the black point up halfway to make the black lines gray so they have less impact on the form when multiplied over it.
5. Click OK to accept the adjustment.
6. Save the file again as `Castle_Form_Painting.psd`.

When you're finished, the form painting should look like Figure 6.41. You can check out the work file for this project in the Chapter 6 DVD materials: `Castle_Form_Finish.psd`. I restored the perspective guidelines from the perspective section for use in the next chapter.

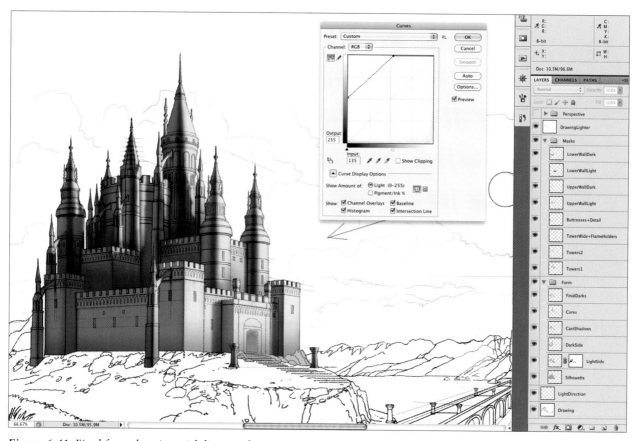

Figure 6.41 *Final form drawing with line overlay*

Assignment: Tone Your Castle Drawing

Using the perspective drawing you created of your own castle in Chapter 5, create a toned version on your own. The steps are as follows:

1. Isolate the silhouette of your castle.
2. Define the light and dark sides. Make sure the sides are tonally distinct—no mushy castles!
3. Create re-usable mask-holding layers defining the major structures of your castle.

4. Add cast shadows. When a shaped architectural element is casting a shadow, like the castle crenellations, use that shape to define the shadow.

5. Add cores to areas where the light side meets the dark side on rounded surfaces.

6. Create a layer to add your final darks, darkening the intersection of forms, downward-facing surfaces, and regions that receive less reflected light.

7. Add a lightened, thinned out version of your drawing set to Multiply at the top of the layer stack so that you can retain your line drawing.

With the form drawing complete, you now have the basis for applying photographic textures to your castle in Chapter 7.

seven

Texturing and Color Correction

In the previous chapters, you *built the foundation of a castle by establishing the perspective, light side, dark side, and shadows. Now you can enhance the realism of the project through the application of photographic textures.*

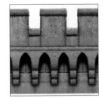

By avoiding the use of photography up to this point, you've sidestepped one of the most common pitfalls of digital matte painting: the montage approach of piecing together photos to make a composition. If you become overly reliant on photographic material, you won't experience the creative freedom of designing a composition from scratch. Starting with photographic images can stymie your artistic vision in the initial design phase. Falling under the influence of a photograph's existing realism, you won't mine the rich vein of imagination that lies within you. By taking the time to work through the basic steps, you won't be a slave to photography. Rather, the reference photos will serve to advance your vision.

Blending Modes

Blending modes give you the ability to blend two layers together in ways unavailable to the traditional/analog artist, and they're one of the unique strengths of working digitally. Therefore, before you begin texturing the castle, it's worthwhile to take a closer look at blending modes. Some of the modes have been referenced in past chapters, most notably Screen and Multiply.

In the Layers panel, open the drop-down menu at the top, and take a moment to acquaint yourself with the different modes (Figure 7.1).

The Six Categories of Blending Modes

In these descriptions, the blend layer is the upper layer and the base layer is the lower layer. With all the blending modes, the opacity of the blend layer will influence how much it shows up over the base layer:

Figure 7.1 Blending modes in Photoshop

Normal Modes The normal modes don't apply a blend, except for the level of opacity.

Darken Modes The darken modes result in a darker blend. Any white on the blend layer leaves the base layer unchanged.

Lighten Modes The lighten modes result in a lighter blend. Any black on the blend layer leaves the base layer unchanged.

Conditional Modes The conditional modes are of special interest to matte artists when adding textures, because they compare the blend and base layers and blend only under certain conditions. The explanations for these modes can be complicated. One great option in Photoshop is to select the blend layer and then press Shift plus the (+) or (-) key to cycle through the modes until you find the effect that you want.

Comparative Modes The comparative modes compare the two layers and alter the blend based on the differences. They aren't used in matte painting.

Color Variable Modes To understand the color variable modes, you need to be familiar with the three variables that make up a color (Figure 7.2).

- *Hue* refers to the color family, such as orange, green, blue or red.
- *Saturation* is the intensity of the color. A bright red has more saturation than a dull red.
- *Luminosity* deals with the lightness or darkness of a pixel, without reference to the color. It generally deals with grayscale images, but it can also be used in reference to a light color as opposed to a dark color.

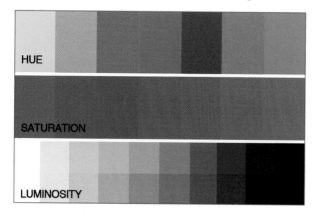

Figure 7.2 The three variables that make up color

The terms *hue* and *color*, which are often used interchangeably, have slightly different meanings. *Hue* refers to the color family but not the saturation or luminosity. These two red squares are the same hue because they belong to the same color family— red. However, they stand in sharp contrast to one another because of the differences in their saturation and luminosity.

Color refers to both the color family and saturation but not luminosity. These two squares bear a closer resemblance than the hue pair, because they share the same color and saturation, even though the luminosity is different.

Blending Modes Used in Matte Painting

Rather than look at all the blending modes, here is a list of the blending modes you'll use for matte painting. For an explanation of the modes not covered, you can consult Photoshop's documentation:

Normal Places the blend layer over the base layer with no blending. This is the default blending mode. With the base layer (Figure 7.3) over the blend layer (Figure 7.4), the result is only the blend layer (again see Figure 7.4) because the base layer is covered up.

Figure 7.3 Base layer

Figure 7.4 Blend layer

Darken Blends the layers to display the darker tone. Darker tones stay the same, whereas lighter tones are replaced by darker ones (Figure 7.5).

Figure 7.5 Darken blending mode

Multiply Multiplies the layers together. The result is always darker. Think of it like holding a transparency in front of a slide projector. If you place a second transparency in front of the first, it will reduce the light and create a darker image that is the combination of both images (Figure 7.6).

Figure 7.6 Multiply blending mode

Color Burn Similar to Multiply, it adds more contrast and saturation to the blend (Figure 7.7).

Figure 7.7 Color Burn blending mode

Lighten Blends the layers to display the lighter tone. Lighter tones stay the same, whereas darker tones are replaced by lighter ones (Figure 7.8). This mode is the opposite of Darken.

Figure 7.8 Lighten blending mode

Screen Multiplies the inverse of the layers together. The result is always lighter. Think of it like a slide projector showing an image. If you shine a second projector on the same area, the result will be a brighter, lighter image that combines both images (Figure 7.9). This mode is the opposite of Multiply.

Figure 7.9 Screen blending mode

Color Dodge This mode is similar to Screen, but the result has more contrast, brightness, and saturation (Figure 7.10).

Figure 7.10 Color Dodge blending mode

Overlay Screens the light pixels and multiplies the dark pixels from the blend layer. This mode is very useful for adding textures, because it both lightens and darkens the image with one layer. The result has more contrast and saturation (Figure 7.11).

Figure 7.11 Overlay blending mode

Soft Light This is a subtler version of Overlay. Overlay can sometimes be overpowering because it adds significant amounts of contrast and saturation. Soft Light adds some contrast but very little saturation. This mode is useful when you don't want to change the color of the base image (Figure 7.12).

Figure 7.12 Soft Light blending mode

Hard Light Similar to Overlay, but the blend layer has much more influence on the final blend. This mode is useful if you want the color and texture of the blend layer to show though clearly (Figure 7.13).

Figure 7.13 *Hard Light blending mode*

Color Applies the hue and saturation of the blend layer to the base layer, leaving the luminosity the same (Figure 7.14).

Figure 7.14 *Color blending mode*

This mode is useful for colorizing elements in a composition. For instance, if you place a layer of blue on top of the blend layer, it turns everything blue, regardless of the underlying color (Figure 7.15). This can be powerful when you're unifying the color of a composition.

Figure 7.15 *Layer of solid blue applied to the base layer with the Color blending mode*

Pass Through Available only when you have a group folder selected. Pass Through keeps the existing blending mode of each layer in the group. Although this is the default for any group, you can override the blending modes of the individual layers by setting the group to a different blending mode.

Texturing The Castle

If you have not worked extensively with photographic textures before, I suggest that you work along with the demonstration using the same file that is shown in the figures. If you are an advanced user, you should read through this chapter, then apply the principles to do the assignment at the conclusion of this chapter, and add textures to the toned castle you created at the end of Chapter 6, "Form."

If you are working along with me, open the file Castle_Form_Finish.psd in the Chapter 6 DVD materials. Keep all the layers created for the form painting to use with the texture files. Make sure you're working in 16-bit for this part of the project. (While doing the perspective drawing, I often change to 8-bit so the file responds more quickly.) Go to the top of the interface, and choose Image → Mode → 16 bits/Channel to make sure your document is in the higher color space. The document will double in size. In professional matte painting, all your work will be in 16-bit.

You need the original background plate from the concept painting to work over. Open `CastlePlate16Bit.psd` from the Chapter 3 DVD materials. Select all, and copy the plate. Paste it into the file below the Form group. It can sometimes be tricky to get a pasted layer to come in below, rather than inside, a group. To avoid that problem, scroll near the bottom of the Layers panel, and select the Light Direction layer. Paste the copy from the original plate, and it will be placed in the correct layer position. Close `CastlePlate16Bit.psd`.

The demonstration file has room added at the top to show more of the sky. You need to move the background plate down to line up with the drawing, which leaves a large white space at the top. Marquee-select the top inch of the background plate, and press Command/Ctrl+J. Then, press Command/Ctrl+T, and stretch the duplicated section of the sky up to cover the white space (Figure 7.16).

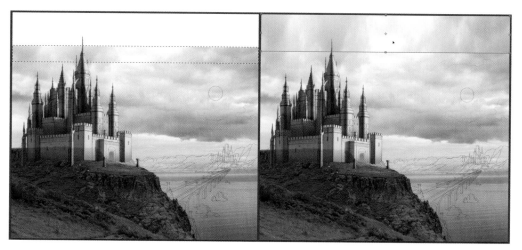

Figure 7.16 *Extend the top of the original plate.*

Merge the stretched sky layer with the original plate, and name the layer **Plate**. You need to smooth the join where the stretched section meets the original plate. Use the cloud brush you created in Chapter 2, "Photoshop Workspace, Tools, and Custom Brushes," to blend the join between the sections. Because you won't be using it, close the Masks group by clicking the triangle to the left of the name. Rename the file `Castle_Texture_Painting.psd`, and save it to your hard drive.

Adding Stone Texture Using Soft Light

One of the reasons the castle still doesn't look realistic is that the tones are too smooth. When you study any photograph, there is variation even in areas you think of as featureless. Photographic surfaces show a small amount of *noise*—the breakup of any solid tone or color into speckles of slightly different tone or color—throughout the image. You'll use the Soft Light blending mode to create a layer with a stone texture on it that will add this natural variation to the castle.

Creating the Weathered Stone Wall Texture

To create the stone texture, follow these steps:

1. Go to the www.cgtextures.com folder in the Chapter 7 DVD materials, and open the photo of a large patch of stone wall called `StoneWall.jpg` (Figure 7.17). It doesn't have enough variation in it, so you'll use blending modes to make it look old and grungy.

2. To add a layer of dirt to the wall, open `BrickWallMixed.jpg`. Copy and paste it into the first wall file (Figure 7.18).

3. Change the blending mode to Overlay. This mode can be overpowering, so set the opacity to 40% to make it blend better. With the Eraser tool, remove some sections so the wall has random sections of dirt and grime. Drag-copy sections to other areas on the wall to get additional randomization.

4. Open the file `DirtyBrick.jpg`. You can use it to add some large blotches and drips to the stone texture. Copy and paste it into the stone-wall file. This time, try the Color Burn blending mode. It gives you some nicely streaked sections, but the result is too dark. Correct this by turning the opacity of the layer down to 20%. The result is a nicely randomized wall showing character and age (Figure 7.19).

Figure 7.17 Base layer for stone texture

Figure 7.18 Second texture to add variation

Figure 7.19 Application of textures to add streaking and weathering

You can compare your work with the demo version of the file on the DVD, `StoneWall All.psd`.

Select all, and Shift+Command/Ctrl+C to copy-merge the textured stone wall section from the file you just created. With the Plate layer still selected, paste it into the castle file. You need to move the texture above the Form group but below the Masks group. This can be tricky, because the layer tends to land inside one of the groups, not in between them. If the layer goes into one of the groups, try again, and drag it in between the two groups. Name the layer **BigTextureSection** (Figure 7.20).

Figure 7.20 BigTextureSection layer between the Masks and Form groups

At the bottom of the Form group, set the Silhouette layer to 100% opacity so that it blocks out the sky and hill. At the top of the Layers panel, turn on the visibility of the Perspective group by clicking the eyeball, and change the opacity of the group to 100%. You'll use the perspective lines to distort the stone texture into perspective.

Texturing the Dark-Side Walls

Begin with the walls on the dark side of the castle. Duplicate the layer BigTextureSection, and rename the copy **DarkSideTexture**. Turn off the visibility of BigTextureSection. Select DarkSideTexture again, and set the opacity to 50% so you can see both the castle and the walls. Choose Edit → Transform → Distort to place the section of wall into perspective. Double-check that the lines of stone match the left-side perspective lines, and press Return/Enter to accept the distortion (Figure 7.21).

Figure 7.21 Distorting texture to cover the walls on the dark side of the castle

Set the opacity of the DarkSideTexture layer to 100%. Doing so causes the texture to block the castle. To make the texture blend with the castle, you must change the blending mode to Soft Light. Now, the pattern of the stone wall covers the facade. However, this texture won't work for the rounded towers and the right-side walls vanishing to the right VP. You need to use a layer mask to confine visibility to the dark-side walls. Open the Masks group, and load in the LowerWallDark and UpperWallDark selections created in the last chapter. Then, apply the combined selections as a layer mask on the new DarkSideTexture layer. As a result, the texture is confined to the dark side of the castle (Figure 7.22).

Texturing the Light-Side Walls

Duplicate the BigTextureSection layer again, turn on the visibility, and rename the layer **LightSideTexture**. Similar to what you did for the DarkSideTexture layer, set the opacity to 50%, and distort the stone texture into shape for the light-side walls using the right-side perspective lines. Set the opacity to 100%, and change the blending mode to Soft Light. Apply a layer mask using the selections from the UpperWallLight and LowerWallLight masks in the Masks group. Now the light side walls are textured.

Figure 7.22 Adding a layer mask to confine texture to the walls

Texturing the Towers

With the walls textured, you can tackle the towers. Begin by adding texture for the tallest castle tower. The stone texture needs to be warped to follow the roundness of the tower using Photoshop's Warp transform. Duplicate BigTextureSection again, turn on the visibility, and call the layer **MainTowersTexture**. Move the stone-wall texture on MainTowersTexture to the right side of the layer so you can grab sections of it for use on different towers.

Texturing the Central Tower

Draw a marquee around the central tower, leaving an extra margin on each side in order to warp the texture around the tower (Figure 7.23).

Figure 7.23 Marquee-select around the central tower

Apply the texture to the tower in three steps.

1. Still on the MainTowersTexture layer, move the marquee you just drew around the central tower over the large texture section on the right side of the layer. Command/Ctrl+Option/Alt+drag to copy a tower-sized piece of the texture to the left. Move it directly on top of the central tower. Leave the blending mode as Normal, and set the opacity to 50% (Figure 7.24).

2. Choose Edit → Transform → Warp. The Warp tool, introduced in Photoshop CS2, has 12 control points that allow you to distort the texture smoothly to match the tower. Unfortunately, you can only grab one point at a time, so you need to pull the points on the left side down and to the right carefully, one by one. Do the same with the right-side points, pulling them down and to the left to curve around the tower. Make sure the vertical points on the sides of the tower are in alignment, or you'll get a wavy stone texture (Figure 7.25).

3. When you're finished, press Return/Enter to accept the warp. Load the Towers1 selection from the Masks group, and apply it as a masking layer to the stone texture. The texture is now confined to the tower.

Texturing the Two Front Towers

Disable the layer mask you just added by Shift+clicking the layer-mask preview. A red X appears over the layer mask. Now, repeat the previous process for the two front towers:

Grab a new section of stone-wall texture from the right, and move it over the left-front tower. Warp it into position so the texture follows the curvature of the tower.

Rather than re-warping a texture, you can reuse sections to cover similarly shaped areas. In this case, when you've warped the texture to fit the left-front tower, you can re-use it for the right-front tower. Command/Ctrl+Option/Alt+drag to copy the section and move it on top of the right tower. Press Command/Ctrl+T to scale it down 5%, because the tower is slightly farther away (Figure 7.26).

Figure 7.24 Place the texture over the tower.

Figure 7.25 Warp the texture to match the perspective.

Figure 7.26 Reusing a texture for similar areas

Enabling the Layer Mask for the Towers

Shift+click the layer-mask preview again to enable it. Now all of the tower textures are confined to the towers. Raise the opacity of the layer to 100%, and set the blending mode to Soft Light (Figure 7.27).

Texturing the Rest of the Castle

Finish adding the stone-wall texture to the rest of the castle. Every surface that is made out of stone should have the texture applied to it, including the remaining towers, the buttresses, the round cylinders above the entrance, and the cylinders/torches in front of the castle entrance. The reason for adding this texture is less about specific detail and more about getting a rustic finish to all stone surfaces to use as a base for the castle.

Grouping All the Texture Layers

Select BigTextureSection, DarkSideTexture, LightSideTexture, MainTowers Texture, and all the layers you created to texture the rest of the castle surfaces. I added three more layers to finish the castle: BigRoundTowerTexture, DetailsTexture, and HighButressesTexture. With all the texture layers selected, Shift+click the Make New Group icon at the bottom of the Layers panel. Doing so places the textures in a new group; name it **TexturesGroup** (Figure 7.28). The visibility of the BigTextureSection layer should still be off.

Cast Shadows and Texture

One more detail needs attention: the cast shadows. With TexturesGroup above the Form area, the Soft Light texture is lightening and adding detail to the cast shadows. You don't want the cast shadows lightened. The shadows will look more natural if you move TexturesGroup inside the Form group, and place it below the FinalDarks, Cores, and CastShadows layers. Close TexturesGroup, and move it between the DarkSide and CastShadows layers in the Form group. Doing so causes the layers of cast shadows to be applied on top of the texture and achieves a smoother result (Figure 7.29).

Turn off the visibility of the Perspective group. The stone texture covers the entire castle (Figure 7.30).

With the basic texture complete, it's time to use photography to add detail to the castle.

Finding Reference Photos

The first question that comes up when you begin to use photography in your paintings is the most obvious: where do you find good reference materials? If you're a world traveler with a library of your own photos in high resolution, look no further than your hard drive. However, most of us need to find other sources of photos.

Google and Copyright

You can turn to Google, do a search on *castles*, and find a plethora of material. That approach comes with some obvious pitfalls. Whoever took and posted the photos online still owns the copyright. If you incorporate the photographs into a project without getting the copyright holder's permission, you may be sued for copyright infringement. If you change an image substantially, chances are no one will know where you got the reference, but it isn't a good practice.

Figure 7.27 Textures set to Soft Light and confined to the towers

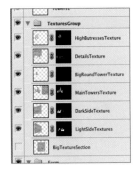

Figure 7.28 Stone textures all grouped together

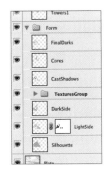

Figure 7.29 TexturesGroup inside the Form group

Figure 7.30 *Castle with a Soft Light overlay of the stone texture*

Resolution Issues

Most of the images available on the Internet aren't of adequate quality or resolution to be useful in a project. For example, if you find a perfect photograph, but it's very small, it will be of limited application. Photos available on the Internet are usually saved as JPEGs and show compression artifacts that require substantial repainting. Flickr is an often-visited source of photo references, but there are copyright issues, plus the size and resolution vary widely. At times, you'll find a great photo—just what you need!—only to discover that it was uploaded at 500 pixels wide when you need 2,000 pixels.

Reference Websites

Luckily, there are websites specifically designed for artists to find high-quality photo references. I contacted my favorite reference websites, and all four agreed to provide photos for use in this project. They're stored in the Chapter 7 DVD materials. These are the sites:

- www.environment-textures.com is a subscription site that charges a little more than $100 a year depending on the conversion rate of the Euro. This site is specifically for texture artists, and all the shots are taken as straight on as possible, showing no perspective. This way, you can add the perspective yourself.

    The site offers nearly 100,000 photos of anything you can think of to use as a texture: landscapes, skies, walls, rocks, windows, buildings, and on and on. I've had a subscription for the last five years. You can find sample reference photos in the www.environment-textures.com folder on the DVD.

- www.cgtextures.com lets you download 15 MB of textures a day for free. After you reach the limit, you must wait 24 hours before you download more photos. For a while, I restricted my use to the daily quota, but I found myself using the site so frequently that it made sense to purchase a yearly membership for $60 to support the site. As a member, you can download 100 MB a day and get access to larger files.

    The site offers a wide array of reference images and some gigantic sky files to subscribers. You can find sample reference photos in the www.cgtextures.com folder on the DVD.

- http://freetextures.3dtotal.com offers a dazzling selection of textures tailored to the needs of texture artists. Usage is free. The site is growing daily, so you can check back periodically to see what has been added. Be sure to check out the sample reference photos in the freetextures.3dtotal.com folder on the DVD.

- www.great-castles.com is one of the best sites on the Internet for researching castles. It's an encyclopedic source of large, quality photos of the castles of Europe. At last count, the site had 129 different castles, some photographed in great depth. The people who run the site love castles and offer the photos as a free resource. By special arrangement with Ron Lyons, Jr., the proprietor of the site, I'm including 40 photos in the www.great-castles.com folder on the DVD.

Levels and Curves in Color Correction

With your reference photos in hand, you'll quickly discover that they're in different color spaces. Before you begin to work with the photos, they will require color correction. The following is a primer on Levels and Curves, the indispensable tools of color correction.

Anatomy of Curves and Levels

You can't use Curves and Levels at the same time, but they share many of the same controls. By pressing Command/Ctrl+L to open the Levels dialog box, or Command/Ctrl+M to open the Curves dialog box, you access control of the open image's entire range of tones and colors.

Let's look at the similarities. On the left side of Levels is the black point input control that matches the black point input on the left side of Curves. The same is true of the midtones and white point controls, which are in both dialog boxes.

There are differences between the two, however. The sliders at the bottom of the Levels dialog control the output levels for the image's brightest brights and darkest darks. In contrast, the slider at the bottom of the Curves dialog functions as a redundant control of the white and black point inputs.

Take a moment to study the controls in Levels and Curves (Figure 7.31).

Behind both Levels and Curves is a graph that resembles a spiky mountain range, known as a *Histogram*, which maps the tones in the image (Figure 7.32). You can tell a lot about an image by looking at its Histogram. In Levels, the white tones in an image are graphed above the white point slider, the midtones are above the midtone slider, and the blacks are above the black point slider. Curves is the same, but the points are on a line rather than a slider. The graphs show how much of each tone you have. For instance, the image with the Histogram shown in Figure 7.32 has no pure blacks: the graph at that point is flat. The graph rises to the maximum around the dark midtones. Another lower spike occurs in the highlights. Above the white point, the graph returns to zero again except for a few very small bumps.

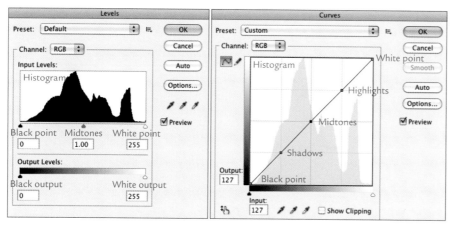

Figure 7.31 *Controls for Levels and Curves*

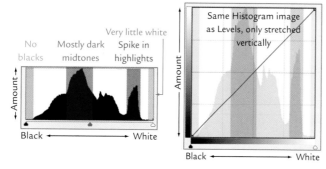

Figure 7.32: *Reading an image's Histogram*

Open the file that displays this Histogram: Castles_of_Great_Britain_612022.jpg in the Chapter 7 materials on the DVD. You'll use it to learn more about Levels and Curves in the following section.

Common Color Corrections

To acquaint you with the most common color corrections in Photoshop, let's look at the same correction done in Curves (shown on the left in the figures in this section) and Levels (on the right in the figures). Each correction will be applied to the castle photo you just opened.

Moving the White Point to the Left

At the white point, the image is completely white, or 255, 255, 255 in the RGB readout. If you move the white point in (to the left in Curves or Levels), you brighten the tones in the picture. Everything to the right of the white point in the Histogram will turn completely white. The only part of the tonal scale left unchanged in this adjustment is the darkest dark or black point.

For the first example, you'll brighten all the highlights and midtones in the image, plus heighten the contrast and saturation, by moving in the white point. Press Command/Ctrl+M to open Curves, and move the upper-right point to the left (Figure 7.33). Click OK, and look at the adjustment. Click Undo to return to the original image.

Press Command/Ctrl+L to open Levels, and move the right slider in Levels to the left (again, Figure 7.33). Click OK, and look at the adjustment. It's the same as the adjustment in Curves. Undo to return to the original image.

The Opposite: Moving the Black Point to the Right

At the black point, the image is completely black, or 0, 0, 0 in the RGB readout. If you move the black point in (to the right in Curves or Levels), you darken the tones throughout the picture. Everything to the left of the black point in the Histogram will turn completely black. The one part of the tonal scale left unchanged in this adjustment is the lightest light or white point.

Image Credit: Corel Stock Photo Library

Figure 7.33 *Lightening an image by moving the white point*

To darken all the shadows and midtones by moving in the black point, go through the process of opening both Curves and Levels to compare the adjustment. Move the lower-left point on Curves to the right, and then move the left slider in Levels to the right. This is the opposite of what you did with the white point. Moving the black point also adds significant contrast and saturation (Figure 7.34). After each adjustment, click Undo to return to the original image.

Figure 7.34 *Darkening an image by moving the black point*

Reducing Contrast

To reduce contrast in the image, move the black point straight up and the white point straight down in Curves. Doing so reduces contrast and saturation and makes the image grayer and duller.

Notice that Levels requires separate sliders to change the Output Levels (Figure 7.35). To reduce contrast, move both these sliders toward the middle.

Figure 7.35 *Reducing contrast and saturation of an image*

The Opposite: Adding Contrast

To add contrast to the image in both Curves and Levels, move the black point to the right and white point to the left. Doing so raises the white point and lowers the black point, adding a double dose of contrast and saturation (Figure 7.36).

Figure 7.36 *Adding contrast to the image by raising the white point and lowering the black point*

Clipping

Whenever you raise the white point or lower the black point, you throw away part of the image and cause sections to turn completely white or black. This is known as *clipping*. You can see the effects of clipping by reopening Levels after applying a correction (Figure 7.37). The Histogram looks quite different. The information in the red areas has been thrown away and replaced by white at the location of the white point and by black at the location of the black point. When you apply a correction, the remaining information in blue is spread across the Histogram. Furthermore, the Histogram is no longer solid, as indicated by breaks in the graph. The breaks show that the tonal values from the middle of the graph have been spread over a larger area, causing gaps in the information. Because you have fewer steps for fine gradations, smooth transitions in the image can become coarse jumps between tones.

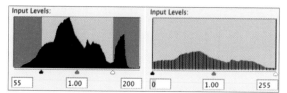

Figure 7.37 *Extreme color correction causes clipping in an image.*

Raising the Midtones

Although correcting an image using the white and black points gets the job done, it's a harsh correction. There is a way to lighten an image without losing part of the tonal range or adding excessive contrast and saturation: you can raise the midtones, which is often a better option. In Curves, add a new point in the middle of the curve by clicking the line, and drag the point straight up. In Levels, drag the middle slider to the left. Both techniques lighten the image without changing the color dramatically (Figure 7.38). Both midtone adjustments leave the white and black points untouched.

Figure 7.38 *Lightening an image by raising the midtones*

The Opposite: Lowering the Midtones

The same goes for darkening an image by pulling the middle of the curve lower, or dragging the middle Levels slider to the right. These two moves offer a less severe way of darkening an image (Figure 7.39).

Figure 7.39 *Darkening an image by lowering the midtones*

Altering the RGB Channels: Raising the Red Channel

In the previous examples, you've worked on all three RGB channels simultaneously, altering the image overall. However, you can adjust the channels one at a time. If an image is too green, you can select the Red channel in the Channel drop-down menu at the top of both Curves and Levels. You can add more red to the image overall by pulling up in the middle of the curve or moving the slider to the left in the Levels. When you add red to the midtones, you lighten the image (Figure 7.40).

Figure 7.40 *Raising the red midtones to add red*

The Opposite: Lowering the Red Channel

If you pull the red curve down or move the Levels slider to the left, you remove red from the image and, in the process, add its RGB opposite, blue-green. This mainly affects the midtones and darkens the image (Figure 7.41).

Figure 7.41 *Lowering the red midtones to reduce red and add green*

The same holds true for the other color channels. Pull up on the Blue curve, or move the Levels slider to the right, to add blue and make the image lighter. Do the opposite, and you remove blue and add its RGB opposite color, yellow. Pull up on the Green curve, or move the Levels slider to the right, to add green and make the image lighter. Do the opposite, and you remove green and add its RGB opposite, magenta-red.

Why Curves?

At this point, you may be thinking "If Curves and Levels do the same thing, and Curves is more complicated, why shouldn't I stick to Levels?" The answer is that you'd be selling yourself short. Curves can do many things that Levels can't. For instance, Curves allows you to make highlights brighter and shadows darker, all in one economical move. You create an S curve to do both (Figure 7.42). With only one midtone slider, there is no way to do this in Levels.

When you get more proficient at color correction, Curves is the tool you'll use most often.

Figure 7.42 *Curves as opposed to Levels*

This section merely scratches the surface of the power of color correction. If you want more control over your images, I highly recommend that you seek out *Professional Photoshop: The Classic Guide to Color Correction* by Dan Margulis (Peachpit Press, 2006).

Dan's book is considered the Bible of color correction, and it imparts important lessons for any matte artist. Several editions of this book have been released, but even the first one has enough information for an advanced degree in image wrangling.

Working with Reference Photos

You'll be working on the castle project with reference photos from many different sources, with a range of resolutions. The photo of St. Vitus Cathedral was used as an inspiration for the demonstration castle, so reopen St_Vitus.jpg in the Chapter 5 DVD materials. This is a low-resolution shot taken with an older digital camera, as you'll notice when you crop in on the tower.

Duplicate the Blue channel, and create a high-contrast matte to separate the building and the sky. Invert the channel, load the selection for the building, and extract the upper-left tower for use on the front towers of the castle.

Copy and paste the tower into the castle file; place it over the textured drawing of the front-left tower. Choose Edit → Transform → Distort. Now, distort the tower to match the drawing. By pulling down on the left side of the distortion box, you make the tower's ellipses line up with the drawing. Scale the tower 95% horizontally and 104% vertically to fit (Figure 7.43). Name the layer FrontTowers, and move it between the Masks and Form groups.

Warping a Tower

Next, open GalataTower.jpg from the Chapter 7 DVD materials. This is a much higher-resolution image, so it will require less overpainting for the project. Again, duplicate the Blue channel, and create a high-contrast matte to extract the tower. Copy and paste it into the castle project.

The tower is larger than you need, so scale it down 36% horizontally and 44% vertically using the Transform tool. Press Return/Enter to accept the transform.

Notice that the ellipses on the tower are flat and don't match the drawing. To fix this, choose Edit → Transform → Warp to warp the tower to match the drawing's ellipses (Figure 7.44). Name the layer MainTower, and move it below the FrontTowers layer between the Masks and Form groups.

Figure 7.43 *Distorting a tower into position*

Figure 7.44 *Warping a tower to match the ellipses in the drawing*

Color-Correcting the Towers

You have two towers correctly sized and distorted to match the drawing, but they're in very different color spaces. The tower on the FrontTowers layer is green and has a cool cast, whereas the large tower on the MainTower layer is brown and has a warm cast. Move the towers on each layer off to the right of the drawing, side by side, so you can concentrate on matching their colors using Curves.

For the green tower, go to the Green channel and pull down the white point to get rid of the overall green cast. Pull down the midtone for the Red channel to get rid of the red in the stains on the tower, and pull up the midtones on the RGB curve to lighten the overall file (Figure 7.45).

For the main tower, pull down the white point on the Red channel, and pull a little less on the Green and Blue channels, respectively. Raise the highlight midtones on the RGB curve to lighten the tower. Now both towers are in the same color family and make an excellent base over which to paint (Figure 7.46).

Finishing the Towers

With your photo reference sized and color-corrected, you need to do some painting to make these pieces a seamless part of the castle. Begin with the front tower.

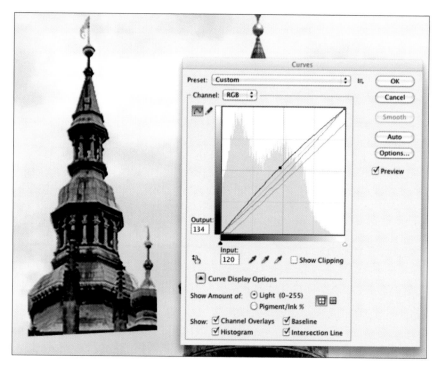

Figure 7.45 *Use Curves to color-correct the green tower.*

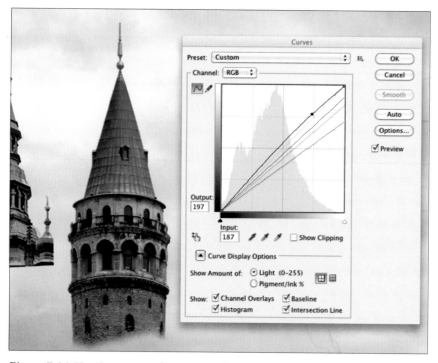

Figure 7.46 *Use Curves to color-correct the main tower.*

This is a three-step process:

1. Look through the reference photos on the DVD for an image that works well for the bottom of the tower. For instance, warwick24.jpg in the www.great-castles.com folder has a detailed tower base. Marquee-select the entire tower, and copy it. Paste it into the castle project, and position it above the FrontTowers layer (Figure 7.47). Scale it down so it fits right below the green tower. Name the new layer TowerBase.

2. On the FrontTowers layer, delete the extraneous right-side tower, and paint over the brown pointed tops that appear in front of the green tower.

3. Return to the TowerBase layer. Because there was bright sunlight on the right side of the original photo, you need to do two color corrections. In the Channels panel, look through the RGB channels to find one channel that separates the sunlit side from the shadow side. In this case, the Red channel has the most contrast. Duplicate that channel, and use Curves to create a high-contrast mask that isolates the light side of the tower from the darker side.

   You also need to remove the yellow cast by pulling the white point to the left on the Blue curve. Remove some of the red by pulling the white point down on the Red curve. Darken the side of the tower overall by pulling down on the RGB midtones and white point (Figure 7.48).

4. With the light side less conspicuous, press Command/Ctrl+D to deselect the light side and correct the entire tower base. Remove more of the yellow and red using Curves, and pull in the black point to make the darks darker. You can also press Command/Ctrl+U to bring up hue/Saturation and desaturate all of the color. When you're finished, the tower base should have the same color tone as the tower top (Figure 7.49).

Figure 7.47 Add a tower base for the FrontTowers layer.

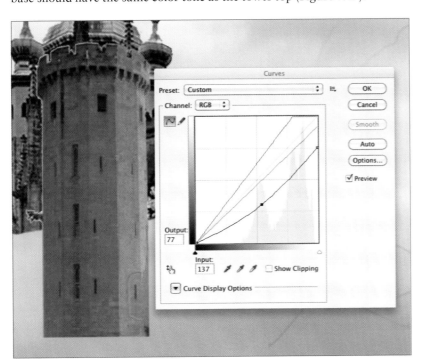

Figure 7.48 Curve correction for the light side of the tower base

5. Now, paint! You have a template for the entire tower, so you need to clean up the soft edges to merge the two pieces. You can alter the photo reference to further refine the image. Don't be restricted by the photo reference: use it as a starting point that can be reworked to match your vision and composition (Figure 7.50).

When the tower base is completed, make sure TowerBase is directly above the FrontTowers layer. Select TowerBase, and press Command/Ctrl+E to merge the layers. The entire front tower should be on the FrontTowers layer.

Follow the same process for the MainTower layer. The original tower photo is of better quality, so you'll have less painting to do to get this looking great.

Figure 7.49
Color-correcting the entire tower base

Figure 7.50
Painting over the photo reference to finish the tower

The main tower top is sized and distorted into perspective, but the tower needs a base. Turn on the visibility of the BigTextureSection layer in TexturesGroup, and select a section of it to use as the tower base. Copy the section out of the layer, and turn off the visibility of BigTextureSection again. Paste the stone texture above the MainTower layer, and warp it into perspective to match the tower top (Figure 7.51).

Line up the base with the tower, and paint the join between the base and top. Feel free to add new details and adjust the tower to your liking. For this final tower, I added a flag and some spiky points, tapered the base of the tower top, added more blue in Curves, and painted a shadow core (Figure 7.52).

If you used more than one layer to create the main tower, merge them all into the MainTower layer. Move both towers into place over the castle.

Figure 7.51
Reusing the warped stone texture to create a tower base

Figure 7.52
Finished main tower

Repeating Details

Architects use design motifs to embellish and unify a structure. Therefore, when you use different photo references, you should decide which details will be a recurring theme. Otherwise, the overly busy edifice won't coalesce into a believable structure. In this castle project, the crenellations are a unifying design motif that can be used throughout the castle. Open `DromolandCastle.jpg` from the Chapter 7 DVD materials; this is a photo of one of the best-preserved castles in Ireland, and you'll borrow some of its detailing for this project. Here are the four steps to create a finished crenellated wall top:

1. Marquee off and copy the crenellations at the top of Dromoland Castle above the entrance. Paste the section of eight crenellations into your castle file. To obtain additional decorative features, note the interesting detail at the top of the left bastion (square corner structure). Marquee off a selection of the arched points, and copy and paste them below the section of crenellations you already pasted in (Figure 7.53).

Figure 7.53 *Combining selections from references to add detail to the castle*

2. The arched points are the wrong size. Scale them larger so a set of two points appears below each square crenellation. Color-correct the detail with Curves to match the color of the two towers.

   There is more to do. The arched stone details under the square crenellations are soft and not in proper perspective. Rather than repaint them all, select one of the lower-arched details and spend your time painting it to your satisfaction. When one looks great, marquee-select it, and duplicate it to the right to cover up one of the unfinished arched details (Figure 7.54). Fix up the join between the two to blend them together.

Figure 7.54 *Color-correct and refine the crenellation details.*

3. Duplicate the two lower-arched details you've doctored to get a complete line of them. Because you've duplicated and reused one arched detail for the entire line, add some defects, stains, and cracks to make each detail look slightly different. Color-correct and paint the top crenellations to give them more finish (Figure 7.55).

Figure 7.55 *Finished crenellations*

With your design work completed, duplicate the crenellations and create an extended section with 14 crenellations. If you've used more than one layer to create the crenellations, merge them all into one and name the layer Crenellations. Marquee-select the line of 14 crenellations, and copy-drag to duplicate it; you want to keep a clean copy to reuse on the rest of the walls.

Turn on the visibility of the Perspective group, and set the opacity of the group to 50% so it isn't so intrusive. Drag the duplicate down to the front-left wall, and, consulting the left perspective lines, carefully line it up with the wall. Use the perspective drawing as a template, and add the same number of crenellations (Figure 7.56).

Figure 7.56 Duplicating and setting crenellations into perspective

Add crenellations to the top of all the walls and bastions. Keep this rule in mind when you're duplicating references: every time you scale or distort a piece of reference, you lose some sharpness and resolution. You'll be tempted to use the same sample to populate every surface, but reusing it too many times will degrade the image. Therefore, after using the same section a few times, go back to the original undistorted section at the top of the file and take a new sampling to keep the material crisp (Figure 7.57).

Either trim the crenellations to size or apply a layer mask. You can turn off the Perspective group.

Figure 7.57 Adding crenellations to all the walls

Finishing the Castle

Now that you've finished two towers and the crenellations, you've acquired the skills and techniques to go off on your own. Finish the castle, and create the bridge. Before you do, let's review the basic procedure governing the use of reference material:

1. Find a piece of photo reference that complements the castle. Marquee-select the portion you plan to use, and copy and paste it into the project.
2. Scale, distort, or warp the image to fit the intended space, following the perspective guides.
3. Color-correct the new addition so it matches the other elements.
4. Paint on top of the image to add the final polish and make it a seamless part of the whole. As a rule, every piece of photo reference requires some degree of overpainting to reach an optimal state.

You have four folders full of excellent photo references for this project, so go through and complete this castle on your own.

Castle Bits

While working on a project, I keep a file open in which to store reference elements I'm using. I paste them into this file before I have manipulated, distorted, or color corrected them so I can re-use them in their original state. This allows me to grab an element that I'm using without having to stop and return to the original file they were copied out of. For your reference, I've included the file for this project, aptly called `CastleBits.psd`. You'll find some ready-for-use details that you can incorporate into the castle (Figure 7.58).

Figure 7.58 `CastleBits` *file with many of the details used to create this project*

When you're finished creating the towers for the castle, select all the layers you used to create them and place them in a new group called **TowersGroup**. This new group should be above the Form group.

Copying the Castle Walls

In the process of texturing the towers, if you've varied at all from your perspective drawing, the Form group will no longer exactly match the textured castle. You'll want to turn off the visibility of the Form group, but when you do, the castle walls disappear. You need to copy all the information from the walls and crenellations onto a new layer. Doing so will also make it easier to color-correct the walls to match the rest of the castle.

Turn off TowersGroup, and turn on the Form group if you turned it off. Turn on the Crenellation layers. The walls should now show up clearly with textures and shadows. Make a selection containing just the castle walls. Shift+Command/Ctrl+C to copy-merge the selection (Figure 7.59). Paste it into a new layer above TowersGroup, and name the new layer **CastleWalls**.

Figure 7.59 Copy-merge the selection containing the castle walls.

Cool down the castle walls in Curves to match the towers. On separate layers, add the castle entrance and whatever details you would like to complete the castle (Figure 7.60). The buttresses on the left side of the castle are on another layer on top of CastleWalls.

Turning Off the Form Group

Select the CastleWalls layer, the layer on which you painted the entrance, and whatever other layers you used to complete the walls, and put them in a new group called WallsGroup. You can now turn on TowersGroup and turn off the Form group. On your own, complete the flame holders in front of the castle, the bridge, the front steps, and whatever flourishes you feel like adding.

After you color-correct the entire castle to a uniform cool coloration, the project now looks like Figure 7.61.

Figure 7.60 *Castle walls complete with an entrance, windows, and buttresses*

Figure 7.61 *Finished photo textures on the castle*

Next, let's turn our attention to darkening the sky, adding the background, and toning the castle.

Figure 7.62 Original concept sketch

Figure 7.63 Use the Gradient tool on the SkyMultiply layer to darken the plate.

Figure 7.64 Darkening the castle to match the sky

Lighting the Scene

Right about now, you may be thinking, "Dude, you have a big blue-gray castle in the picture that looks nothing like the concept sketch (Figure 7.62). What gives?"

What has happened is that the project is evolving in stages. To do the texturing, you don't want to be preoccupied with the lighting. You'll now add dramatic lighting to the piece and finish it.

Darkening the Sky

Open the concept sketch, CastleConcept_Horror.psd from the Chapter 3 DVD materials. You'll use it as a reference while you tint the sky.

Create a new layer called **SkyMultiply** above the Plate layer, and set the layer blending mode to Multiply. Select the Gradient tool, and choose a dark blue like the one at the top of the sky in the concept painting with an RGB setting of 15, 60, 75. With the Gradient tool set to Foreground To Transparent, drag down from the top to darken the sky and up from the bottom to darken the ocean and hill. Check the concept sketch to see that you have a similar level of darkening (Figure 7.63).

Darkening the Castle

The castle is too light for the night setting. At the top of the Layers panel, above WallsGroup and TowersGroup, create a new layer. Set the layer blending mode to Multiply, and name the layer **CastleBlueMultiply**.

Fill the entire layer with a dark blue with an RGB reading of 24, 55, 70. Make a selection containing the castle, bridge, and flame holders, and make it into a layer mask for the CastleBlueMultiply layer. Now the dark blue color will be confined to the selected area of the castle that is white in the mask. Depending on how dark you want the castle, the color may be overpowering; adjust the opacity of the layer to around 70% (Figure 7.64).

One of the great things about a layer mask is that you can paint into it. This allows you to control what sections of the layer show through. The light side of the castle is much too dark because of the Multiply layer you just applied. Load the selections for the light side of the castle from the Masks group: LowerWallLight, UpperWallLight, Towers1, and Towers2. Then, with a soft variable-opacity brush with black selected in the Color Picker, paint into the layer mask to block some of the CastleBlueMultiply layer and let more of the light-side walls and towers show through.

Adding Flames

At this point, the castle looks unoccupied. It's time to add some life by adding lights. The flame holders should be ablaze, so add a new layer set to Lighten. Name the layer **Flames**. For the fire effect, paint a center core of pure yellow and add a ragged edge of red (Figure 7.65).

The flames cast a warm light on nearby surfaces, allowing you to add some contrasting orange to an otherwise cool composition. Add a new layer on top of the CastleBlueMultiply layer, and set the blending mode to Overlay. Name the layer **OrangeOverlay**. With a soft round brush with variable opacity and orange selected in the Color Picker, paint pools of warm light around the base of the flame holders. The Overlay blending mode is a powerful way to add colored light to a surface. It colors the layer with which it's blending but still allows the underlying texture to show through.

Figure 7.65 Adding flames

Load the selection for the light-side lower walls. In the vicinity of the flame holders, paint warm light on the castle wall and towers near the entrance. Add pools of light on the bridge as cast by the flame holders. Select CastleBlueMultiply, OrangeOverlay, Flames, and any other layers you used to tone the castle, and place them in a new Group named **Toning+Details**. This group should be above WallsGroup and TowersGroup.

When you're finished, the castle should look like Figure 7.66.

Creating the Sky

You'll create the sky through a layering process, arranging different sections of clouds on top of each other to achieve a complex sky. You can find the photo reference for the sky on the DVD in the www.cgtextures.com folder. Open

Figure 7.66 Adding warm light from flames to nearby surfaces

Figure 7.67 Adding a photo reference of clouds

Figure 7.68 Tint the clouds to match the plate.

FullskiesSunset0106_1_L.jpg, and copy it into the project just above the SkyMultiply and Plate layers. Name the new layer **Sky**. Position and scale it behind the castle until you find a section of the clouds you like. In order to concentrate on the sky, turn off the visibility of the castle (Figure 7.67).

Fill the sky with the same dark blue color you used to multiply the Plate layer, with the fill blending mode set to Multiply and opacity set to 60%. The sky will look too yellow, so use Curves to add some blue in the midtones, and raise the white point to add more contrast in the cloud tops. The cloud cover is beginning to resemble the concept sketch (Figure 7.68).

Moonlight

Add the moon either by painting it or by using the moon in the CastleBits.psd file. Name the layer **moon**. With the moon in place, duplicate it, and move the duplicated moon below the original in the Layers panel. Select all, and blur the copy of the moon with a Gaussian blur set to a radius of 32 pixels to add a glow. Name the blurred moon **MoonGlow**.

Adding a rim of clouds around the moon will intensify the drama of the sky. For this task, select the clouds on the left that have a slight curve to them (Figure 7.69).

Press Command/Ctrl+J to copy the strip of clouds, and name the new layer MoonClouds. Choose Edit → Transform → Warp, and warp the clouds around the moon to create a rim-lighting effect. Applying an extreme warp like this twists the image dramatically; but as long as your reference is of good quality, the distorted version will still be sharp (Figure 7.70).

Figure 7.69 Add the moon as the primary light source, and select an area of clouds for reuse.

Figure 7.70 Warping clouds to add rim lighting

Highlighting the Clouds

Using the Dodge tool  set to Midtones, at a very low opacity, paint over the edges of the clouds surrounding the moon. The Dodge tool highlights and adds contrast to the existing tones. To complete the spiraling of clouds around the moon, grab a section of clouds from the left side of the sky, and distort them above the moon to create a tunneling effect. Feel free to rearrange the clouds and paint into the sky to get the most dramatic effect you can. When you're finished, select all the layers making up the sky, including the moon, and place them in a new group called **SkyGroup**.

The Background Elements

The concept sketch has a mountain range in the background that you'll now add to your composition. The www.environmental-textures.com folder contains several reference shots you can use. As before, copy the section of reference you want, color-correct it, and then multiply blue over it to match the rest of the scene.

You can build the background castle from sections of the foreground castle that are scaled and rearranged. Paint a path leading down to the bridge connecting the two castles. As a final touch, make a new layer behind the mountains, and paint a red glow with a large soft brush (Figure 7.71). Select all the layers you used to create the background, and place them in a new group named **B-group**.

Figure 7.71 Finished sky with a red glow, and the background mountain range

Figure 7.72 *Final castle for 3D projection*

The Top Painting Layer

Many matte artists add a final layer at this point on which to make any last-minute corrections. This final layer sits above all the others. Let's add such a layer now, and call it **TopPainting**. You can paint directly on this layer instead of returning to the lower layers of the project. If you try to work on a layer below CastleBlueMultiply or OrangeOverlay, you'll find it difficult because those layers have a powerful effect on the underlying pixels. A top paint layer is where you can tweak any layer requiring work and bring the entire composition up to your standards of finish.

The final castle should resemble Figure 7.72.

The final demonstration file is included on the Chapter 7 DVD: `Castle_Final_Textures.psd`.

Assignment: Texture and Finish Your Castle

Using the form drawing you created of your own castle in Chapter 6: "Form," add photographic textures and finish your castle matte painting. Follow these steps:

1. Add a stone texture to your entire structure using the Soft Light blending mode to create a varied base tone.
2. Find photographic reference to complement your design, and color correct, scale, and paint over it to enhance your vision of the castle.
3. Add a dramatic sky.
4. Use layers of color set to Multiply, or Overlay, to tint and enhance the mood of your scene.

Your finished castle matte painting will be used in the next chapter, "Preparing Your Photoshop File for Camera Projection in Maya."

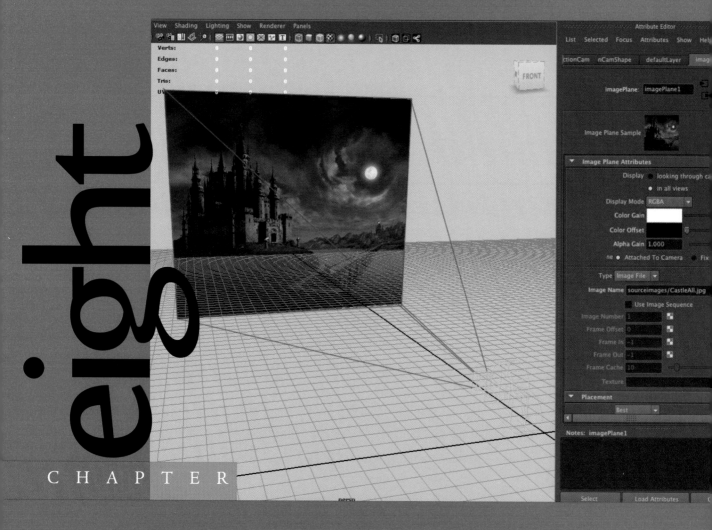

eight

CHAPTER

Preparing Your Photoshop File for Camera Projection in Maya

You will use the castle *painting you created in Chapters 3–7 to learn an advanced matte painting technique called* camera projection. *Camera projection uses a digital camera to project a painting onto 3D geometry.*

In this chapter, you'll learn how to prepare your Photoshop files for use in Maya. You'll also learn how to set up an image plane as reference for creating the 3D geometry.

What is Camera Projection?

Camera projection shines an image onto blank 3D forms that are shaped to match the elements in the image. In this project, six elements from the castle matte painting—the hill, castle walls, turrets, bridge, sky, and water—will have a corresponding 3D shapes created to receive the projected image. You'll model and carefully line up these shapes with the painting. The magic occurs when the scene is re-photographed using a moving camera while leaving the projector in the same spot. It will look as though the painting has come to life in full 3D.

Doing camera projection in Maya involves multiple steps, and initially it can seem intimidating. Don't worry—the next three chapters will take a detailed look at the process with corresponding graphics. Make sure you follow the steps in sequence. If you miss a step, you may find that your projection won't work, and it can be frustrating to figure out exactly where you went wrong.

This demonstration uses Maya 2011, but any version of Maya will work. Also, most other 3D programs, including Cinema 4D, 3D Studio Max, and LightWave, offer similar functionality.

Getting Started in Camera Projection

The first step in camera projection is to prepare your painting for use in Maya. Unless you are a very experienced Maya user, I recommend that you work along with the demonstration using the same file shown in the figures. At the end of the chapter, you will be asked to prepare your own castle painting the same way. Open the demonstration castle painting completed at the end of Chapter 7, Castle_Final_Textures.psd (Figure 8.1).

Next, you'll break up the painting into the smallest number of layers that will produce acceptable results. When you prepare your own file for camera projection at the end of the chapter, you'll probably want to add more layers: for instance, having a separate piece of geometry for each tower and flying buttress. For the first runthrough, however, it's a good idea to keep it simple and to concentrate on the central elements of the painting. This demonstration will be made from six pieces of geometry:

- Three simple cubes for the bridge, the castle walls, and the castle towers
- Two planes for the sky and the water
- One cube with many subdivisions so that you can practice using the Sculpt Geometry tool

Figure 8.1 Final Photoshop painting from Chapter 7

Reduce the File to Six Layers

You'll reduce the Photoshop file to six layers—one for each element in the project. The file created at the end of the last chapter has far too many layers, and will be impossible to bring into Maya without substantial layer reduction. You keep the original, multi-layer version in case the director asks for changes or revisions, so save the file you will reduce under another name, Castle_6_Layers.psd. Change the file from 16-bit to 8-bit by choosing Image → Mode → 8 bits/Channel.

> Even though you will be required to work in 16-bit for professional projects, importing 16-bit files into Maya is more complicated. In order to keep this first camera projection as simple as possible, you will work with an 8-bit file.

You must reduce your painting file to only six layers. Study this diagram to see the six layers you'll be using (Figure 8.2).

Figure 8.2 Diagram of the castle broken up into six layers

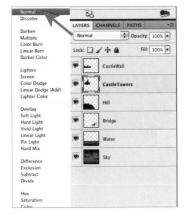

Figure 8.3 All Photoshop layers must be set to Normal for the blend mode.

Make sure the blending mode for each layer is set to Normal (Figure 8.3). The layers where you used a blending or transfer mode to get a particular effect will not import into Maya with the effect intact. For instance, where you applied a stone texture to a wall or tower using the Soft Light transfer mode, you must merge the texture and the wall together so that the final layer is set to normal.

After you reduce the layers to the minimum needed for this first camera projection, delete all the alpha channels and paths (Figure 8.4). Now you're ready to prepare the files for Maya. You can open the final file, ready for Maya on the DVD, Castle_ 6_Layers_Demo.psd, to compare to your reduced version.

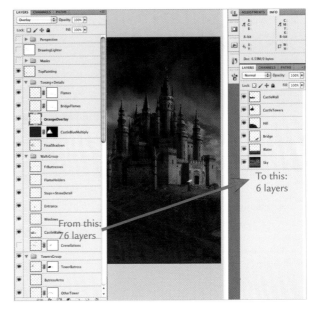

Figure 8.4 Reduce the number of layers, and delete all alpha channels and paths.

Figure 8.5 Make the Hill layer the only visible layer

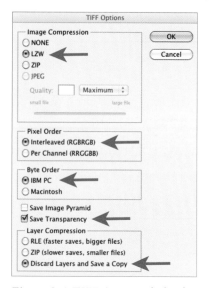

Figure 8.6 TIFF Options dialog box

Figure 8.7 Layers and Channels panels for the prepared TIFF color file

Preparing the Color Channels

To prepare the color channels in Photoshop for use in Maya camera projection, each layer must be individually written as a separate file. In Photoshop, display one layer at a time so that the checkerboard transparency pattern is behind the image. Let's start with the Hill layer. Turn off all of the layers except Hill (Figure 8.5).

Choose File → Save As. The Save dialog opens. It's important to name each file distinctively so that you can recognize the files when you get into Maya. Because this is the hill, name the file `Hill.tif`. Choose TIFF from the Format drop-down list. Uncheck Layers in the Save Options area, and click Save. The TIFF Options dialog box opens.

Choose the following options (Figure 8.6):

- Image Compression: LZW
- Pixel Order: Interleaved
- Byte Order: IBM PC
- Save Transparency: select, and click Yes in the dialog box that opens asking if you want to save the transparency information
- Layer Compression: Discard Layers And Save A Copy

Click OK in the upper-right corner to close the TIFF Options dialog box.

When you've completed the first layer, open it and make sure it matches these settings (Figure 8.7):

- There should be only one layer, called Layer 0.
- There should be no alpha channels.
- A checkerboard pattern should be visible in the background to show transparency. If the background is filled with solid white, the TIFF settings aren't correct.

You'll need to create a color file for each layer in the Photoshop file. Because you have six layers, repeat the previous process six times. Name the TIFF color files the same as the layer names in your castle painting file.

Preparing the Alpha Channels

The next step is to prepare an alpha channel for each layer. You deleted all the alpha channels from the castle painting file, so you'll create new alpha channels for each of the six color files you created previously. Maya works best if you save the alpha channels as separate files.

You'll use these files in Maya to indicate what part of the image needs to be transparent. In most other 3D programs, black means transparent and white means opaque. In Maya, this standard is reversed, with white meaning transparent and black meaning opaque; so, the alpha channels you create in Photoshop must be inverted for Maya.

> If you're using 3D Studio Max or Cinema 4D, you won't invert the alpha channels.

In the Photoshop file, make sure only the Hill layer is visible; select the Hill layer in the Layers panel if it isn't already selected. Choose Image → Apply Image. The Apply Image dialog box appears. Choose the following options (Figure 8.8):

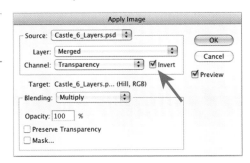

Figure 8.8 *Apply Image settings for the alpha channel*

- Source: the document you're working on
- Layer: Merged
- Channel: Transparency
- Invert: select
- Blending: Multiply

Click OK to accept these options.

By selecting Invert, you change black to white and white to black so that the alpha channel will work properly with Maya transparency.

Save the resulting black-and-white file as a TIFF using the same settings you used for the color channel (Figure 8.6). There is one significant difference: Save Transparency is grayed out, because there is no transparency in the image (Figure 8.9). Save the alpha channel with the same name as the color file, but append _alpha to the name: Hill_alpha.tif. Carefully following this naming convention will be extremely helpful when you're trying to figure out where the files go in Maya. Make sure Discard Layers And Save A Copy is selected in the TIFF Options dialog box.

Figure 8.9 *Final prepared Hill layer alpha channel*

By using Image → Apply Image, you fill the pixels of the layer with black. You want the layer's color back, so undo the Apply Image using Command/Ctrl+Z.

Now, do the same thing for each layer. Because you have 6 layers, you'll end up with 12 separate files: one color file and one alpha channel file for each layer (Figure 8.10). You'll have an alpha channel file for the Sky layer, but it will be solid black because there are no transparent areas.

You need one final file: prepare a file with the entire painting on it. This complete image, containing all the layers, will be your reference while modeling in Maya. You can save it as a TIFF file or as a JPEG.

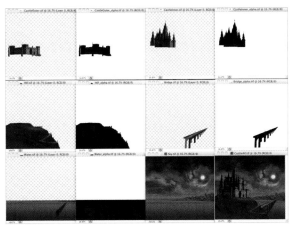

Figure 8.10 *One color file and one alpha file for each layer, and one reference file*

Check the File Size

Double-check to be sure none of your files are noticeably larger than other files. If there is one unusually large file, you may have mistakenly saved the TIFF file with all its layers, in which case it won't work in Maya (Figure 8.11). Reopen the file, and resave it with Discard Layers And Save A Copy selected in the TIFF options.

Name	▲	Date Modified	Size	Kind
Bridge_alpha.tif		Today, 1:30 PM	184 KB	Adobe...FF file
Bridge.tif		Today, 1:26 PM	442 KB	Adobe...FF file
CastleAll.jpg		Feb 7, 2010 3:35 PM	762 KB	Adobe...EG file
CastleAll.tif		Today, 1:32 PM	4.7 MB	Adobe...FF file
CastleTowers_alpha.tif		Today, 1:25 PM	188 KB	Adobe...FF file
CastleTowers.tif		Today, 1:33 PM	860 KB	Adobe...FF file
CastleWalls_alpha.tif		Today, 1:27 PM	180 KB	Adobe...FF file
CastleWalls.tif		Today, 1:31 PM	778 KB	Adobe...FF file
Hill_alpha.tif		Today, 1:50 PM	156 KB	Adobe...FF file
Hill.tif		Today, 1:23 PM	17.9 MB	Adobe...FF file
Sky_alpha.tif		Today, 1:29 PM	139 KB	Adobe...FF file
Sky.tif		Today, 1:24 PM	2.9 MB	Adobe...FF file

Figure 8.11 One file is much larger than the others.

Setting Up for Camera Projection

If you're new to Maya, it's a good idea to watch the Essential Skills Movies that appear when you first start Maya. If they don't come up, choose Help → Learning Movies. There are seven movies, each about a minute long, and they will provide you with the Maya basics to do this lesson.

Set the Project Folder

After you open Maya, set up a new project by choosing File → Project → New to create a new project folder (Figure 8.12). Name the new project Castle_Project. You'll use this project folder for the entire camera projection, so locate it somewhere convenient on your hard drive.

Figure 8.12 Open Maya, and set up a new project file.

Click Use Defaults, and then click Accept (Figure 8.13). Doing so creates a new project folder to organize your files. Notice that because you chose Use Defaults, Maya creates many different folders inside your project folder—including images, mel, scenes, and sourceimages—which will hold the different assets you create for the project. You should now move all the color and alpha channel files for the castle layers into the sourceimages folder in the Castle_Project folder you just created.

Save your Maya file to the scenes file in the Maya project folder directory. Maya files can be saved as either Maya Binary (.mb) or Maya ASCII (.ma) files. Save the file as a .ma file.

Create a Projection Camera

Next, create a new projection camera to use to line up your geometry. To do so, choose Create → Cameras → Camera, and click the box to the right of Camera menu item to open the Create Camera Options dialog box (Figure 8.14).

Figure 8.13 Create a new Maya project folder.

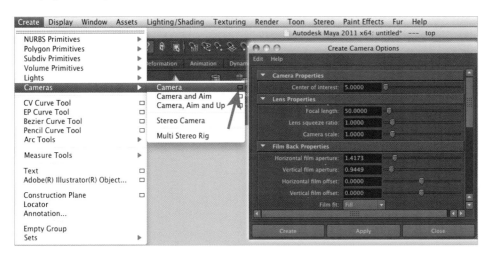

Figure 8.14 Create Camera Options dialog box

You need to estimate the focal length of the new camera. Because you're working on a painted scene, you don't have a focal length with which to work. However, since the demonstration file was not created using extreme vanishing points, you can make an intelligent guess regarding the focal length. Start by entering 50 mm for the focal length under Lens Properties. You can leave the rest of the properties at their defaults for the time being. Click Create to close the dialog box.

Choose Window → Outliner to open the Outliner, which lists all the objects, lights, and cameras in the scene (Figure 8.15). Double-click the default camera name, camera1, and rename it **projectionCam** because you'll be projecting the painting from this camera.

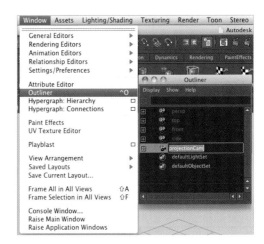

Figure 8.15 Maya Outliner window

Set the Rendering Parameters

Open Render Settings to input your rendering parameters. To do so, on the top menu, click the icon that resembles a clapboard with two dots next to it ▣ .

Choose the following (Figure 8.16):

- File Name Prefix: Castle_Project.
- Image Format: Maya IFF. Usually, you'll want to render out to a file sequence rather than a QuickTime movie. If you render out to a movie and the render crashes, you lose all your work.
- Frame/Animation Ext: name.#.ext.
- Frame Padding: 4.
- Start Frame and End frame: 1 and 200.
- Alpha Channel (Mask): deselect, because you won't need the alpha channel in your render.
- Width and Height: the width and height of your original Photoshop file. This size should exactly match the TIFF files you prepared for each layer.

One of the most common errors I see in file setup by students is not matching the Width and Height to the actual file size of the images to be projected. Double check that this dimension matches the original Photoshop file!

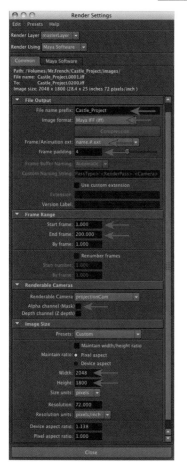

After you enter the width and height of your painting, Maya automatically calculates the device aspect ratio by dividing the TIFF file by dividing the TIFF file's width by the height. In this case, it's 2,048 divided by 1,800, or 1.138.

Set the Film Aspect Ratio

You need to use the device aspect ratio from the Render Settings dialog box in another place: the number must be entered in the Film Aspect Ratio setting in the projectionCamShape node. Leave the Render Settings dialog box open, and move it to one side while you adjust the film aspect ratio.

To open the projectionCamShape node in the Maya Attribute Editor, do the following:

1. Select projectionCam in the Outliner by clicking the name.
2. Choose Window → Attribute Editor. The Attribute Editor lists the parameters of any object you have selected.
3. The projectionCamShape attributes appear in the Attribute Editor.
4. Move down to the Film Back rollout, and enter the number from the Render Settings Device Aspect Ratio setting into the Film Aspect Ratio field (see Figure 8.17).

The device aspect ratio and film aspect ratio are determined by the dimensions of the castle painting and the TIFF files you prepared. Double-check to see that these two numbers are the same, and correct them for your files if necessary. If the values aren't the same, the projection won't line up!

Figure 8.16 Maya Render Settings dialog box

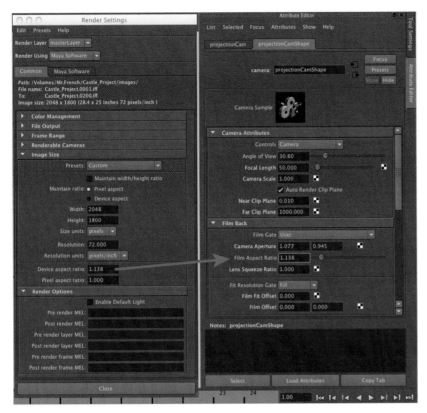

Figure 8.17 *Device aspect ratio and film aspect ratio*

Turn off the Default Light

You must attend to one last detail in the Render
Settings dialog box: you need to turn off the
default light. To do so, deselect Enable Default
Light (Figure 8.18). You may need to expand or
scroll down in the Render Options rollout to get
to this setting, because it's at the bottom.

You don't need the default light. You'll use the
lighting from your painting, not Maya's 3D lights, to
illuminate your scene. Close the Render Settings dialog and the Outliner.

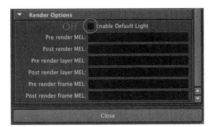

Figure 8.18 *Turn off Enable Default
Light*

Adding the Image Plane

Now you'll add an image plane to projectionCam to use as a reference for modeling. An
image plane is attached to a particular camera, and it serves as a backdrop for that camera.
The image is fixed to the camera at a distance you set, so it moves when the camera moves
in any direction (Figure 8.19). By default, the camera doesn't have an image plane attached
to it.

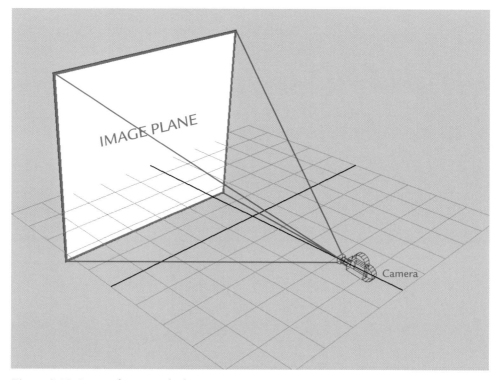

Figure 8.19 Image plane attached to a camera

Assign the Image Plane to the projectionCam

You need to assign the full castle painting as the image plane, or backdrop, for projectionCam. Depending on how your interface is set up, you may have 1–4 viewport panels visible. Click inside any one of the viewport panels. At the top of each viewport panel is a menu—a unique set of controls that only pertains to that view. In the viewport menu, choose Panels → Perspective → projectionCam to set that viewport to see the scene from projectionCam (Figure 8.20).

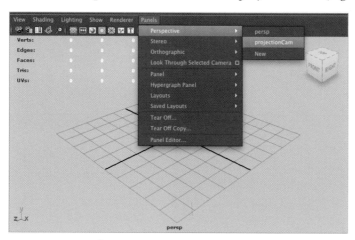

Figure 8.20 Set the viewport to projectionCam.

Even though you set the viewport to projectionCam, you still need to select the camera. From the viewport menu, choose View → Select Camera to select the projectionCam camera (Figure 8.21). You could have done this through the Outliner window, but this way is handier because you don't need to leave the view to select your camera.

At this point, you can add the image plane. With your camera selected, choose View → Image Plane → Import Image, and import the flattened version of the painting showing all the layers. You may have saved this as either a JPEG file or a TIFF; either will work (Figure 8.22). You'll use this plane to line up the geometry.

Figure 8.21 *Select projectionCam to add the image plane.*

Figure 8.22 *Import the image plane.*

Turn on the Resolution Gate

With projectionCam still selected, choose View → Camera Settings → Resolution Gate. Turning on Resolution Gate gives you some extra space around the image in the viewport (Figure 8.23). This ensures that you can see the entire image.

Image Plane Attributes

You should position the image plane so it fills the view of the camera entirely. To do so, choose View → Image Plane → Image Plane Attributes → imagePlane1 (Figure 8.24).

Figure 8.23 *Turn on Resolution Gate.*

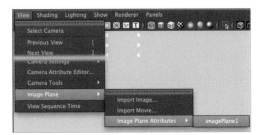

Figure 8.24 *Image plane attributes*

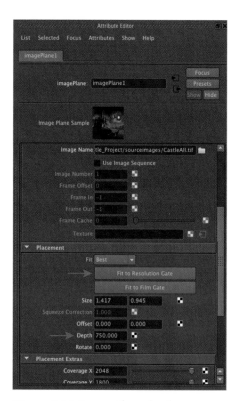

Figure 8.25 Image plane depth

Figure 8.26 Grid Options dialog box

With the image plane attributes open, scroll down to the Placement rollout, and click Fit To Resolution Gate. By adjusting Depth to 750, you move the image plane further out to make room for the geometry you'll add to the scene (Figure 8.25).

> The view of the castle painting in the projectionCam viewport won't change, because no matter how far away or near the image plane is, it always fills the viewport.

Positioning the Camera Using the Reference Grid

You now must position the camera in reference to the grid. If the grid isn't showing, make sure Display → Grid is selected. Then, in the viewport menu, make sure the grid icon is selected ◈.

The grid is initially too small. You can enlarge it by choosing Display → Grid and selecting the box alongside the menu item to open the Grid Options dialog box. Set Grid Lines Every to 10 and Subdivisions to 1 units to make the viewports more readable. Extending Length And Width to 1000 will help you find the horizon line (Figure 8.26).

You need to move the camera around until the grid aligns with the horizon in the picture. The image plane blocks part of the view of the grid, so look beyond the image plane on both sides to find the furthest visible line on the grid. Make sure the grid is positioned right on the horizon line (Figure 8.27).

Now your Photoshop files have been readied for Maya, and the full painting is loaded onto an image plane. You can check what your project should look like at this point on the DVD in the folder `Castle_Project_Chapter_8`. The Maya project file, located inside of the scenes folder, is called `Castle_Project_Chapter_8.ma`. Move the `.ma` file from the DVD into the scenes folder in the `Castle_Project` folder you created earlier in the chapter. When you open this file, choose File → Project → Set and navigate to the `Castle_Project` file in order for the file to find the `CastleAll.jpg` image for the image plane. All the color and alpha channel files should be in the `sourceimages` folder. You can compare yours to the files I set up on the DVD.

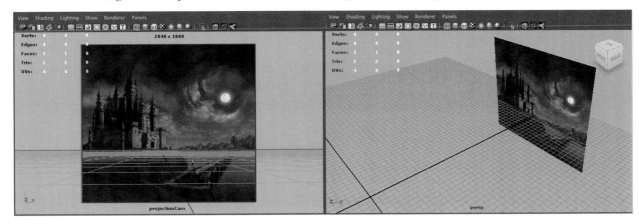

Figure 8.27 Maya image plane setup

Assignment: Prepare Your Castle for Camera Projection, and Set Up the Maya File

Having followed along using the demonstration file, you should now do the same process using your own castle painting finished in Chapter 7. To prepare the painting for camera projection, do the following:

1. Collapse your many layered castle painting file down to a minimum number of layers, with each layer representing a major element in the painting. Suggested layers for the painting are:

   - Two layers for the castle.
   - One layer for the hill the castle is placed on.
   - One layer for the water.
   - One layer for the sky.
   - Additional layers can be created for other major elements in your castle painting.

2. Prepare a color channel, and an alpha channel for each layer.
3. Prepare a file showing the complete painting to use on the background plane.

   Once you open Maya, follow these steps:

1. Set the Rendering Parameters
2. Set the Film Aspect Ratio
3. Uncheck enable Default Light
4. Add the Image Plane
5. Line up the grid to the Image Plane
6. Save your file as CastleProjectStart.ma

   In the next chapter, you'll start modeling the geometry for the camera projection.

Matte Artist Profile: Dylan Cole

Dylan Cole is one of the most exciting talents to enter the world of matte painting in a long time. I first noticed his work on *Daredevil*, where he is credited as the sole matte artist on the production. The matte paintings were breathtaking, and I thought, "There is a guy to watch." His list of films is impressive, including *Lord of the Rings: Return of the King*, *I, Robot*, *The Aviator*, *Superman Returns*, *The Road*, and *2012*. He has recently extended his work into concept art, and worked on *Avatar*, *Tron Legacy*, and *Alice in Wonderland* in that capacity. A wonderful communicator and teacher, he has three training DVDs on matte painting available from Gnomon workshop.

Figure 8.28 Dylan Cole

David Mattingly Welcome Dylan! Thanks for agreeing to be part of *The Digital Matte Painting Handbook*. First, tell me about your upbringing and background.

Dylan Cole Thanks for having me. I was born and raised in Southern California, Vista specifically. My dad was a carpenter and my mom stayed at home until I was in middle school. Then she resumed her career in banking. My dad had learned a lot about drawing from his father. Being a practical carpenter, he believed if you could draw it, you could build it...and if you could build it, you could draw it. Obviously not to be taken literally, but more of a sense of accuracy and pre-planning. I learned all of the fundamentals of perspective from my dad by the time I was 11. I think that was a huge help for me.

I was always interested in art. I was the little kid that would draw cards for their parents for every holiday, though how many moms got Star Destroyers and X-wings on their Mother's Day cards? My mom still has all of that stuff and it cracks me up to see. Definitely some good blackmail material there. It wasn't until I was about 10 that I got more serious about drawing and realized I had a talent for it. I was getting really into comic books so I was drawing that type of stuff for a while until, I got more involved with painting in high school. I went from wanting to be a comic book artist to possibly a sci-fi book cover illustrator. It wasn't until I got the *Art of Star Wars* books that I realized exactly what I wanted to do. Seeing those matte paintings solidified it for me. It was the perfect mix of art, film, and technology. And there was a romantic simplicity to it just being a painting that you created projected up on the screen.

DM Who are your most important artistic influences? When you go to a museum, who is the one artist you always have to seek out?

DC In addition to a ton of matte artists, such as Albert Whitlock, Michael Pangrazio, Syd Dutton, and Robert Stromberg, I love the Hudson River School artists, such as Frederic Church and Albert Bierstadt. My other favorites are the Orientalists, such as Weeks and Gerome. To be able to see some of the work in person was a thrill. The first time I went to the Met in New York, I didn't have much time so I made a beeline straight for the Hudson River School guys. It was the first time I had a seen a Church or Bierstadt in person and it was amazing.

All of the paintings shown in Dylan Cole's profile were done for a gallery show, and not for a specific motion picture. However, they are done in a style identical to his matte paintings.

Figure 8.29 *The River Bathers*

DM Where did you go to school? How important do you think going to art school is for a matte artist?

DC I actually went to UCLA as a Fine Arts major. I wanted more of a university atmosphere. I don't think the art department was a perfect fit for me. It was much more about contemporary fine art and it is a wonderful school for that. I wanted a bit more technical instruction about drawing and painting. So I am largely self taught in those respects. It was great in that I had the freedom to explore many different styles and mediums. My observation of nature and other artists combined with my dad's perspective instruction formed the foundation of my art education. I then got an internship at ILM while I was at UCLA that opened up my eyes to digital matte painting. At the time I knew it was happening, I just had my head in sand and wanted to do it all traditionally. I had just bought a new computer and opened up Photoshop for the first time; I was inexperienced to say the least. So I learned a lot in that summer from some of the best matte artists in the world. Thankfully with my traditional skills I picked up digital painting fairly quickly.

I think art school is very important for a matte artist. Matte painting draws on so any disciplines that it is good to be able to explore all of those, such as drawing, painting, design, photography, 3D tools, even a bit of sculpture. I don't think it is absolutely necessary if you are very driven, but it is a huge help. Plus one of the best things about art school is hanging out and learning from other artists. You also have a built-in network for your career.

Figure 8.30 *Surf Fishing at Sunset*

DM How did you become interested in matte painting? What was your first job as a matte artist? The first time I took note of your work was when *Daredevil* came out, and I was impressed by the beauty and complexity of the matte shots. You seemed to be the only matte artist on the movie—did you do all of the shots?

DC Thanks! Well, I first became interested in matte painting when I saw the *Art of Star Wars* books. Such great work by Michael Pangrazio, Chris Evans, Ralph McQuarrie, Frank Ordaz, and Harrison Ellenshaw. I remember being especially impressed with the Death Star hangar paintings from *Return of the Jedi*. Those shots still hold up well today. I loved the idea that some of the most iconic things of my childhood were just paintings created by an artist on glass or masonite.

My first job as a matte artist was at Illusion Arts on *Time Machine*. I actually didn't do any final matte shots, I was more of a concept artist. I was only there for a little over a month, but I learned a lot from Syd Dutton and the other artists there. It was a great experience. After a stint in Prague as a concept artist on *A Sound of Thunder*, I was at Rhythm and Hues working on *Daredevil*. It was my first time doing final matte paintings for film. I had a blast. I did not do all of the matte paintings, but I did a lot of them. Alex Yerxa did some as well. I did 21 matte paintings in about 12 weeks. Young enthusiasm goes a long way!

I was then off to Weta to work on *Return of the King* as a senior matte painter at the age of 23. I was incredibly excited.

DM You have worked both traditionally and digitally. Speed and economic realities aside, which do you prefer?

DC Well, sadly I was never able to work traditionally as a professional. I really wish I could have done that. I love aspects about both. I love the tactile and emotional quality of working traditionally. I love the paint under the fingernails and actually being physically tired after working on a painting for a long time. However, I love the freedom and speed of digital tools. I feel I can create anything in just a few days and that is very empowering and a lot of fun! I actually have hardly painted traditionally at all in the last ten years. It makes me sad, but I am creatively fulfilled working digitally.

DM When working digitally, what software to you use? How much 3D do you use in your work? Do you do your own compositing?

DC I use Photoshop for most of the work that I do. That is my main tool. I have also been steadily using a lot more 3D in my work. I use Cinema 4D because it is easy to use and has some fantastic camera mapping tools. I don't do my own compositing, but I have done some animating of my paintings in the past, such as the big plume on Mt. Doom in *Return of the King*.

Figure 8.31 The Industrialist Monks

DM What advice do you have for aspiring matte artists?

DC I would say to learn the fundamentals of drawing, painting, design, and composition. These will help you immensely and separate you from the photo-monkey variety of matte artists or those that can only work in 3D. Also, be brutally honest with your work. Figure out what isn't working and why. I also find it helps to do a lot of quick sketch-paintings to learn about color and composition. Detailing is laborious, but fairly easy. I think the important part is composition and color. It is all about mileage, you have to get all of the bad paintings out before you can do the good ones!

DM You have worked both at studios and as an independent. Which do you prefer, and what are the plus and minuses of each?

DC I currently work as an independent from home and I definitely prefer it. I get to work on many different projects at once and I get to sit at home in my underwear if I want. I also have the freedom to move my schedule around so I can run errands or do anything else I need. However, in order to get to this point, I had to establish a good reputation by working at facilities. I definitely miss the social aspects of facilities. It is a lot of fun to work and learn from other artists. There is also a nice mental separation of work and home. The problem with working at home is that you are always at work!

DM In the history of matte painting, there have been some amazing painters. I was wondering if you had a favorite, and why.

DC Ooh, that is hard. I would have to say Albert Whitlock and Michael Pangrazio. Albert Whitlock just blows my mind with how convincing his stuff was and how ambitious his shots were. He knew how to lead the eye through the painting and make you focus on the subject. I also really like his paint handling. I think he perfected the photo-impressionism style of matte painting. And I love Michael Pangrazio for the same reason. He had a wonderful looseness that worked very well and he knew how to create iconic compositions. I also enjoy all of Mark Sullivan's work. Beautifully executed and composed.

DM I noticed that you recently have been working as a concept artist. Could you talk about transitioning from matte painting to other jobs?

DC I was a concept art director on *Avatar* and that was a wonderful experience creating these alien environments. I would work in a very similar manner to my matte painting, it was just a bit looser and quicker. It was the one-day version of the painting and it was a lot of fun because you solve color, composition, and design, you just don't have all of the detail perfected. It is also a lot more creative because you are designing the world instead of working off of someone else's design.

Figure 8.32 *Vasilios vs. Elizar*

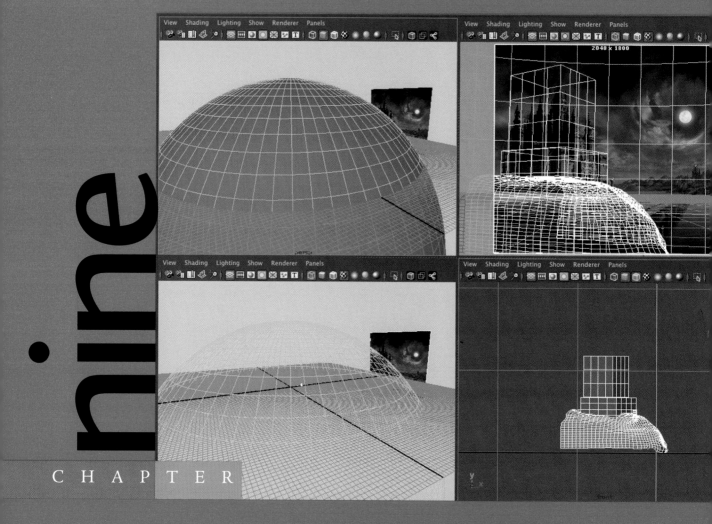

CHAPTER

Building Geometry for Camera Projection in Maya

Now that you've prepared your *image and alpha files for use in Maya and added an image plane as reference, it's time to build the geometry for your 3D castle. A feature film matte painting would use hundreds of geometric shapes, but this exercise will keep it simple and limit your work to six elements. The castle walls and towers will consist of two stacked cubes: the water will be a plane, the bridge and hill will be delineated by two deformed cubes, and the sky will be a section of a sphere. This streamlined construction will enable you to get familiar with the concepts and learn how to create a moving matte painting.*

Lining Up the Reference Box

If you are not familiar with Maya, or have not done camera projection before, I suggest that you work through this chapter using the demonstration files provided so that your work will match the figures. At the end of the chapter you will create geometry for the castle you finished in Chapter 7. Advanced Maya users should read through this chapter to familiarize themselves with the concepts, then go right to the assignment.

If you were working along with me, find the `Castle_Project_Chapter_9` folder on the Chapter 9 DVD materials. Open `Castle_Project_Start_Chapter_9.ma`, inside of the `scenes` folder. This is the file completed in the last chapter, with the image plane aligned to the grid. When you open the file, choose File → Project → Set, and double check that the project is set to the `Castle_Project` folder on your hard dive. If it is not, navigate to that folder, and press Set. Whenever you open a Maya file, it's good policy to make sure the project is set to your current project folder. That way, any files you create while working will be saved to the project folder. Rename the file `Castle_Project_Geo.ma`, and save it to the `scenes` folder.

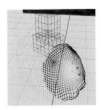

The first piece of geometry you'll build is the most important. All other sections of the castle will be based on it. Start with one cube to represent the castle walls. You'll adjust the focal length based on how this cube lines up with your reference painting. First, you need to set up your Maya file so that all new geometry created in the project appears in the same location. Choose Create → Polygon Primitives → Interactive Creation, and make sure Interactive Creation isn't selected. If it's checked, select it again to uncheck it. Now, create a cube by choosing Create → Polygon Primitives → Cube. Click the box to the right of Cube to open the Polygon Cube Options dialog box. Set Width, Height, and Depth all to 5 and give the cube four divisions on each dimension (Figure 9.1). Because Interactive Creation is turned off, the cube appears automatically in the center of the grid.

If you ever can't find a particular piece of geometry, you can select it in the Outliner and press F on the keyboard. Maya will fill the current viewport with just that object.

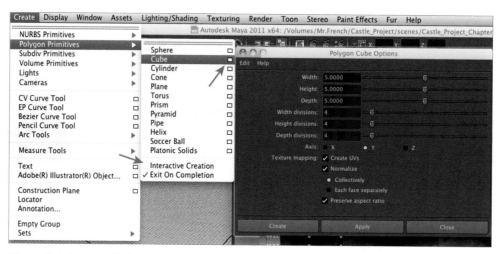

Figure 9.1 Polygon Cube Options dialog box

In the last chapter, you added a projection camera called projectionCam. Then, you added an image plane with the reference painting. Now, you'll align the newly created cube with the painted castle on the projectionCam image plane. You'll primarily handle this task from the projectionCam viewport; this is also where you'll project the textures. Getting the cube to line up with the base of the painted castle is tricky: it's the most difficult part of this process.

You'll use the Maya Transform tools, which are located on the left side of the interface. They are Select ▨ (keyboard shortcut Q), Move ▨ (W), Rotate ▨ (E), and Scale ▨ (R).

Depending on what version of Maya you're using, the icons may look slightly different.

Let's get started. You need to move the cube. To do this, select the Move tool. Now, click the cube and move it between the projectionCam and the image plane. In order to have space for the ocean and background mountains, there should be four times as much distance from the cube to the image plane as there is from the cube to the camera (Figure 9.2).

Leave the camera where it is, and move the cube around until you can see it from the projectionCam viewport. Press R to select the Scale tool. Scale the cube so it's roughly the size of the painted castle wall, and rename it **CastleWall**. You can also use the default perspective camera—Panels → Perspective → Persp in the viewport menu—to position the cube, and you can move the camera to see the scene from different angles.

Move, rotate, and scale the box so it lines up with the bottom wall of the castle. The Maya grid shows you the location of the horizon line in the scene. Use the horizon line to match the vanishing points (VPs) of the cube to the VPs of the walls of the painted castle (Figure 9.3). You can review how to determine where the VPs are in Chapter 4, "Perspective Basics."

You may need to change the focal length. Here is how you can tell if this is necessary:

- If the VPs on the cube are too far out and are flatter than the painted castle walls, you need to shorten the focal length.
- If the VPs on the cube are too close in, and the lines angle in more than the painted castle walls, you need to make the focal length longer.

A shorter focal length will require you to move the camera closer to the cube, and a longer focal length means the reverse (Figure 9.4 and Figure 9.5). Thus, when you change the focal length, you must change the camera position accordingly. Save your `Castle_Project_Geo.ma` file now.

You can compare the two different focal lengths in the Chapter 9 materials on the DVD in the `scenes` folder in the Maya project folder `Castle_Project_Chapter_9`. The file is called `35mm_vs_50mm_Chapter_9.ma`. The proper focal length for this project is somewhere between these two examples. I'll leave it to you to determine what works best.

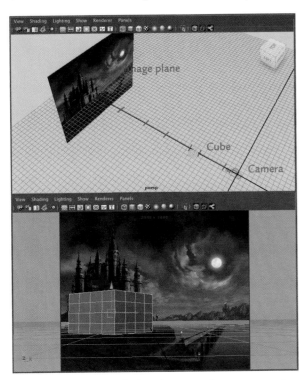

Figure 9.2 *Position the box between the camera and the image plane.*

Figure 9.3 *Line up the box to the VPs in the painting.*

Figure 9.4 *A longer focal length (50mm) makes the VPs flatter.*

Figure 9.5 *A shorter focal length (35mm) makes the VPs angle in.*

Re-open `Castle_Project_Geo.ma`. Take the time to set up this first cube properly. As mentioned previously, you'll position everything else in the scene in relation to this cube, so get it to match the painting as precisely as possible. If the cube is off a little, the projection will still work. However, the closer the match, the better the final result.

After you've aligned the geometry and found both the correct positioning and focal length for projectionCam, you don't want to be able to move it. You'll lock all the channels on the camera using the Channel Box, Maya's primary tool for editing and controlling objects in a scene. To open the Channel Box, click the Channel Box icon 📋 in the upper-right corner of the interface. Two or three icons are displayed next to the Channel Box icon.

Because the Channel Box shares space with several other windows, you may need to click the Channel Box icon several times until the Channel Box window becomes visible below the icon. Because the Channel Box and the Attribute Editor share the same window, you can use the keyboard shortcut Control/Ctrl+A to open and switch between them.

With projectionCam selected and the Channel Box open, you see all of the camera's transformation properties. These include translate, rotate, and scale for all the axes, and visibility. Click at the top and drag down to select all the transform properties; they turn blue when selected. In the Channel Box, choose Channels → Lock Selected (Figure 9.6). When locked, the properties turn dark gray. You won't be able to move this camera again unless you unlock the properties.

With the first cube lined up to the painting on the image plane, you can duplicate it, resize it, and move it into position as the castle towers (Figure 9.7). Rename the duplicated cube **CastleTowers**. To keep this project easy to understand, you're using a single cube to represent all the towers. Even with this simple geometry, the castle will have a convincing 3D appearance.

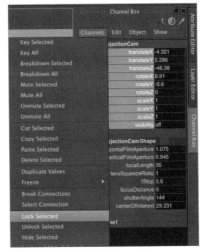

Figure 9.6 *Lock the projection camera.*

Figure 9.7 *Duplicate the first box to create the rest of the castle.*

Sculpting the Foreground Hill

Choose Create → Polygon Primitives → Cube, and select the box next to Cube. Add another cube for the foreground hill, with Height, Width, and Depth set to 5 and with 20 subdivisions on each dimension to give you some geometry to sculpt (Figure 9.8). Rename this object **Hill**.

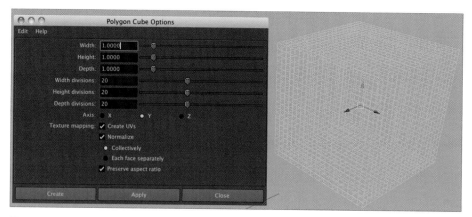

Figure 9.8 *Create a cube for the foreground hill with 20 subdivisions in each direction.*

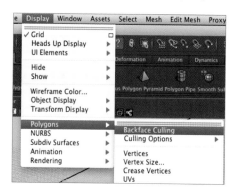

Figure 9.9 *Backface culling*

With 20 subdivisions on the cube, it will be difficult to see what you're sculpting. To make dense objects easier to work with, choose Display → Polygons → Backface Culling (Figure 9.9). Doing so turns off the visibility of the back sides of the cube and only shows the geometry that faces toward you.

You can further simplify the scene on a per-viewport basis by clicking the grid icon ◈ at the top of each viewport to turn the grid on or off.

Move the 20-sectioned cube under the castle cubes, and rotate it to match the castle's angle (Figure 9.10). Make sure it's large enough to cover the entire hill.

The Sculpt Geometry Tool

You'll now use Maya's Sculpt Geometry tool to shape the hill. If you want to work over a copy of the project that's already set up to this point, open `Fgr_Hill_Chapter_9.ma` in the scenes folder in the Chapter 9 materials on the DVD. Again, save it to the `Castle_Project` folder on your hard drive, and confirm that the project is set to that folder to keep the project organized.

To open the Sculpt Geometry tool, go to the drop-down menu in the upper-left corner of the interface. What appears in the main menu changes according to what task you're performing in Maya. Choose Polygons from the drop-down menu, which adds Mesh to the main menu; then, select Mesh and click the box to the right of Sculpt Geometry Tool (Figure 9.11).

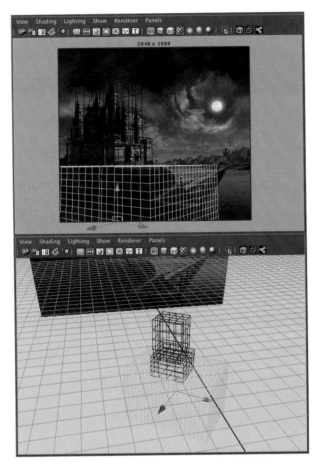

Figure 9.10 Positioning the geometry for the hill

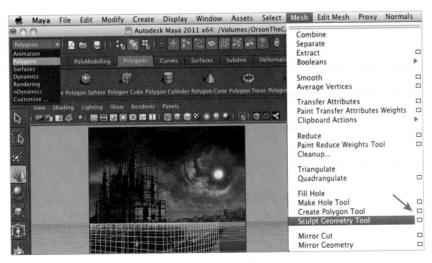

Figure 9.11 Opening the Sculpt Geometry tool

Open the Tool Settings panel for the Sculpt Geometry tool by clicking the Tool Settings icon in the upper-right corner ▦ . You may need to click it a couple of times until Tool Setting appears (Figure 9.12). You'll only look at the Brush and Sculpt Parameters rollouts, but this panel has many more rollouts that you should explore on your own.

The Sculpt Geometry tool functions like a brush to shape the polygons that make up the cube. You can control whether the tool Pushes 🖰 , Pulls 🖰 , Smoothes 🖰 , Relaxes 🖰 , Pinches 🖰 , or Erases 🖰 the polygons.

The main Brush controls are the upper radius, Radius(U); the lower radius, Radius(L); and Opacity. The Radius sliders work like Size Jitter does in Photoshop, controlling the size of the brush according to how hard you press when using a digitizing tablet. The Radius(U) diameter is the largest the brush can be when you press hard, affecting a larger area. The Radius(L) diameter is the smallest the brush can be when you press softly, affecting a smaller area. You can resize the upper radius by holding down the B key and pressing and holding the middle mouse button. Dragging to the right makes the brush larger, and dragging to the left makes it smaller.

Figure 9.12 *Sculpt Geometry tool interface*

It's helpful to turn down the brush's opacity to move the vertices into position gradually. High Opacity makes the brush affect the vertices forcefully, whereas a smaller number makes the brush work in a more gradual manner. A setting of 0 gives the brush no effect. Try 0.25 as a starting place, and go over an area repeatedly to move the vertices in a controlled fashion.

If you haven't worked with the sculpting tools before, set aside time to experiment with each one. Don't worry about making mistakes. You can use the Erase tool in Sculpt Parameters to remove any modifications you make to the geometry.

Begin shaping the foreground hill with the Sculpt Geometry tool (Figure 9.13). Use the Push, Pull, and Smooth operations to shape the hill. You may find that this tool produces some odd shapes and spikes, especially if you have the opacity set too high. If this happens, use the Smooth tool to even them out.

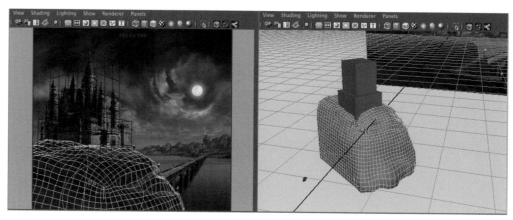

Figure 9.13 *Using the Sculpt Geometry tool*

Component Mode

Each piece of geometry is made up of different components, including edges, faces, and vertices. A *vertex* occurs wherever two or more straight lines intersect. Vertices are the points that make up the object.

You can model the cube by moving the components of an object manually. Choose the Select tool from the left menu, and select the hill. Press and hold the right mouse button to display the components menu. You can choose between all of the object's different components. In this case, choose Vertex, and release the mouse button. Magenta dots appear where the vertices occur on the object. Now you can push and pull the vertices manually to achieve sharp detail (Figure 9.14).

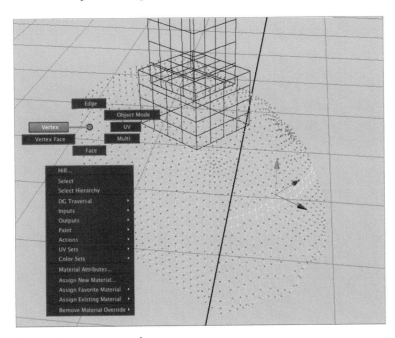

Figure 9.14 Vertex mode

You can move, scale, and rotate the vertices rather than the entire object. Vertex mode lets you work on discrete sections of the object; it's extremely useful for adding fine details.

Soft Selection Mode

While in Vertex mode, you can also use the Soft Selection tool to move areas more uniformly. Choose Window → Attribute Editor, or click the Attribute Editor icon in the upper-right corner ▤ .

In the Attribute Editor, scroll down until you can select Soft Select. The vertices that you've selected turn yellow and move the most. The vertices surrounding the selection are now soft transforming vertices, and they will also be affected by the transform tools. You can change the size of the affected area by changing the Falloff Radius setting. The closest soft transforming vertices are colored red and move progressively less as the distance increases from the selected yellow vertices. Even further away, the vertices are dark brown, moving less and less. Finally, the original magenta vertices don't move at all (Figure 9.15).

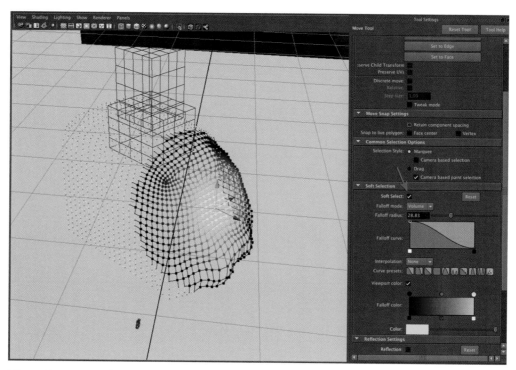

Figure 9.15 *Using the Move tool and Soft Selection*

Now you're on your own. Use this set of tools to shape the hill to match the reference.

Adding the Sky

At this point you have a castle made of two boxes and a sculpted hill atop which the castle will sit. It's time to add the sky. Create a sphere by choosing Create → Polygon Primitives → Sphere, and select the box to the right of Sphere. You should get The Polygon Sphere Options dialog box. If you get the Polygon Sphere tool instead, you need to turn off Interactive Creation. In the Polygon Sphere Options dialog, set Axis Divisions to 80, Height Divisions to 40, and Radius to 100 (Figure 9.16). Click Create to close the dialog box.

The sphere needs to be much larger so that it almost touches the image plane with the castle painting but doesn't cover it. Make sure the sphere centers on the camera and covers the area between the camera and the image plane entirely. Move the sphere down so the rounded top of the sky dome is visible in projectionCam (Figure 9.17).

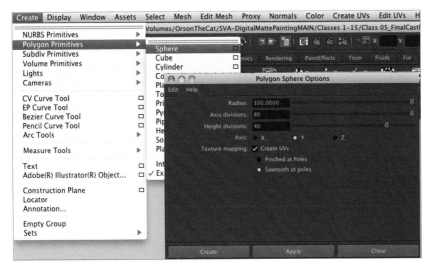

Figure 9.16 Create a polygon sphere for the sky.

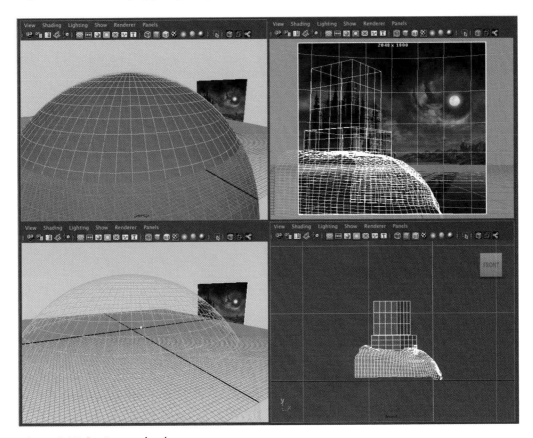

Figure 9.17 Setting up the sky

Large portions of the dome are unused. To delete them, change to Component mode and select Faces. Delete any faces that projectionCam can't see, but leave an outside border of faces as a safety margin (Figure 9.18). To exit Component mode, press and hold the right mouse button, and select Object Mode.

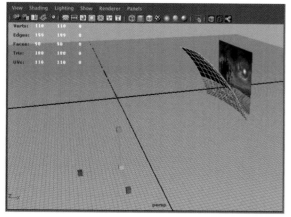

Figure 9.18 *Positioning the sky geometry and deleting unneeded faces*

Centering the Pivot

Every object transforms—scales, rotates, and moves—from a center pivot. Whenever you select a transform tool, the cursor appears on the center pivot of that object. After you've deleted the unneeded faces, the center pivot is positioned far away from the section of the sky you're using, because it was the center pivot for the entire sphere. To re-center the sky pivot, choose Modify → Center Pivot. Doing so places the pivot in the middle of the remaining section of the sky dome.

Adding the Remaining Geometry

You're getting near the end of this process. All that remains is to make a plane for the water with 20 sections in each direction and Width and Height set to 500. Scale and position it so it fills the space between the castle and the sky where the water would be. Name it **Water**.

Make a really long, stretched cube for the bridge on your own. Be sure to name it also. When you're finished, you have six pieces of geometry (Figure 9.19). This is the minimum number of layers to make this scene work.

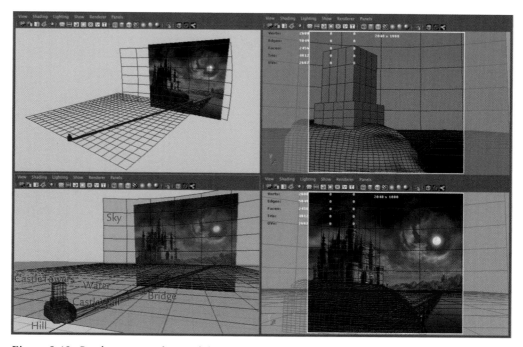

Figure 9.19 *Castle scene made up of the minimum number of objects*

You can check out what the project should look like at this point in the Chapter 9 materials on the DVD. The file is named `Final_Geometry_Chapter_9.ma`.

Assignment: Build Geometry for Your Castle

Now it is your turn to build geometry to match your own castle by following these steps:

1. Using your painting on the image plane as reference, carefully line up a cube to match the perspective of your castle.
2. Once you are satisfied with the position of the box, lock your projectionCam so that it can't be accidently moved.
3. Create a cube with 20 subdivisions to sculpt the foreground hill using the Sculpt Geometry tool, Component mode, and Soft Selection tool.
4. Add a sky using a sphere with the unneeded faces deleted.
5. Build geometry for any other major elements in your composition.

With the basic geometry in place, you'll advance in the next chapter to texturing the shapes. After that you will animate a new camera and bring your painted scene to three-dimensional life.

Matte Artist Profile: Michele Moen

Michele Moen is one of the most respected female matte artists in the history of the industry. While matte painting has been a male-dominated field since its inception, Michele was a trailblazer, admired for her professionalism and incredible talent. She also is one of the nicest people in the industry. Hired on as an apprentice to legendary matte artist Mathew Yuricich during the production of *Blade Runner* (1982), she quickly rose to become a much in-demand matte artist. Her credits include 2010 *(1984)*, *Ghostbusters (1984)*, *Babe: Pig in the City* (1998), *Armageddon* (1998), *Mars Attacks* (1996), *The Fifth Element* (1997), *Gladiator* (2000), *Superman Returns* (2006), *I Am Legend* (2007), and *Star Trek* (2009). Michele has extended her career into concept art, and worked in that capacity on two *Chronicles of Narnia* films: *Prince Caspian* (2008) and *Dawn Treader (2010)*. I worked with Michele on *Dick Tracy* (1990), and, unbeknownst to her, I positioned my easel so I could watch her paint a complex three-point perspective cityscape. I was, and still am, in awe of her painting ability. Every year more women appear in the end credits of movies as matte artists, and they benefited from Michele as a role model who opened the door for them.

Figure 9.20 Michele Moen

David Mattingly Hi, Michele. Thanks for agreeing to be part of *The Digital Matte Painting Handbook*. First, tell me a little bit about yourself.

Michele Moen I was born in and lived in Northern California for my first ten years. My parents were both creative sort of bohemian intellectuals.

I wanted to be a writer all the way up through high school until I had one particular art teacher at Santa Monica High who strongly encouraged me to apply to an art school upon graduating. I wish I could remember her name to thank her because if it hadn't been for her, I probably wouldn't have gone to Art Center College of Design or even pursued a career in art. All it takes sometimes is a little nudge from one very special person.

DM   Who are your most important artistic influences? When you go to a museum, what artists do you seek out?

MM   John Singer Sargent and Joaquin Sorolla are my absolute favorite painters. I also look for Jean-Leon Gerome and Ilya Repin, and the photographer, Sebastiao Salgado. I have many favorite painters, but I tend to seek out the painters of realism. Architecture, landscapes, and people are my favorite subjects.

DM   Where did you go to school? How important do you think going to art school is for a matte artist?

MM   I went to Art Center College of Design and started off with a major in advertising but eventually changed my major to illustration. I was living on my 28-foot converted navy whaler sailboat during my first term and had some disastrous homework assignments trying to do color swatches under a single incandescent light bulb swaying from the motion of the water. I highly recommend art school for any type of creative position. If you have the opportunity to go to school, by all means go and get it out of the way. There are some foundation courses that are a necessity; perspective, composition and the process of design, and basic color theory.

DM   How did you become interested in matte painting? What was your first job as a matte artist? You worked with Matt Yuricich early in your career, and I wonder if you could share some memories of working with him.

MM   My goal after finishing art school was to move to New York and illustrate. Seriously! I had never heard of matte painting and I had only taken one Film History Appreciation course. Somehow, events changed my course and after some L.A.-based freelance illustrating jobs at ad agencies I took my portfolio in to a studio called Entertainment Effects Group in Marina Del Rey to show the art department, hoping to get a storyboard or illustrator position. By chance, Matthew Yuricich was there getting ready to start on a movie called *Blade Runner* after finishing *Close Encounters of the Third Kind* (1977). He looked at my portfolio that had some indication that I could handle a brush and asked me if I'd like to wash some brushes for him. That doesn't sound glamorous but I was in awe of so many artists working in a studio on a movie that I would have said yes to any job offered. I started work as a matte painting apprentice for the legendary Matt Yuricich. (I still had no idea what a matte painting was.) Matt was also mentor to matte painter Rocco Gioffre. I continued to work with Matt in the same studio location after Doug Trumball and his E.E.G. left and Richard Edlund moved in with a team of ex–Industrial Light and Magic staffers, becoming Boss Film Studios. Richard was and always has been a huge proponent of matte painting. I remained at Boss for 17 years, working with Matt until he retired and then taking over as head of the matte department. Richard promoted me all the way through my matte painting career and will remain my hero and friend.

I still talk to Matt Yuricich by phone every few months and he's always been a treasure trove of great stories. He'd drive in at 3:30 in the morning to avoid the traffic, turn on his favorite foot-tapping polka music and paint before we all came in at 9. Most of the departments would meet in the screening room for an hour of dailies and by 11:30 Matt would hang up his dark colored painting smock, change into a nice shirt and go out to lunch. The dark colored aprons didn't reflect into the matte painting so the color of the paint wouldn't be affected. At first before I "graduated" to my own matte painting assignment, I'd sit on a stool behind him, ask questions and watch him paint and then, before he went home for the day, he'd show me an area on his painting that I should work on. I would often draft out the perspective and line drawing needed for the particular matte shot, prepare his specific palette of oil colors, and have all his many brushes washed and drying for the next morning. He had a mirror set up the same distance away from the painting that the camera would be when the painting was shot and he'd check the mirror throughout the day to spot bad perspective or odd juxtapositions. Matt's general advice was to paint and to draw, continually. Paint landscapes, paint anything; the more you look at the world around you and try to reproduce it, the better artist you will become—the more you do it, the better you get. It's a craft and perfection comes with practice.

DM You have worked both traditionally and digitally. Speed and economic realities aside, which do you prefer?

MM As much as there is a romance to the traditional method of matte painting, I could never really go back. The studios won't go back either. I paint in oils now when I'm not working on a film. There are so many possibilities in creating jaw-dropping sequences digitally that I'd now have to prefer the digital methods. It is still story-telling no matter how it is accomplished and there are always challenging opportunities to be innovative and creative.

Figure 9.21 Matte painting for the independent film Interstate *(2007)*

DM When working digitally, what software to you use? Do you do your own compositing?

MM When working digitally, I use Photoshop. Sometimes I will quickly compose a shot and develop a color mood in Corel Painter because it forces me to jump right in and paint on just one or two layers. In Photoshop I tend to add up too many layers that eventually become a huge, tangled 3 GB file if I'm working in 16 bit.

Image credit: Copyright Universal 2002

Figure 9.22 Matte painting for the Scorpion King *(2002). Left side: start frame; Right side: end frame.*

At one point I focused on compositing my own shots. I did composite a few shots on *The Scorpion King* (2002). Compositing gets you that much closer to complete control of the final shot and it gives you a greater sense of pride. But, personally, I don't have the patience to continue with compositing. I like working with compositors and often the studios are small enough to encourage working with each other.

DM   You are one of the few women to become a noted matte painter. Could you talk about how that has affected your career?

MM   In the end, it's really all about the work you produce. Of course there are times I have felt special being a woman in film! I remember walking into my first Academy Board meeting and I was the only female at a large table of about 35 male VFX and Special Effects Supervisors. I grew up with brothers and find it quite comfortable working with mostly guys. If you do a good job, and remain flexible, it doesn't matter what gender you are. It's also a team effort and, although there will always be a better artist walking through the door, a positive and professional work attitude will always get you a recommendation for the next job. Word of mouth recommendations are usually the way we get hired so those first few jobs are important in establishing contacts and developing a reputation. When I first started, the more established guys would tell me I'd never last in this business because I was too nice and I giggled. There is a trade off that should not be ignored; the hours can be long and while on a project, your life becomes that project whether it be a three-day commercial over a holiday weekend ending in one sleepless night or a 10-hour day, 6 days a week, 15-month job in an industrial warehouse over an hour's commute from home each way. Or, there might be an invitation to travel to India or Singapore to work for a year or two. Another factor to consider is that this is a very competitive field with constantly changing technology. We all have to continually learn new skills and software to compete and that sometimes means taking courses on the weekend after having worked the 55 hour week. We can never sit back and coast.

Figure 9.23 Matte painting for Star Trek *(2009)*

DM   Who is your favorite matte painter? Also, could you mention some matte shots from the past that you particularly admire?

MM   My favorite matte artist is Matt Yuricich because he was my mentor and is my friend. Albert Whitlock was the master at applying impressionistic brush strokes to create a scene that appeared as original photography. I was inspired by Peter Ellenshaw's paintings from *Mary Poppins* (1964). Some of the originals hung on the wall at Disney as we painted on *Dick Tracy*.

Favorite matte shots: the changes in technology make it really difficult to have one favorite for very long. (There's another way at looking at this question of favorite matte shots; if a matte painting is done correctly it'll go by unnoticed.) The one major aspect that keeps coming back to me is composition. It can be the most beautifully rendered, detailed image and if it isn't graphically composed or designed well to read in a few seconds, it fails. At various times I've been very impressed with certain paintings; Matt Yuricich's work on *The Robe* (1953) and *Ben Hur* (1959) with architecture that had to be painted "squeezed"; how could anyone draw perspective squeezed and distorted?

Paul Lasaine's and Craig Mullens' sense of design and composition; they both have a classical aesthetic. Their sketches and matte paintings can be flipped, flopped, made black and white and they still read well. Rocco Gioffre's digital matte paintings contain the traditional tricks of movement that make the shots look real. Steve Messing is a relatively new and incredibly talented digital matte artist who has almost been a well-kept secret, but, not for long. Dylan Cole does some amazingly vast and dramatic landscapes that inspire me. Bob Scifo, Mark Sullivan, Michael Pangrazio, Robert Stromberg, Yusei Uesugi, Chris Evans all remain my favorites as consistently excellent artists. Robert Stromberg has the ability to design and compose a digital matte painting that doesn't necessarily look finished or overly-rendered and overly-detailed yet immediately reads as realism on the screen.

DM What matte shot did you have the most fun doing?

MM The most fun matte shot was the huge *Dick Tracy* pan with famous guest artists. Peter Ellenshaw, Harrison Ellenshaw, David Mattingly, Paul Lasaine, Michael Lloyd, Tom Gilleon, Lucy Tanashian, and I all painted on one painting. The day Peter Ellenshaw walked into our department at Disney, he studied our very long pan painting that we had been working on, picked up a house painting brush filled with paint and wiped a large section of our painting out and re-composed the painting. It wasn't working and he fixed it and taught us to stay focused on the composition and the story we were telling. We were not creating a personal painting meant to hang on a gallery wall.

CHAPTER

Projecting Textures in Maya

Camera projection is the basis *of all advanced matte painting today. This is the last of three chapters devoted to camera projection. When you complete this section of the book, you'll have a working knowledge of how to set up a camera projection and animate a scene.*

Camera projection requires a great deal of setup. In the previous chapters, you created the image files to map the geometry, oriented the image plane, and built geometry to represent the objects in your scene. After all that work, it's time for the big payoff. In this chapter, you'll project textures onto the geometry, create a new camera to animate, and render a 3D animation of your scene.

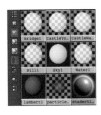

Adding Materials to Geometry

Unless you have an advanced knowledge of Maya, it would be a good idea to work along with this chapter using the demonstration files. If you are already a Maya master, read through the material, then do the assignment at the end of the chapter.

If you are working along with me, open Castle_Project_Start_Chapter_10.ma on the Chapter 10 DVD materials. When you open the file, choose File → Project → Set and set the project to the Castle_Project folder you created on your hard drive in Chapter 8. Be sure to save the Maya scene file to the scenes folder in Castle_Project. All the image files you created in Chapter 8 should already be in the sourceimages folder in Castle_Project on your hard drive. If they aren't there, move them; or you can copy and use the files in the sourceimages folder in the Chapter 8 DVD materials. With that bit of housekeeping out of the way, you can begin projecting your painting.

Setting Up the Sky Projection

Let's begin with the sky, because it's a large section that you can use to make sure the texture is lining up properly. In order to use your painted texture in camera projection, you need to turn it into a material to use as a projection map.

Select the Sky geometry, right-click and hold. Drop down to the lower menu, and select Assign New Material (Figure 10.1).

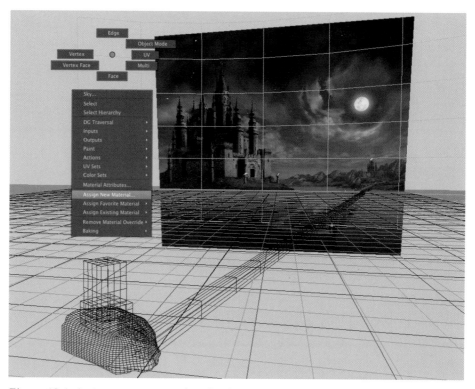

Figure 10.1 *Assign a new material to the sky.*

The Assign New Material dialog box opens. Maya offers many different shading options. At left, under Maya, select Surface to reduce the number of choices, and choose Lambert (Figure 10.2).

Figure 10.2 *Select Lambert from the list of materials.*

When you choose Lambert, the material immediately opens in the Attribute Editor; it's called *lambert*, followed by a number. Two tabs appear in the Attribute Editor. Select the tab with the lambert name, not the Shading Group tab that has *lambert* followed by *SG*. You'll use Lambert material for all the projections because it has no reflections or highlights. All the reflections and highlights have already been painted into the image files, so you don't need them from the material. When you want reflections and highlights, you can use more complex materials like Phong and Blinn. At the top of the Attribute

Editor, change the name of the new Lambert material from *lambert*, followed by a number, to **Sky**. Because you already have a piece of geometry named Sky, Maya renames it Sky1 for you.

The Lambert material is a neutral gray by default, as shown in the Color box in the Common Material Attributes rollout. You need to load the Sky.tif color file—the painting of the sky—into the material color channel. Maya uses channels in materials to control how an object looks. There are channels for color, transparency, incandescence, bump mapping, and many other attributes. You can fill these channels with textures built in to Maya, such as noise, color ramps, and even fractal granite, but in this case you'll fill them with the matte painting. In the Attribute Editor, click the checkerboard box to the right of Color in the Common Material Attributes rollout (Figure 10.3).

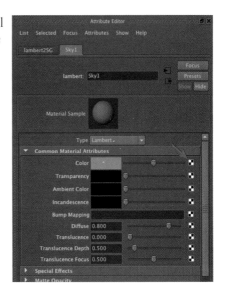

Figure 10.3
Lambert material
Attribute Editor

Doing so opens the Create Render Node dialog box. *Nodes* are the building blocks of materials. They have attributes, or properties, which define how the image will look. In Maya, there are many kinds of nodes: surfaces, transforms, and 2D textures are examples of nodes. In this case you'll use 2D textures for all the projections. So, to reduce the number of options displayed, click 2D Textures at left. Right-click File, and choose Create As Projection from the pop-up menu. You're creating 2D textures as projections, which enables you to project your painted images onto the 3D geometry (Figure 10.4).

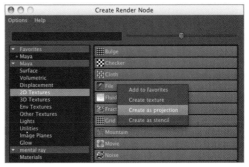

Figure 10.4 *Maya*
Create Render
Node dialog box

A projection node opens in the Attribute Editor, named *projection* followed by a number. Each time you create a new projection node, it's numbered one increment higher. Choose the following attributes (Figure 10.5):

- Under Projection Attributes:
  - Proj Type: Perspective.
- Under Camera Projection Attributes:
  - Link to Camera: projectionCamShape (the camera to which all the geometry is aligned)
  - Fit Type: Match Camera Film Gate
  - Fit Fill: to Fill
- Under Effects:
  - Filter: 0

Click the icon to the right of Image ▣.

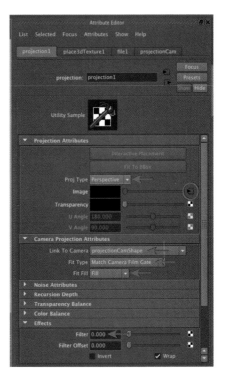

Figure 10.5
Projection
Attributes

The file node opens in the Attribute Editor. Set Filter Type to Off to avoid having a white glow around the image, known as *fringing.* Now, click the folder icon to the right of Image Name to load the Sky.tif image (Figure 10.6).

The Open dialog box appears. The images you created in Chapter 8 should be in the sourceimages folder in the Castle_Project folder on your hard drive. Select Sky.tif, and click Open (Figure 10.7).

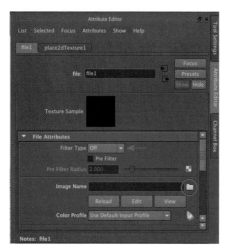

Figure 10.6 *Adding an image to the material*

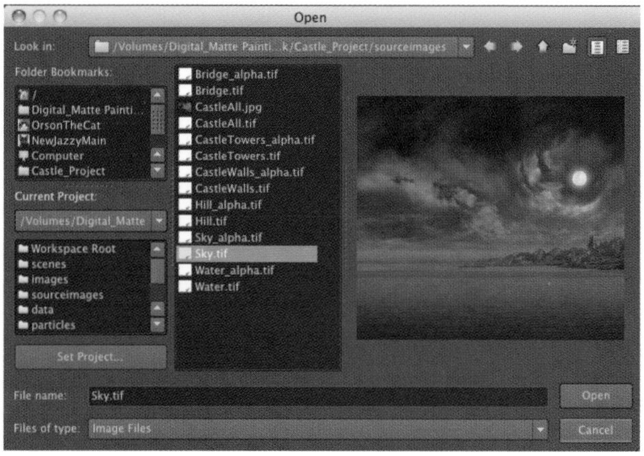

Figure 10.7 *Loading in the sky image*

Figure 10.8 *Go To Output Connection button*

Returning to the Attribute Editor, click the Go To Output Connection button twice (Figure 10.8). Doing so returns you to the main Sky1 Lambert Attribute Editor.

Next, you'll add the transparency channel for the sky. Below the color channel, click the checkerboard to the right of Transparency (Figure 10.9).

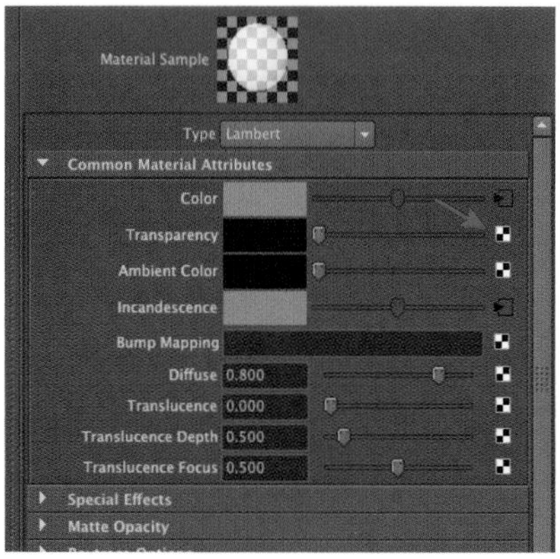

Figure 10.9 *Open the Create Render Node dialog box to add a file to Transparency.*

The Create Render Node dialog box opens. Right-click File again, and select Create As Projection. Doing so opens a new projection node for the transparency channel. In the Projection Attributes rollout, set everything exactly as you did in Figure 10.5.

Click the boxed arrow to the right of Image, and the File node opens. Set Filter Type to Off, and click the folder to the right of Image Name. When the Open dialog box appears, choose Sky_alpha.tif, and click Open. All the alpha channel files should be appended with _alpha to match the corresponding color files.

Back in the Attribute Editor, click the Go To Output Connection button (Figure 10.8) twice to get back to the main Sky1 Lambert Attribute Editor. Scroll down, and expand the Hardware Texturing rollout. For Textured Channel, choose Combined Textures. Set Texture Resolution either to High (128×128) or Highest (256×256) (Figure 10.10). Your choice between these two texture resolutions will depend on how much memory is in your computer.

Figure 10.10 *Setting the parameters for Hardware Texturing*

Owing to a bug in Maya, the options in Hardware Texturing often aren't available when you first create a texture. If you can't select Combined Textures or increase Texture Resolution, save and exit Maya. When you reopen the file, those selections should be available.

That completes the process of loading in the color and transparency attributes as projections. Save the project as Castle_Project_TextureSky.ma. You need to use the exact same image of the sky for the Incandescence material attribute. You could go through this process again, but there is a faster way to assign a map for a second time in the same material. To do that, you'll learn about the Maya Material Editor.

Introduction to the Material Editor

Other 3D programs intuitively call the dialog box where you create materials the Material Editor. Maya has a special name for it: Hypershade. Don't let this confuse you. Whenever you encounter the term *Hypershade*, think "Material Editor on steroids." Hypershade is where you control the incredible variety of surfaces and materials available in Maya.

To open the Hypershade dialog box, select Window → Rendering Editors → Hypershade (Figure 10.11). The top menu may look slightly different than the one shown in Figure 10.11 depending on which menu you've selected in the main menu bar.

Because you already created it, the Lambert material for the sky appears in the top menu, represented by a ball (Figure 10.12).

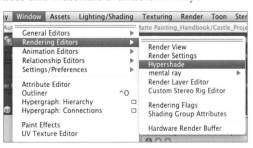

Figure 10.11 *Opening the Hypershade dialog box*

Figure 10.12 *The Hypershade dialog box*

One more Maya term to learn: materials in Maya are also called *shaders*. Hypershade contains three default shaders:

- lambert1
- particleCloud1
- shaderGlow1

Don't assign these three default shaders to anything new in the scene—always make new shaders. These three are reserved for objects that haven't had materials assigned to them, and adding textures to them can cause problems with the scene.

Figure 10.13
Graphing the Sky1
material network

Using Hypershade to Reuse a Projection

Rather than create another projection to add the sky image to the incandescence channel of the Sky1 shader, you'll use the Hypershade dialog box to use the same projection node twice.

Here's how you do it. Right-click and hold on the Sky1 ball; a menu appears surrounding the cursor. Choose Graph Network below the ball (Figure 10.13).

In the work area below the Materials tab, the Sky1 material displays the nodes connected to it. A lot of nodes are shown that we won't discuss in this chapter—you'll need a full Maya course to understand what they do. Concentrate on the two projection nodes you set up for the Color and Transparency attributes. First, let's check which projection node is handling which attribute.

1. Hold the cursor over the line connecting the projection1 node and the Sky1 ball. Text appears that reads *projection1.out-Color -> Sky1.color.* This shows that the projection node is inputting the color from the sky image file into the color channel of the Lambert material (Figure 10.14).

2. Do the same thing over the connection between the projection2 node and the Sky1 ball. The text reads *projection2 .outColor -> Sky1.transparency.* This projection node is inputting the transparency from the sky alpha channel into the transparency channel.

You'll use the incandescence channel to light the scene. You turned off all the Maya lights, so even though you have an image file loaded into the color channel, the geometry will still render black. It's like a pitch-black night—even if there is color all around you, you can't see it without light. You'll reuse the same file you used to color the geometry to provide the lighting by *incandescing* or glowing the same color.

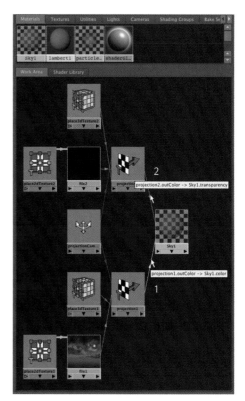

Figure 10.14 *The projection nodes inputting attributes into the Sky1 Lambert material*

You can reuse the projection1 node created for the color channel instead of creating a new node. Middle-click and hold down on the projection1 node, making the node lighter, and then drag over to the Sky1 ball and release. A new drop-down menu appears, showing many of the attributes available for this material. Select Incandescence to connect the image from the projection node to the Incandescence property of the Sky1 material (Figure 10.15).

As a result of this connection, the Sky1 ball becomes much lighter, because the sky image file is now illuminating it. If you hold the cursor over the line between projection1 and Sky1, you'll notice it now has two lines of text: the original and *projection1.outColor -> Sky1.incandescence*. The line also gets thicker to show that two properties are coming into the material from the same projection (Figure 10.16). This technique is not only easier than going through the entire process of setting up another projection node for the new attribute, but it also simplifies the Maya file.

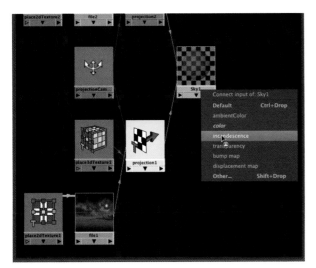

Figure 10.15 *Connecting the Incandescence property from the projection1 node*

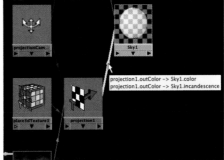

Figure 10.16 *Incandescence connected to the Sky1 material*

Checking Your Projection

The sky projection is complete. Because you have one material loaded, check to make sure everything has gone correctly. Look through the projectionCam viewport. Now, turn the sky projection texture preview on and off in the viewport by pressing the numbers 4 and 6 on your keyboard (Figure 10.17):

4 shows a wireframe preview, which allows the image plane to show through.

6 shows a texture preview, which blocks out the image plane. The texture preview is burned out because you have Incandescence on.

> Make sure you don't have X-Ray turned on for your viewport by going to the viewport menu and confirming that Shading → X-Ray isn't selected. If X-Ray is on, the textures will be see-through, and it will be harder to tell if they're properly positioned.

4   6

Figure 10.17 *Press 4 for wireframe, and the image plane shows through. Press 6 to see the textured sky.*

Maya's texture preview isn't perfect, but you'll be able to tell if the textured geometry lines up with the image plane.

Figure 10.18 *Rendering selected from the drop-down menu in the upper-left corner*

Because Maya texture previewing isn't completely accurate, you should do one final check to make sure the sky projection is lined up properly: you need to do a full-size test render. Make sure Rendering is selected in the upper-left corner drop-down menu, just below the main menu bar (Figure 10.18). This drop-down menu changes what appears on the main menu bar to offer different options for animation, polygons, surfaces, dynamics, rendering, and more. If Rendering isn't selected, the Render menu item doesn't appear.

Choose Render → Test Resolution → Render Settings. Doing so sets Test Resolution to 100 percent of the resolution you specified in Render Settings Image Size, and the same size as the image files you're projecting (Figure 10.19). As the project moves on, you can choose a smaller size to render your tests to save time, but do this test at full size.

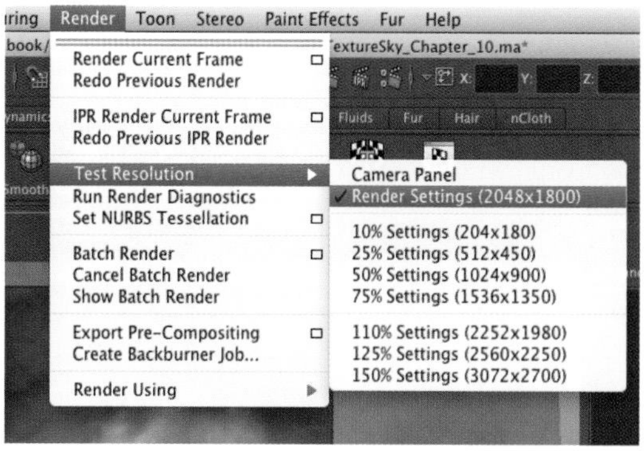

Figure 10.19 *Test resolution for the sky projection*

The preview render uses the currently selected viewport. Select the viewport showing the view from projectionCam. Click the Render The Current Frame icon on the right side of the top icon menu. Doing so opens the Render View dialog box, and Maya renders a preview of your scene. Choose File → Save Image in the upper-left Render View menu to save the file. Open both the test render and the Sky.tif file for comparison. Copy and then paste the Sky.tif image on top of the render, and confirm that the two skies line up perfectly (Figure 10.20). The other geometry renders as black because those elements don't yet have materials assigned to them.

Figure 10.20 *Sky plate compared to the full-size test render. They must match exactly.*

If the positioning of the sky in the sky plate doesn't match the sky on your test render, the projection isn't lined up. Before you add any more materials to the geometry, you need to figure out what went wrong. Backtrack through the steps in setting up the projection to find which setting is incorrect.

The most common error in misalignment is the failure to match the number in the Render Settings dialog box's Device Aspect Ratio to projectionCam's Film Aspect Ratio. That ratio is determined by dividing the width of the image file by the height.

To double-check the numbers, open the Render Settings dialog box. On the Image Size rollout, note the number in the Device Aspect Ratio box. Now, select projectionCam. In the Attribute Editor, on the Film Back rollout, make sure Film Aspect Ratio matches (Figure 10.21). If not, the projection won't line up.

Figure 10.21 *The Device Aspect Ratio value must match the Film Aspect Ratio value.*

Maya sometimes rounds numbers after you type them in and press Return/Enter. If you type **1.138** into Film Aspect Ratio, Maya will round it to 1.14. This is acceptable rounding in this situation.

Save your project to preserve what you've done. You can check how the scene should look at this point by opening Castle_Project_TextureSky_Chapter_10.ma in the Chapter 10 DVD materials.

Eighteen Steps for Defining Projection Materials

You're now ready to add the materials to the other geometry in your scene. Save the file as Castle_Project_AllTextures.ma. This process is exactly the same as what you did for the sky. Because this is a repetitive process, the following is an 18-step checklist for defining a projection material:

1. Right-click the geometry, and choose Assign New Material (Figure 10.1).
2. When the Assign New Material dialog box opens, choose Lambert (Figure 10.2).
3. The Attribute Editor opens. Give the material a name that matches the object to which it will be assigned (Figure 10.3).
4. Click the checkerboard ▣ to the right of the material attribute to which you're adding an image map. You'll add images to Color, Incandescence, and Transparency. Note that after an image has been added to an attribute, the checkerboard turns into a box with an arrow ▣ to indicate that it has content.
5. The Create Render Node dialog box opens. You can reduce the number of choices available by clicking 2D Textures at left (Figure 10.4).
6. Right-click File, and select Create As Projection from the pop-up menu.
7. The projection node attributes open in the Attribute Editor (Figure 10.5).
8. On the Projection Attributes rollout, set Proj Type to Perspective.
9. On the Camera Projection Attributes rollout, set Link To Camera to projectionCamShape.
10. Set Fit Type to Match Camera Film Gate.
11. Set Fill Type to Fill.
12. On the Effects rollout, set Filter to 0.
13. Back on the Projection Attributes rollout, click the arrow to the right of Image to open File Attributes (Figure 10.6).
14. On the File Attributes rollout, set Filter Type to Off (Figure 10.6).
15. Click the folder to the right of Image Name.
16. The Open dialog box opens. Navigate to the sourceimages folder, select the image file for projection, and click Open (Figure 10.7).
17. At the top of the Attribute Editor, next to the filename, are two boxed arrows (Figure 10.8). Click the bottom Go To Output Connection button twice to return to the main Lambert parameters in the Attribute Editor. Repeat steps 4 through 17 until you have image files in Color, Transparency, and Incandescence (Figure 10.9).
18. When all your image files are loaded in, you need to turn on the texture preview in the viewports. On the Hardware Texturing rollout, for Textured Channel, choose Combined Textures. Set Texture Resolution to either High or Highest (Figure 10.10).

You can speed up the process when assigning the same image to two different attributes by using the Hypershade dialog box and by right-click + dragging and dropping from the projection node (Figure 10.13 through Figure 10.16). Note that you can't reuse the same projection node for the Transparency attribute. That will only work when you're using the same map for two different attributes, and the alpha and color files are different.

When you've mastered these 18 steps, setting up projections will go quickly.

Textured Preview of the Entire Scene

After you've added materials to all the geometry in the scene, press 6 to see the scene in textured preview (Figure 10.22). If the scene looks good in the preview, it's time to do another test render.

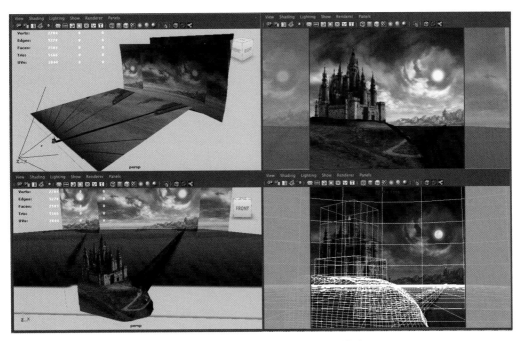

Figure 10.22 *Four viewports with all the texture projections added*

Select the projectionCam viewport, and click the Render Current Frame icon in the top icon menu. If all the geometry is properly textured and aligned, it's time to add the animated camera. Save the file to preserve your fully textured version. You can check your file against the version in the Chapter 10 DVD files, called `Castle_Project_AllTextures_Chapter_10.ma`.

Adding the Animated Camera

In this section, you'll add a new camera to animate and capture your scene in motion. Save your file again as `Castle_Project_CameraMove.ma`. Select the original projectionCam that you used to line up the geometry, and duplicate it using Command/Ctrl+D. The new camera is called projection-Cam1. Because the original projectionCam is locked to prevent you from moving it, you need to unlock the new camera in the Channel Box/Layer Editor in order to animate it. Select the new camera, rename it **animationCam**, and select all the attributes. Either right-click the selected attributes or go to the Channels menu in the Channel Box/Layer Editor, and choose Unlock Selected (Figure 10.23).

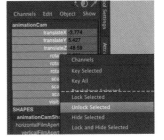

Figure 10.23 Unlock the animationCam attributes in the Channel Box/Layer Editor.

Make sure you only unlock the new camera, not your original projectionCam. If you move the original projection camera, your projected textures will no longer line up with the geometry, and the illusion will be destroyed.

Inserting Keyframes

For anything to change over time in an animation, you must insert keyframes. Keyframes record any change made to the scene between set points on a timeline. In this case, you'll add a keyframe for the start position and the end position of the camera.

At the bottom of the interface is a timeline showing the 200 frames of the animation. With animationCam selected in its original position, keyframe it at frame 1 by pressing S on the keyboard. Now, move to frame 200 by dragging the cursor to the right along the time-line. Push in until the castle is larger in the frame. At the same time, move a bit to one side to show more change in the surfaces of the castle. Press S to set a new keyframe manually.

Notice that there is now a small vertical red line at frame 1 and at frame 200 in the timeline, indicating that keyframes are set on those frames (Figure 10.24). You can use Autokey to have Maya set keyframes for you automatically by clicking the key icon in the lower-left corner ▦. The key turns red when Autokey is active ▦. After you've set one keyframe on any parameter, Maya will then set a keyframe for you whenever you move to another frame and change that parameter.

Projection camera (do not move!)

New animated camera

Figure 10.24 Keyframing animationCam

When you animate the camera, don't make your move too wild. This isn't the time to release your inner Michael Bay. A gentle push-in works best for camera projection (Figure 10.25). If you move too far off axis, the projection will tear and distort.

Save the project. To check out how your project should look with the camera move, you can open `Castle_Project_CameraMove_Chapter_10.ma` in the Chapter 10 materials on the DVD.

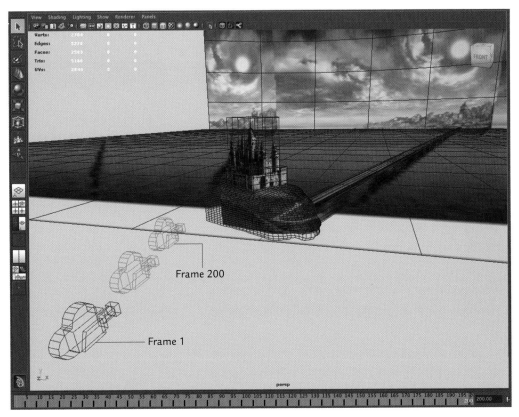

Figure 10.25 *Camera move from frame 1 to frame 200*

Rendering a Sequence

You'll render out a 200-frame sequence to see the final camera projection. First, you need to choose a camera from which to render. Open the Render Settings dialog box by clicking the icon in the top icon menu ■. On the Renderable Cameras rollout, from the Renderable Camera drop-down menu, select animationCam. Make sure Alpha Channel (Mask) and Depth Channel (Z Depth) are unchecked (Figure 10.26). Now the camera you keyframed will be rendered.

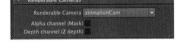

Figure 10.26 *Select animationCam on the Renderable Cameras rollout.*

Resize the Final Output

Next, you should resize the final output. If you render now, the sequence will be the same size as the original castle image files, which is too large for this first test. On the Image Size rollout, select 720 × 480. Notice that Device Aspect Ratio changes to 1.500 (Figure 10.27).

When you look through animationCam, notice that your framing has changed. With this new size, you may want to adjust the camera position on the first and last keyframes.

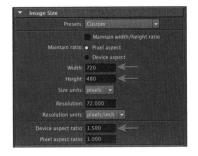

Figure 10.27 *Select the final size to render out the image sequence.*

Batch Rendering

The filename should already be set to CastleProject, so you're ready to render. Select Rendering from the drop-down menu in the upper-left corner if it isn't already chosen. Choose Render → Batch Render. Even though little changes on screen, Maya is hard at work: it's rendering the sequence in the background. To track the render's progress, consult the lower-right corner, where the boxed line of text shows what percentage of each frame is completed (Figure 10.28). If you set up the project correctly, all the frames should be placed in the `images` folder in the `Castle_Project` folder on your hard drive.

Figure 10.28 Rendering information during a batch render

You shouldn't change Image size or Device Aspect Ratio on the projectionCam. Doing so would throw off the projection alignment. However, you can render any additional cameras you add at any resolution needed.

Now you have 200 still frames of your render, but how will you view them? You could use a compositing package such as After Effects to make them into a movie, but every copy of Maya has a utility called FCheck that you can also use.

Inside the folder containing the Maya application, double-click the icon for FCheck. In FCheck, choose File → Open Sequence, and navigate to your 200 rendered images. Select one of the images, and click Open. It will take a moment for all the files to be loaded, and then the sequence will play.

You can see how the final project should render out by checking the movie `CastleProjectBoxes.mov` on the DVD.

Final Troubleshooting

Here are some common mistakes regarding camera projection, and their solutions:

Problem The castle looks too bright and has weird shadows on it (Figure 10.29).

Figure 10.29 Castle with Enable Default Lights on

Solution Make sure Enable Default Lights is deselected in the Render Options section of the Render Settings dialog box.

Problem You see a white fringe around your castle (Figure 10.30).

Solution Make sure filtering is removed from all the projections by setting Filter under Effects to 0 in the projection node and Filter Type under File Attributes on the image to Off.

Problem At the end of the camera move, two sets of towers are visible (Figure 10.31).

Filtered   Unfiltered

Figure 10.30 *Filtering added vs. filtering removed*

Figure 10.31 Projections on the back faces of geometry showing

Solution You're seeing the projection continue through the front side of the cubes and project onto the back. You'll have to delete the back sides of the cubes. You don't see the double projection at the beginning of the camera move because the front and back projections are right on top of each other. The further animationCam moves from the position of projectionCam, the more you see the back-side projection. This won't be a problem if the geometry is carefully modeled to the contours of the castle; but because you just used cubes, the back is visible.

Problem At the end of the animation, the flame holders on the bridge look like they're leaning to the left (Figure 10.32). What happened?

Solution Because there is no geometry to catch the projection of the upright flame holders, they're projected onto the top of the bridge. This is fine for the initial camera position; but by the time animationCam moves to the left, the projection from projectionCam is distorted. Actual geometry in the shape of the flame holders will fix this problem.

Figure 10.32 The flame holders distort to left at the end of the animation.

Problem   The reflection of the bridge bends to the right at the end of the animation (Figure 10.32). That doesn't look right.

Solution   The reflection looks fine on frame 1. By frame 200, your view is distorted because the reflection is painted into the water plate. Fixing this requires more advanced Maya knowledge than it's possible to go into in this book. In a nutshell, you need to do a separate render with the water set to a reflective material to get an optically correct reflection from the bridge. Then, you need to composite the reflection into the scene as a final step, using a program like After Effects.

The Final Animation

Here are the start and end frames of the final camera-projected castle (Figure 10.33 and Figure 10.34).

Notice how the different sections of the project change size in relation to each other. This is due to *multiplaning*. As you alter your viewing position, the objects that are closest to you move or change size more than the objects that are farther away. This is a naturally occurring phenomenon. For example, as you drive down a highway, the light posts in the foreground zip by, whereas the mountains in the distance appear not to change at all. Meanwhile, the hills a couple of hundred feet away move, but not nearly as fast as the light posts. These objects are multiplaning against each other.

Figure 10.33 Start frame. Notice the size of the castle in relation to the sky.

Figure 10.34 End frame. Notice that the castle has scaled much larger than the sky.

In the context of your matte painting, the castle gets much larger in frame as the camera pushes in, but the sky stays virtually the same size because it's much farther away. The perspective in the scene also changes as your eye level moves in relation to the geometry.

If the camera move is too extreme, you'll see the telltale distortions on your projections. If that occurs, you need to back off on the camera move. Take note where the tearing starts to occur, and set the ending keyframe before that point.

You've completed your first advanced matte painting project. Take a moment to pat yourself on the back!

Six is probably the fewest layers you can use and get reasonable results. When you've mastered this first simple version, you should go back and add more detail to the castle. The procedure is the same, although you'll have more objects in the scene and, as a result, more detail. If you model every wall crenellation and tower detail, your final product will look even better. Here is a diagram of how you can break the castle into 14 layers and add additional geometry for even more convincing results (Figure 10.35).

Figure 10.36 shows a wireframe view of the project with more geometry. You can check out this more complex version of the project in the Chapter 10 DVD materials in the project folder `Castle_Project_More`. Inside that project, in the `scenes` folder, is `Castle_Project_More_Chapter_10.ma`. You need to set the project to this folder so that this scene can find a new set of textures; to do so, choose File → Project → Set, and set the project to the `Castle_Project_More` folder. This project has a new set of textures, because it's been broken into more pieces and the perspective has been reworked on the painting to match the new geometry.

You can see the project rendered out with some additional bells and whistles in the file `CastleProjectMore.mov` on the DVD.

Castle High Towers
Castle Inner Walls
Castle Entry
Castle Back Wall
Castle Front Wall
Castle Flying Buttresses
Foreground Hill

Sky
Moon Glow
Moon

Mountains
Back Castle

Bridge
Flame Holders
Water Plane

Figure 10.35 Diagram of the castle in 14 layers

Figure 10.36 Castle scene with more geometry for added detail

Assignment: Assign Textures and Create an Animation Using Your Own Castle

Having worked through the project with the demonstration file, it's time to repeat the process with your own castle. Follow these steps to complete the project:

1. Add a projection material to your sky.
2. Confirm that the projected file is properly aligned by doing a full sized test render and comparing it to the sky file in the sourceimages folder.
3. If the sky is lined up properly, add texture projections to all of your geometry by following the 18 steps for defining projection materials.

With your projection materials added to all of the geometry, add a camera move to the scene.

1. Duplicate the projectionCam, and name the duplicate animationCam.
2. Unlock animationCam in the Channel Box.
3. Set a keyframe for animationCam at frame 1.
4. Move to frame 200, and push animationCam in closer to the castle, and slightly to one side. Set a second keyframe.
5. Render out your sequence.

For more convincing results, do the following:

6. Add more geometry to more exactly match your castle and other elements in the scene.
7. As needed, prepare a new .tif file to project on to the new geometry.

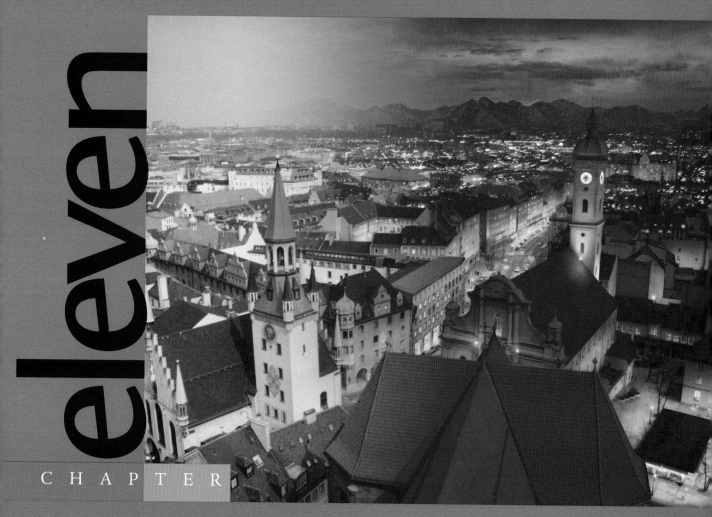

eleven

Lighting Techniques

One of the common tasks *of a matte artist is to take a plate and change the direction of the lighting. One example is to take a scene photographed in the daytime and alter it to serve as a nighttime shot. This exercise will bring into play all the skills you've learned so far. It requires adjusting the color temperature of the plate, taking elements from other photos and placing them in the scene, and hand painting. You'll start with a daytime shot of Munich, Germany, and turn it into a sparkling urban nighttime landscape.*

Day-for-Night

Directors often shoot scenes in the daytime that are later changed to night scenes, a technique called *day-for-night*. Why not just shoot at night? Although many advances have been made in film sensitivity with the advent of digital filmmaking, it's still harder to shoot at night and achieve a proper exposure. Directors often shoot in the daytime and rely on matte artists and compositors to make the transformation in post-production.

Open the file `MunichOldTown_BK1066.tif` in Photoshop. This will be your starting point (Figure 11.1).

Save the file to your hard drive as `DayForNightCity.psd`. Select all, and press Command/Ctrl+J to duplicate the layer and make a copy of the original image. Rename the new layer **Plate**. Add a border around the file to serve as a work area by choosing Image → Canvas Size. Enter **12.24** inches by **8.827** inches to add an extra inch on each side. When you're setting up a file for a complex painting, having a border is useful because you can see the edges of the elements you add and shift them around if you change your mind about the placement.

Image Credit: Corel Stock Photo Library

Figure 11.1 Daytime Munich Germany

You need to add a black mask to block off the border area. Click into the layer thumbnail for the Plate layer to load the selection, and press Shift+Command/Ctrl+I to invert the selection. Now only the masked area is selected. Make a new layer above Plate, and name it **BlackMask**. Fill the selection with black. Doing so creates a mask over your work area that you can turn on and off and use to reframe the plate if needed. Press Command/Ctrl+D to deselect all.

Preparing the Daytime Plate

Before you begin to turn your plate into a night scene, you need to do some prep work to get it ready for relighting.

Adding a New Sky

Create a new layer above Plate but below BlackMask, and call it **Sky**. The sky is a flat blue in the plate. Add cloud formations to make the scene more picturesque. Turn off the BlackMask layer while you're painting the sky so you can paint beyond the edges. Use DaytimeSky.jpg from the DVD materials as a starting point, and revise and extend it using the cloud brush you created in Chapter 2, "Photoshop Workspace, Tools, and Custom Brushes." Paint beyond the edge of the plate so you have the latitude to move the clouds when the scene is composited (Figure 11.2).

Figure 11.2 Add clouds to the plate.

Adding a Mountain Range

With the sky completed, create a new layer above Sky where you'll add a mountain range to define the horizon better. Name the new layer **Mountains**. This mountain range was created by patching together reference photos in the www.environmental-textures.com folder from the Chapter 7 ("Texturing and Color Correction") section of the DVD. The range is hard lit from the side, so you'll need to paint over the mountains to match the lighting in the plate (Figure 11.3). The work file for the mountains, MountainRange.psd, is included on the DVD.

Figure 11.3 Add a line of mountains on the horizon.

Select both the Sky and Mountains layers, and Shift+click the Create New Group icon at the bottom of the panel. Select this new group, and rename it **Sky+Mountains**. Trace around the buildings that intersect with the horizon to create a selection, and apply the selection as a layer mask to Sky+Mountains to integrate the group with the plate (Figure 11.4).

Figure 11.4 Use a layer mask to integrate the mountains into the edge of the city.

Removing Cast Shadows

The sun is casting hard shadows on the orange foreground roof and the middle left steeple. These shadows need to be removed for the night version. At night, most of the illumination will come from the street, and the roofs will receive only soft reflected light. Create a new layer called **DaytimePainting** above the Sky+Mountains group. To patch the hard shadow on the foreground roof, copy a selection of the lit area of the roof to the left of the shadow.

Paste the copied section over the hard cast shadow. You'll need to distort the pasted section to make the roof tiles line up. Eliminate all the cast shadows shown in green so you have a clean plate over which to work (Figure 11.5). Select the Plate and DaytimePainting layers and the Mountains+Sky group, and Shift+click the Create A New Group icon. Name the new group **Daytime**. Now your daytime plate is ready for conversion to night.

Figure 11.5 *Eliminate cast shadows.*

Preparing the Nighttime Plate

Make the BlackMask layer visible so you have clean edges on the frame. Create a new layer just below the BlackMask layer, and call it **BlueMultiply**. Fill the layer with a dark blue (an RBG readout of 55, 80, 115 in the Color Picker). Set the layer blending mode to Multiply. The composition immediately looks more like a night scene, but it's too dark (Figure 11.6).

Figure 11.6 *Dark blue multiplied over the entire composition*

For the rest of the chapter, the mask around the edges of the composition won't be shown in order to allow for larger figures, but it's still there.

Creating Mattes to Add Directional Lighting

Because light will be coming up from the street, the rooftops will receive the least light. First, you'll create a matte that selects just the rooftops. Turn off the BlueMultiply layer so you can see the plate clearly. Now, marquee off just the tops of the roofs. As you move far into the background, it will be more difficult to delineate the rooftops, so limit your work to where the roofs are easily defined. I live in a city with a lot of flat roofs; when I look across the city at night from a high angle, I see lines of lights from the streets, divided by sections of dark rooftops. Add to the existing selection to include some of those lines of dark roofs in the distance. Create a new layer called **RoofTops**, and fill the selection with bright red (Figure 11.7). This mask-loading layer will hold the roof-top selection for later use.

Next, you need a layer with just the front faces of the buildings. These buildings will be lit from the street level up, so you need a mask-holding layer with that selection. Create a new layer, name it **BuildingWalls**, and marquee around the building faces in the foreground. You can be sloppy where the faces intersect the roofs, because you already have a mask for that, and you can subtract it from the selection. When the selection is complete, fill it with green (Figure 11.8).

Figure 11.7 *Create a mask for the rooftops.*

Figure 11.8 *Create a mask for the building faces lit from the street.*

Create a mask for the towers and the front of the foreground churches. Name it **Towers+ ChurchFronts,** and fill it with blue (Figure 11.9). It's useful to have a separate matte for these structures because they will be rendered separately from the rest of the city.

Figure 11.9 Create a mask for the towers and the church fronts.

You need one more mask for the street and the areas where light rises up from distant streets and courtyards. Loosely marquee around the areas where the street shows, and subtract the existing masks from the selection. Add to the street selection by going through and selecting those areas where light would climb up the sides of buildings or show from distant streets. The more areas you define, the more detailed and beautiful the city will look. Make a new layer, rename it **Streets+Courtyards,** and fill it with purple (Figure 11.10).

Figure 11.10 Create a mask for the street and the light wells.

Figure 11.11 shows what the file should look like with all the masks defined. Some areas aren't covered by a mask, but you have enough to create an effective night scene.

Figure 11.11 All the masks visible

Preparing these masks may seem like a lot of work, but you'll use them again and again during this project to light the scene.

Select all the mask-holding layers, and click the Create New Group icon. Rename the group **MaskHoldingLayers**, and set the opacity of the group to 0% (Figure 11.12).

Figure 11.12 Group the mask layers, and set the opacity to 0.

Painting Into the BlueMultiply Layer Mask

With all the masks set up, it's time to begin painting. Return to the BlueMultiply layer, and turn it on. Add a layer mask. You'll paint into the mask to block the areas that are lit from the street. When you paint into the layer mask, white reveals the BlueMultiply layer and black blocks it. Press D to reset the Color Picker to the default black and white. You can switch between black and white by pressing X. Make sure black is loaded in the Foreground color slot.

First, load in two selections, BuildingWalls and Streets+Courtyards, by Command/Ctrl+clicking into the layer thumbnail previews. Using a soft round brush with the opacity set to 50%, paint where light would rise up from the street. It would be brightest at the street level where storefronts, streetlights, and car headlights provide illumination. The building fronts closer to the roofline get less light. The main street in the center of the composition should be the brightest area, because it appears to be a major retail hub.

In the distant areas, where light wells up from the streets and courtyards, use the Radial Gradient tool to add light that diminishes as it rises to the rooftops.

After you add light to the BuildingWalls and Streets+Courtyards selections, load in Towers+ChurchFronts. Paint and use the Radial Gradient tool to cast light up the sides of the church towers. The tops of the towers shouldn't receive light because they're far above the street level.

While you're painting, it's often useful to view the layer mask separately so you can visualize more clearly what areas are blocked. View the layer mask by Option/Alt+clicking into the mask preview thumbnail (Figure 11.13). You can continue to paint in the black-and-white layer mask.

When you want to see the RGB version, Option/Alt+click in the thumbnail preview again. With the layer mask for BlueMultiply applied, your composition should look like Figure 11.14.

Figure 11.13 Option/Alt+click into the layer mask thumbnail to view the mask separately.

Figure 11.14 BlueMultiply layer blocked by the layer mask to show areas illuminated by the street

Creating a Mask for the Building Windows

If you look at the layer mask for the BlueMultiply layer, you'll note a loss of building detail. Your piece will have more form if you restore some of the windows in the foreground buildings. Turn off the BlueMultiply layer for a moment and, in the Channels panel, check out which of the RGB channels offers the most contrast and shows the windows most distinctly. The Blue channel is the clearest, so duplicate it. On the duplicate, create a high-contrast matte by opening Curves and pulling in the white and black points until the windows are black against white. Some of the background windows still look gray, so marquee around them and run another curve until you isolate as many of the windows as possible. Your final high-contrast matte should look like Figure 11.15.

Figure 11.15 High-contrast duplicated Blue channel to isolate windows

Command/Ctrl+click into the high-contrast matte thumbnail to load the selection. The selection is the reverse of what you need, so invert it using Shift+Command/Ctrl+I. Now, return to the BlueMultiply layer, and turn it on. Option+click into the layer mask, and paint with white into the mask to restore some of the window detail (Figure 11.16). Paint only into the areas where you have windows; otherwise, you risk adding more of the BlueMultiply layer than you want to.

Figure 11.16 Final BlueMultiply layer mask

Creating a Warm Overlay Layer for the Street Lights

The cool lights are beginning to work, but the streetlights need to be warm. Create a new layer above the BlueMultiply layer, and rename it **StreetOverlay**. Command/Ctrl+A to select all. Fill the layer with a warm yellow-orange (RGB setting of 250, 190, 90 in the Color Picker). Set the layer's blending mode to Overlay. The streetlights warm up—but, unfortunately, so does everything else.

You need to confine the warm color to the lit areas. Load the selection from the layer mask for the BlueMultiply layer by Command/Ctrl+clicking into the mask thumbnail. Invert the selection, and apply it to the StreetOverlay layer as a layer mask. By applying the inverse of the BlueMultiply layer, you warm up only the areas that aren't being affected by the cool blue (Figure 11.17).

Figure 11.17 *An orange overlay layer warms up the city lights.*

Silhouetting the Mountains

The background mountains should be darker to silhouette against the sky. We tend to think of the night sky as black; but actually the sky is the brightest element in almost any scene, except for the Sun, the Moon, or artificial lights. You could create a new layer to darken the mountains, but you'll get the same effect by painting into the BlueMultiply layer with a neutral dark blue.

Load the selection from the Mountains layer, and darken the area where the mountains meet the sky, softly blending the transition to where the city starts. Invert the selection, and paint a lighter blue on the horizon just behind the mountains. Now they should stand out nicely (Figure 11.18).

Figure 11.18 Darken the mountains on the BlueMultiply layer, and lighten the sky behind them.

Adding Life to the City

You now have the plate toned with warm and cool layers, but it doesn't have the sparkle of life that lit windows provide. Adding this will involve some handwork; but rest assured, you won't have to place every window individually.

The Window Bank

Find a photo of an illuminated building at night, and copy a selection of the windows. Paste them into a new layer just above BlueMultiply, and call it **WindowBank**. While working on this project, I kept a file open as the repository for any sections of photos I might reuse. If you want lit windows to insert without searching for a photo reference, open the file CityBits.psd on the DVD, copy the layer WindowBits, and paste it into the WindowBank layer.

Move all the windows out of the way by placing them on the foreground rooftop. Copy one window, and paste it above WindowBank into a new layer called **Windows**, and then set the layer blending mode to Screen. You can now light the buildings by distorting the lit window to cover any unlit window. The temptation will be to use the same window over and over again. But going back to the window bank and choosing a new, slightly different window will add realism through randomization (Figure 11.19).

You can also distort a group of lit windows into place across the face of a building, but be careful to match the placement of the original windows from the daytime scene. After you have the windows in place, you can add more variety by making a selection from the layer and painting into the windows.

Create a new layer above Windows, and name it **Storefront**. Add some lit storefronts on the ground floor of the buildings in the main shopping area. You can take them from any nighttime photo of a commercial district, or use the examples in my window bank. Distort and edit the reference to fit the storefront shapes. The square building to the right of the church looks like a food stand, so place some lit windows around the outside. Finally, add a lit balcony to the church (Figure 11.20). When you're finished adding lights to the window, turn off the visibility on the WindowBank layer. You can always turn it on again if you decide to add more windows.

Figure 11.19 *Using the Window Bank to populate the city with windows*

Figure 11.20 *Add lit storefronts and a balcony.*

Adding the Distant Lights of the City

When you look across a large, sprawling city at night from a high vantage point, you see millions of dazzling lights in the background. I don't have any night shots of Munich, but I live just outside of New York City, and I have some night shots from the top of the Empire State Building. You can use my reference shots to add background lights to this scene.

Create a new layer above the Storefronts layer, and rename it **CityLights**. Go back to the CityBits.psd file, and copy NightCity1 from the file. Paste it into the new layer, and set the blending mode to Screen. Move the top edge of the lights to rest below the mountains. This immediately adds depth and grandeur to the scene (Figure 11.21).

Figure 11.21 Add background city lights.

Using a Layer Mask to Edit the Lights

Because these lights are from another city, you'll need to add a layer mask to make the lights conform to this project. Select the CityLights layer mask, and load the Towers+ChurchFront selection. Paint into the layer mask with black to block any lights that appear on top of the towers. Load in the RoofTops selection from the MaskHoldingLayers group, and paint into the selection to stop the lights from showing on rooftops. Now, paint into the layer mask to get the lights to line up with the streets on the plate. Block out any lights that look out of place, such as those bleeding into the foreground retail area. You can be very loose while painting your mask; if you make a mistake, paint over it with white, and the lights will show through again.

Figure 11.22 shows the loose treatment for the layer mask for CityLights.

Figure 11.22 Layer mask for the CityLights layer

Using the `CityBits.psd` file or your own city lights reference, add more background lights. It would be difficult to hand-place all the lights throughout the city, but photographs offer natural randomization that you can control with the layer mask; you can then specifically place lights where needed (Figure 11.23).

Figure 11.23 City lights finished

Lighting Up the Towers

Towers in old cities are often illuminated at night. Let's add lights to both the foreground towers. For the left tower, add two spotlights mounted on the roof to light up the tower steeple. With the Lasso tool set to a 6-pixel feather, draw the inverted cone shape of the light falling on each side (Figure 11.24).

Create a new Curves adjustment layer above the StreetOverlay layer. You want to work with all of the existing corrections applied and this curve correction applied on top of them. Pull the midtones up very high while retaining the dark details on the tower (Figure 11.25).

The light wouldn't extend beyond the side of the tower or light up the front small spire. Paint black into the layer mask for the Curves adjustment layer to confine the correction. Next, soften the top of the light beam at the top of the tower (Figure 11.26).

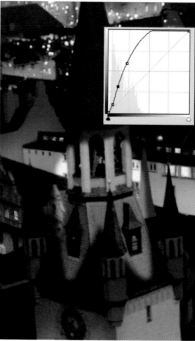

Figure 11.24 Draw the shape of spotlight falling on the tower.

Figure 11.25 Adjustment layer curve for lighting the tower

Figure 11.26 Edit the layer mask

Paint into the Curves layer mask to show light climbing up the clock tower. Also, lighten the front of the foreground church to separate it from the building in front of it. The layer mask for the two towers and the church front should look like Figure 11.27.

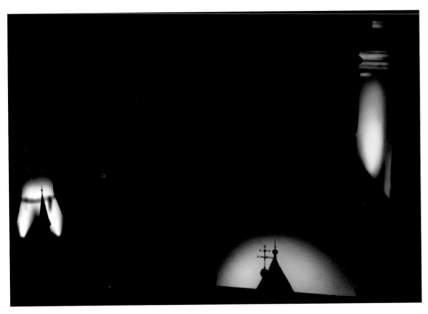

Figure 11.27 Layer mask for the towers and the church front

Top Additions with a Paint Layer

Start a new layer on top of the Curves adjustment layer you just created, and name it **PaintLayer.** Paint some spotlights on the left tower steeple to provide a source for the beams. The clock tower would benefit from an illuminated clock face, so either paint that in or copy the clock face out of the `CityBits.psd` file. Distort the clock face to appear on the side of the tower. You can warm up the light on the towers and church front by painting into the StreetOverlay layer (Figure 11.28).

Figure 11.28 Towers and church front with adjustments added

Light Flares

Small light flares enhance the realism of a night scene. I never use Photoshop's Lens Flare filter for the purpose it was intended for, because its effects are so recognizable and overused. However, prepared in a special way, it's very effective for adding small flares and glows.

Start a new Photoshop file that's 300 × 300 pixels, and fill it with black. Choose Filter → Render → Lens Flare, and select the first option, 50-300mm Zoom. Center the cursor exactly in the middle of the preview so that none of the little light elements go off to the side, and set Brightness to 100. Click OK, and you have a rendered lens flare.

Open Curves, and raise the white point by 25 points to get a brighter center. Still in the Curves dialog, select Green from the Channels drop-down menu, and pull the middle of the green curve up to lessen the bright red. Click OK to accept the curve adjustment. Select all, and apply a gaussian blur of 2 pixels to get rid of the spiky detail. Marquee around the flare while excluding the outer ring, and feather the edge by 10 pixels (Figure 11.29).

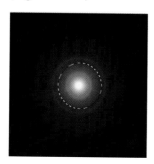

Figure 11.29 *Lens flare for glows*

Copy and paste the flare into a new layer. Rename the layer **Flares,** and set the blending mode to Screen. You'll use this glow over and over to give your city sparkle. This is one instance when you can reuse a reference to your heart's content.

Marquee copy+drag the lens flare to copy it to different locations on the Flares layer. Look in the street with the main retail area, and drag the flare over one of the streetlights. It's too large, so scale it down to 10% of the original size. Using the scaled-down flare, Option/Alt+move to copy it many times to cover every streetlight. As you move away from the foreground, you'll need to scale down the glow to fit the light. Because the flare is blurry, you don't need to be concerned with losing sharpness. However, should it start to look too soft, go back to the original flare, copy it, and scale it to size.

Like tinsel on a Christmas tree, many tiny flares will add pizzazz to the scene. Every car headlight should have one. You can add random flares to brighten up an otherwise dull area. Because buildings often have exterior lights mounted on their sides, let your imagination dictate where you want more sparkle. For instance, you can add a flare to indicate the source of light on the clock tower as well as the front of the church.

Add a new layer named **TopGlows** above the Flares layer and set the blending mode to Screen. Manually paint a streak of white in front of every headlight to show where the light is pooling on the street, and paint a light beneath every streetlight (Figure 11.30). You can paint in more light in the courtyards and distant street on the TopGlows layer to add atmosphere.

Figure 11.30 *Lens flares and glows added*

Relighting

You're almost finished! There are still some areas that require manual relighting. For instance, the clock tower is lit from below, but the shadow pattern suggests it's lit from above. There is nothing to do but manually reverse the direction of the light.

Load the Towers+ChurchFronts selection from the MaskHoldingLayers group, and Shift+Command/Ctrl+C. Doing so copies all the pixels in the selection, including both towers and both church fronts. Paste it above PaintLayer in the same position you copied it from. Select the new layer, and press Command/Ctrl+E to merge it with PaintLayer. Go through and lighten all the surfaces that face down, and darken all the surfaces that face up. You'll need to do that for both towers and church fronts. The top of the tower is lost in the blue of the sky, so color-correct it to make it warmer (Figure 11.31).

A lot of places in the composition could benefit from relighting, but I'll leave them for you to discover and paint. Make all your painted revisions on PaintLayer so you can paint without having to deal with the color corrections applied by the BlueMultiply and StreetOverlay layers. Also, this way you know where all of your final corrections are located.

Figure 11.31 *Reverse the light direction on the clock tower.*

The Night Sky

You need to attend to one last detail: the sky looks out of place, because it's no more than a darkened version of the daytime sky. Add a new layer above the BlueMultiply layer, and name it **Sky.**Using the Clouds brush, paint some moody, streaky clouds (Figure 11.32).

Select all the layers that make up your nighttime plate, but not the MaskHoldingLayers group or the Daytime group, and place them in a new group called **Nighttime**. Now you can lower and raise the opacity of the Nighttime group as a whole to see a gradual transition from day to night. You can check out the final file on the DVD, DayForNightProject.psd.

Figure 11.32 *Nighttime version of the plate*

Assignment: Take Your Own Plate From Day to Night

Try out these techniques using an image of your own choosing, or for an extra challenge, use a photograph you took yourself.

Starting with a daytime photograph, do the following:

1. Duplicate your original image so you are working over a copy.
2. Add a one-inch black border around the image to give yourself a work area.
3. Patch over, or paint out any cast shadows that are apparent in the photo, since nighttime scenes usually will not show hard cast shadows.
4. Create re-usable mask-loading layers for the rooftops, building sides, and any architectural elements in your scene that require relighting.

5. Add a new layer on top of your daytime version, and fill it with dark blue. Set the layer to Multiply, and apply a layer mask. Use the selections from the mask-loading layers to paint black into the layer mask to block the dark blue in areas that will be illuminated.

6. Add a new layer on top of the dark blue layer, and set it to Overlay. Fill the layer with a warm color. Apply a layer mask on top of that, fill the mask with black, and paint white into it to reveal areas illuminated by artificial light.

7. Use lit windows and storefronts from reference photos to populate your structures with nighttime lights.

8. If your scene needs it, add background lights taken from a reference nighttime scene, and use a layer mask to confine the lights to where they are needed.

9. Use flares to add zest to any bright artificial lights in your scene.

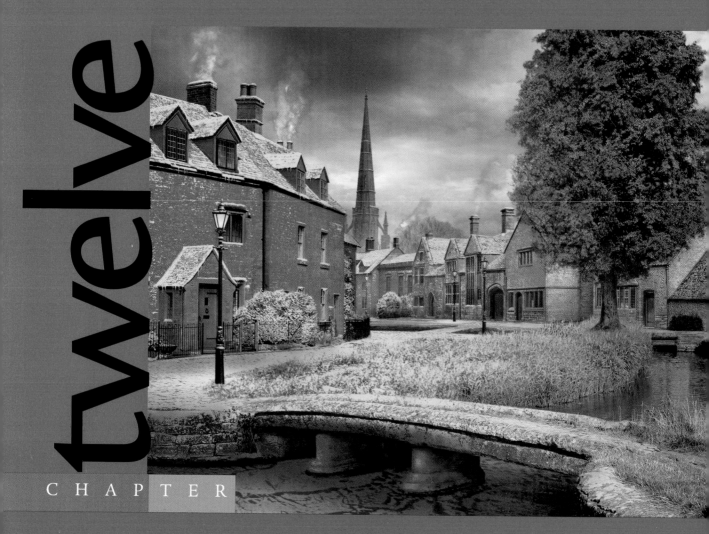

twelve

Changing Seasons

Matte artists are often tasked *with taking a scene photographed in one season and converting it to another. The most common example involves converting a summer scene to winter. Why do this? Because snow is extremely difficult to deal with on a production schedule. If you have a wonderful snow-covered day, changes in the weather can quickly turn your winter wonderland into a slushy mess, and maintaining continuity in the look of the snow is difficult. Also, if the production requires a dramatic change in the time of year, rather than suspending production for months and waiting for the season to change, a wise director will seek out the skills of a matte artist to effect the transformation. After all, nothing better illustrates the passage of time than a cross-dissolve between a bright summer day and a shot of the same scene blanketed with snow against a wintry sky.*

For this project, you'll take a plate of a European country village and remove all modern elements so it looks like it would have in the 1800s. Then, you'll convert the summer scene to a cold and snowy December day. Finally, you'll tone the plate to evoke dusk just as lights are coming on.

The Summertime Plate

In Photoshop, open 683043.jpg from the Chapter 12 DVD materials. The photo of a rural country village will be the plate for this exercise.

Duplicate the Background layer, and rename the new layer **BackgroundRev**. Just as in the previous project, it will be useful to have a work area around the edge of the image. Press D on the keyboard to load the default black and white colors into the Color Picker. Choose Image → Canvas size, and add an extra inch around the sides. Command/Ctrl+click into the layer thumbnail for BackgroundRev to load the layer selection and invert it. Create a new layer called **Mask** at the top of the project, and fill the selection with black (Figure 12.1).

Figure 12.1 The plate with a one-inch mask all around

Image Credit: Corel Stock Photo Library

Removing Anachronistic Details

What a beautiful country village, perfect for a production set 150 years ago. I can just see Tiny Tim and Bob Cratchit walking across the bridge on their way to church. Wait a second—there were no TV antennas in Charles Dickens' era! Press Command/Ctrl+D to deselect the mask, and select the BackgroundRev layer to revise the plate to capture the look of the time.

First, remove the offending television antennas, the white handrail on the far bridge, and all the figures in modern dress. You can do this using the Clone tool; or select, duplicate, and move adjoining areas to cover the parts you don't want. Next, soften the hard shadows on the supports for the foreground bridge and under the eaves of the roofs on the buildings. The Clone tool works particularly well for this, because you want to keep the edges soft. Finally, close the open windows in the top dormers of the left building by duplicating and distorting the open windows into the closed position (Figure 12.2).

Figure 12.2 *Revise the plate to remove all the details that would look out of place in the 1800s.*

Painting Out the Summer Tree

You'll need to paint out the big leafy tree in the middle of the view and substitute for it a bare-branched version appropriate for December. If you look closely, the tree in the plate is actually two trees: a smaller one in the foreground and the larger one behind it. This is visually confusing, so you'll eliminate the small tree in the foreground. However, you must extract and save the large tree on a separate layer for use in the summer version.

You could use the Lasso tool to marquee around the tree, but the detail in the tree leaves would be difficult to select. You can get the top part of the tree using a high-contrast matte with much less effort. Still working on the BackgroundRev layer, duplicate the Blue channel in the Channels panel, and select the new channel. Open Curves, and pull the black point to the right to Input 128 and the white point to the left to Input 210. Doing so makes the tree completely black and the sky completely white (Figure 12.3).

To extract the tree, you need the tree white and the sky black in the high-contrast matte, so press Command/Ctrl+I to invert the channel. Click RGB

Figure 12.3 *Create a high-contrast matte from the Blue channel to isolate the top of the tree.*

at the top of the Channels panel to return to working on the color image of the scene. Using the Lasso tool, select around the bottom of the large tree, including the trunk but omitting the smaller tree. Click back on the high-contrast channel you just created to select it again. Press D to load the default white and black into the Color Picker, and then press X to load white into the background color. Press Delete to fill the selection of the bottom of the tree with white (Figure 12.4).

Figure 12.4 Select the bottom of the tree, including the trunk, and press Delete to fill the selection with white.

Invert the selection by pressing Command/Ctrl+I, and paint black into the channel to isolate the bottom of the tree. When you're finished, only the white silhouette of the tree should be visible in the channel (Figure 12.5).

Load the selection, and click into RGB at the top of the Channels panel to return to the color version of the scene. With BackgroundRev still selected, press Command/Ctrl+J to move the tree onto a new layer. Name the layer **SummerTree**. Parts of the smaller tree are still visible, so either patch the left side of the tree using sections of the existing tree, or manually paint out the smaller tree. When you're finished, you should have the summer tree cleanly separated on the SummerTree layer.

Even though the big tree is on a separate layer, it's still visible on the BackgroundRev layer. Turn off the SummerTree layer for the moment, and return to the BackgroundRev layer. Paint out the big tree on that layer. You don't need to be too careful while doing this, because you'll replace the sky a little later. Just make sure you have blue sky where the tree used to be on the BackgroundRev layer (Figure 12.6).

Turn the SummerTree layer back on. The composition would be stronger if the tree wasn't smack dab in the middle, bisecting the view. Move the tree to the right to create a more pleasing composition. Back on the BackgroundRev layer, block in some rough tones to cover the remains of the tree where the buildings are located (Figure 12.7). You'll replace those buildings with more interesting architecture in the next step.

Figure 12.5 Invert the selection, and paint black around the base of the tree to get a clean selection channel.

Figure 12.6 *Paint out the big tree on the BackgroundRev layer.*

Figure 12.7 *Paint out the background building, and move the tree to the right.*

Replacing the Background Buildings

With the big tree moved, there is now a nice space where you'll add a more complex string of buildings, giving the scene more depth. Open 301074.jpg from the DVD, and marquee around the string of buildings, including their chimneys. Copy the selection, and paste it into the village scene on a new layer directly below the SummerTree layer. Name the layer **NewHouses**, and scale the new buildings down about 35% so they fit with the other buildings along the canal. The perspective on the new buildings doesn't perfectly match the other buildings in the plate (Figure 12.8). You'll correct that in the next step.

Figure 12.8 Paste in the new buildings, and scale them down 35% to fit into the plate.

Create a new layer called **Perspective** just below the Mask layer. Using the large buildings on the right as reference, draw lines of convergence in red to establish a vanishing point (VP) on the right side of the composition. Do the same using the smaller buildings to the right to find a left VP, and draw lines of convergence in green. The buildings aren't parallel to each other because they follow the curve of the canal, but you'll use the VPs to find the horizon line. With two VPs identified, draw the horizon line through them in blue. Return to the NewHouses layer, and distort the buildings into place using the horizon line as reference. You need to adjust the faces of the individual buildings to make them follow the curve of the canal, and you also need to color-correct them to match the surrounding buildings (Figure 12.9).

Turn off the Perspective layer. Add a cathedral spire in the background to indicate that there is a city center beyond the village in the plate. Open 301055.jpg from the DVD. Marquee around the spire, and copy and paste it into a new layer behind the NewHouses layer. Name the layer **ChurchSpire**. Scale the spire down by 58% to fit into the background, and flip it horizontally so it matches the light in the scene. The cathedral reference is soft, so paint over it to sharpen it and restore detail. You'll need to remove tree branches from the original photo and paint out the streetlight. The spire has a reddish coloration, so use Curves to color-correct it and make the color more neutral. Add a layer mask where the cathedral intersects the buildings on the left (Figure 12.10).

Figure 12.9 Replace the background buildings.

Figure 12.10 Use the reference photo on the left to add a cathedral spire in the background.

Image Credit: Corel Stock Photo Library

The trees in front of the cathedral need some work. Add a new layer called **TreesBkSummer** above the ChurchSpire layer, and paint a line of treetops to separate the cathedral from the village (Figure 12.11).

Figure 12.11 Add trees in front of the cathedral to separate it from the village.

The central patch of grass looks rather shabby, with a brown section near the sidewalk and unkempt reeds along the canal. Create a new layer on top of the SummerTree layer, and name it **GrassPatch**. You can either hand-paint the section or find a suitably groomed section of grass that you can graft into the area. You should also get rid of any remnants of the smaller tree, and groom the reeds along the edge of the canal (Figure 12.12).

Figure 12.12 Clean up the grass in the center section.

Replacing the Sky

Some puffy clouds would make this scene more bucolic and heighten the summertime effect. You need to create a matte that separates the sky from the revised plate. To do that, turn off the SummerTree layer and duplicate the Blue channel for a second time. Apply a high-contrast curve to the channel to get the village as black as possible and the sky as white as possible. You'll need to do some cleanup on the channel to get it completely black and white. Click back on RGB at the top of the Channels panel.

You can either find attractive clouds to intensify the feeling of a summer afternoon or use SummerSky.jpg from the DVD. Create a new layer above the BackgroundRev layer, and name it **SummerSky**. Paste the sky into the SummerSky layer, and scale it to fit. In the Channels panel, load the selection from the alpha channel you created to isolate the sky, and apply the selection as a layer mask to the SummerSky layer. The mask prevents the sky from showing on top of the village.

Click the chain-link icon [icon] between the sky and the layer mask to unlink [icon] the sky and the mask. Select SummerSky by clicking the layer thumbnail. Now you can move the sky around and try different positions without having the mask move with it. It's a nice way to try different skies or combine several skies to get just the right effect, because the mask stays in the same place while you rearrange the clouds (Figure 12.13).

Figure 12.13 *Replace the sky.*

Light-Wrapping the Tree

Finally, because the tree was cut out of the original plate and moved, the leaves have hard edges that won't blend well with the sky. Load the selection from SummerTree, choose Select → Modify → Border, and create a 4-pixel border. Soften the border by adding a 3-pixel feather by choosing Select → Modify → Feather.

Turn off the SummerTree layer so that only the sky and buildings are visible. Shift+Command/Ctrl+C to copy a sliver of sky that will surround the tree like an aura. Light tends to bend around the edges of objects and soften those edges; this natural phenomenon is known as *light wrap*. Turn the SummerTree layer back on, and paste the copied sliver of sky on top of the tree. Name the layer **LightWrap**, and set the blending mode to Lighten. Turn the layer on and off to see the effect. The light-wrap effect is too obvious, so experiment with setting the opacity of the LightWrap layer at somewhere around 40%.

The edges of the tree are now softer and blend into the sky (Figure 12.14). Select both the SummerTree and LightWrap layers, and place them in a group called **SummerTreeGroup**.

Figure 12.14 *Light wrap on the tree: left side off, right side on*

Final Details

The paths in front of the homes are poured concrete, a modern material that is out of place in an earlier era. For a more authentic look, open CobblestoneTexture.jpg from the DVD and copy and paste it into a new layer above the GrassPatch layer. Name the layer **Cobblestone**, and set the layer blending mode to Multiply so you retain some of the underlying texture.

Position the texture over the walkways and on the top of the bridge. Rather than delete the unneeded sections of cobblestone, turn off the layer for a moment. Marquee-select the top of the bridge and all the walkways. Turn the Cobblestone layer back on, and apply the selection as a layer mask. Now the texture is confined to the areas you selected (Figure 12.15).

Figure 12.15 *Add a cobblestone texture to the path.*

Period lampposts would add a nice touch. You can use the lamppost in 301080.jpg as a starting point. Marquee around the lamppost from that file, and copy and paste it onto a new layer above the Cobblestone layer. Name the layer **LampPosts**. Duplicate it along the edge of the canal as a repeating motif. On the same layer, add a bridge across the canal where you replaced the houses behind the big tree (Figure 12.16).

Figure 12.16 Add lampposts along the canal and a small bridge.

With all the elements in place, go through and color-correct anything that doesn't fit in. The buildings on the left looked too light, so marquee-select them. Turn off the LampPosts layer so you can work on just the buildings. Shift+Command/Ctrl+C to Copy Merged the entire section. Paste the copied buildings back in the same position on a new layer just above the NewHouses layer. Name the layer **DarkenHouses**. Use Curves to give the structure more form by darkening all the sides that are facing away from the light (Figure 12.17).

Figure 12.17 Select and duplicate the left-side buildings, and then darken and revise the lighting.

Turn the LampPosts layer back on now that you're finished revising the left-side buildings. When you're satisfied with the look of the plate, make a new group called **SummerVersionGroup**. Select all the layers except Mask, Perspective, and Background, and place them in SummerVersionGroup.

Your finished summer plate should look like Figure 12.18. You can open SummerPlate .psd on the DVD materials to compare it with your results.

Figure 12.18 Finished summer version

The Wintertime Plate

You'll want to keep the summertime version and work over a copy. Duplicate SummerVersion-Group, and rename the duplicate group **WinterVersionGroup**. Make sure WinterVersion is above SummerVersionGroup in the Layers panel.

Inside WinterVersion, turn off SummerTreeGroup, because you'll use it only as reference.

Adding a Winter Sky

To get the mood started for the winter version, replace the sky. Inside WinterVersionGroup, select the SummerSky layer, and rename it **WinterSky**. Because you replaced and reworked all the buildings, you no longer need the layer mask on the sky. Select the layer mask on WinterSky, and delete it. Now you can replace the summer sky. CGTextures.com has provided an appropriate sky on the DVD named FullskiesOvercast0028_1_L.jpg. This is a large panoramic sky, so you can move it around and try different sections.

In this demonstration, no single section of the sky worked perfectly, so I took sections of different areas and combined them. I found a brighter section to go behind the church steeple and named the layer **SkyHighlight**. I selected a darker area for use at upper right and named the layer **LfSkyBit**. When I was finished, I selected all these winter sky sections and combined them into a group called **WinterSkyGroup** to keep them organized (Figure 12.19).

Figure 12.19 *Insert a winter sky.*

Adding Snow

Rather than a heavy snowfall, this winter version will have a light dusting of snow to retain the texture of the objects in the scene. Keep in mind these two rules when you're painting a snowy winter scene:

1. Winter scenes are far less colorful than the summer versions.
2. Snow lands and sticks mainly on horizontal surfaces.

Removing All the Green

Turn off the LampPosts layer, because you'll deal with those elements separately. Start a new layer between the Cobblestone and LampPosts layers, and name it **Snow**.

The summer plate has a lot of green showing, so the first step in changing the season is to get rid of as much of the greenery as possible. Choose Select → Color Range. Use the eyedropper to select a green from the center grass patch. Hold down Shift, and select more shades of green. This technique adds each additional color to the selection, and it previews the selection in black and white in the Color Range dialog box. If you click a color and it adds more of the scene to the selection than you want, press Command/Ctrl+Z to undo that addition. Subtract a color from the selection by pressing the Option/Alt key while clicking the color with the eyedropper. Use the slider to add to and subtract from the range of the selection. When you've selected as much of the green as possible, while selecting a minimal amount of the buildings, sky, and bridge, click OK (Figure 12.20).

If you use the selection that the Color Range tool creates without revision, you'll find that the selection has many small holes in it. To get a solid selection, you need to use the Lasso tool to hand patch what Color Range gives you, including the entire center island of

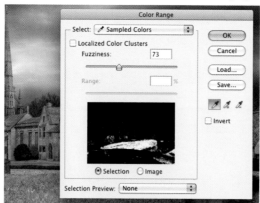

grass and all the bushes and greenery. If parts of the buildings were selected, subtract them from the selection using the Lasso tool.

You need to copy all the green in the selection onto a new layer. Shift+ Command/Ctrl+C to Copy Merged the selected areas, and paste it into the Snow layer. Press Command/Ctrl+U to open the Hue/Saturation dialog box. Pull the Saturation slider all the way to the left to remove all color (Figure 12.21).

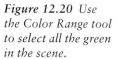

Figure 12.20 Use the Color Range tool to select all the green in the scene.

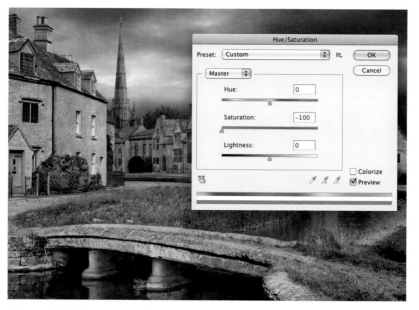

Figure 12.21 Desaturate the greenery in the scene.

Brightening the Grass

With all the color removed, Command/Ctrl+M to open Curves. Apply an extreme curve by pulling the white point far in to the left, and pull the midtones up slightly. The grass instantly looks like it's been coated with a frosting of snow (Figure 12.22).

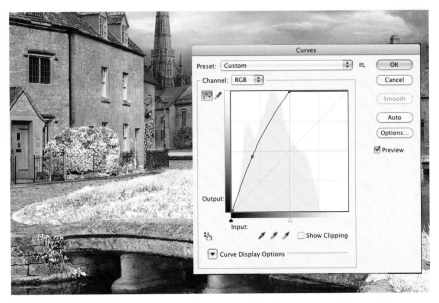

Figure 12.22 *Curve the desaturated grass and bushes to cover them with snow.*

Adding Snow to the Roof Tops

Turn off the Snow layer for now. Create a new layer below the Snow layer, and name it **DesaturateRoofs+Path**. Hand-select all the rooftops and the cobblestone textured pathways with the Lasso tool. You'll handle this differently than the grass and bushes. With the rooftops and pathways selected, Shift+Command/Ctrl+C to Copy Merged everything in the selection, and paste it into DesaturateRoofs+Path. Completely desaturate this new layer with Hue/Saturation (Figure 12.23).

Figure 12.23 *Create a new layer with the desaturated roofs and paths.*

Command/Ctrl+click into the layer thumbnail for DesaturateRoofs+Path to load the layer selection. Make a new layer above it, and name it **SnowOverlay**. Fill the selection in SnowOverlay with white. Next, set the layer blending mode to Overlay (Figure 12.24).

The texture of the tile roofs and the cobblestone paths is preserved, and the surfaces look like they're covered with snow.

The roofs of the houses on the left and the back roofs in the center of the composition near the cathedral are darker than the other roofs, but the snow on all the rooftops should

Figure 12.24
SnowOverlay layer selection filled with white and set to the Overlay blending mode

be of a similar value. Select them on the DesaturateRoofs+Path layer, and pull in the white point using Curves to brighten them to match the other roofs. The more you move the white point input levels to the left, the more snow appears to be on the roofs (Figure 12.25).

Turn on the Snow layer again to admire the start of the snowstorm (Figure 12.26).

Figure 12.25 *Left side before Curves adjustment, right side after*

Figure 12.26 *The rooftops, paths, and greenery are all covered with snow.*

Select the DesaturateRoofs+Path, SnowOverlay, and Snow layers, and place them all in a new group called **SnowGroup**.

Freezing the Canal

At this time of year, the canal should be icy but not frozen solid. Select the Snow layer, and use the Lasso tool to select the area of the canal, carefully excluding the bridge and abutments. Open the file 184022.jpg from the DVD. It shows water just on the verge of freezing, with some patchy patterning of snowfall on the surface. Select the entire photo, and copy it.

Return to the Snow layer, and Shift+Option/Alt+Command/Ctrl+V to paste the ice photo into your composition and create a new layer just above the Snow layer. Doing so automatically applies the selection you made previously of the canal as a layer mask. Name the layer **CanalSnow**. Notice that the layer mask isn't linked to the layer because the chain link isn't visible between the thumbnails. You can move the photo reference around to find a position that works. Choose Edit → Transform → Distort, squash the ice vertically, and distort it so the pattern of the ice follows the edge of the canal on the right side.

To fill in the left side under the bridge, you need to find a section of ice that isn't used on the right. Right-click the CanalSnow layer mask thumbnail, and select Disable Layer Mask to turn off your mask and see all of the ice reference. When the layer mask is disabled, a red X appears over the mask ⬚ . Lasso-select another section of the ice, and Option/Alt +Command/Ctrl+drag to duplicate it to fill the left side of the canal.

To restore the mask, left-click the disabled mask preview (Figure 12.27).

Figure 12.27 Turning the layer mask on and off to see the underlying reference

Color-Correcting the Canal

The color of the canal ice is too green, and it needs more contrast. Select the layer thumbnail for CanalSnow, and open the Hue/Saturation dialog box. Drag the Saturation slider to -85 to desaturate the layer. The ice should have more contrast, so open Curves and drag the white point input to 225 and the black point input to 38 (Figure 12.28).

Even though this is an overcast winter day, the ice would sit in the canal better if there were cast shadows from the bank and bridge. On the CanalSnow layer, use the Lasso tool to marquee around where the shadowed areas should appear on the ice. Add a Curves adjustment layer. Because you had a selection made when you applied the adjustment layer, it has a layer mask attached to it. Pull down the white point on the Curves adjustment to where it

Figure 12.28 Add contrast to the ice reference.

approximates a shadow. Name this adjustment layer **CanalCurves**. Refine the shape of the shadow by painting into the layer mask with a soft brush. None of the shadows should be sharp, because it's overcast. When you're finished, place both the CanalSnow layer and the shadow adjustment layer into a group called **CanalWinterGroup** (Figure 12.29).

Figure 12.29 Add shadows to the canal ice.

The Winter Tree

The only part of the summer tree that you can use in the winter scene is the trunk. Duplicate that onto a new layer named **WinterTrunk**. You can hand paint the winter tree if you like, or find a photo of a bare tree. The people at 3DTotal.com were kind enough to provide a tree with an alpha channel; it's on the DVD, named Winter024.psd. This tree works well, but it's much wider than the summer tree, and the silhouettes don't match. Turn on the summer tree at 40% opacity, and, using it as a reference, scale and pull in the branches of the winter tree so the bare branches reach just to the edges of the summer version (Figure 12.30). Name the layer with the bare tree **WinterTree**.

Figure 12.30 Revise the photo reference of a bare tree to match the silhouette of the summer tree.

Adding Snow to the Winter Tree

The winter tree should have snow on the top surfaces of the branches. A simple way to add that coating is to Command/Ctrl+click into the layer thumbnail for WinterTree to make a selection of the tree, and then nudge the selection down 2 pixels with the arrow keys. Choose Select Inverse, and Command/Ctrl+J to copy the top edge of the tree branches onto a new layer. Apply a curve to the new layer, pulling in the white point until the tops of the limbs turn white. Name this layer **TreeSnowTop1**.

The branches get thicker in the center of the tree, so they need more snow. Return to the WinterTree layer, and make a selection of the tree again. Using the arrow keys, move the selection down 5 pixels and choose Select Inverse. Choose the Lasso tool, and feather it 55 pixels. Hold down the Shift+Option/Alt keys, and use the Lasso tool to draw around the center of the tree selection where the fatter branches are located. Doing so leaves the tiny tips of the branches unselected so they won't get more snow. Command/Ctrl+J to copy the tops of the inner branches to a new layer, and apply a curve to turn the branches white. The inner branches should now have more snow. Name the second layer of snow **TreeSnowTop2**. The snow-covered branches show some residual color from the tree, so desaturate both snow layers using the Hue/Saturation dialog (Figure 12.31).

This is looking good, but the snow didn't land anywhere on the center of the trunk. Duplicate TreeSnowTop2, and move it to the left and down so the snow pattern covers the center of the trunk. Rename the layer **TreeSnowCenter**. Make a selection from the WinterTree layer, invert the selection, and apply the selection as a layer mask to TreeSnowCenter so the snow only shows in the center of the tree. Unlink the image and the mask so you can move the snow around until you get a position that you like (Figure 12.32). Select all the layers for the tree, and place them in a group called **SnowTreeGroup**.

Figure 12.31 Add snow to the tops of the bare tree's branches.   *Figure 12.32 Add snow to the middle of the winter tree.*

Adding Detail With High-Contrast Mattes

Next, you'll add snow to the fronts of the buildings. Snow will stick to a structure wherever there are uneven sections of bricks on the facade. Rather than hand-painting this detail, you'll extract the information using a high-contrast matte. Look through the RGB channels to see which one shows the brick pattern most clearly. The Green channel has the most contrast, so duplicate that channel.

Apply a curve to the duplicated channel, pulling the white and black points into the center until the rough pattern on the brick walls is isolated in black and white. You'll need to do this process several times, because the same curve won't work for all the buildings. The building on the left has a nice pattern on it, but the building next to it is almost completely white and requires a different curve (Figure 12.33).

You'll only use the texture on the walls, not on the sky, ground, roofs, or canal. Marquee around the unneeded areas, and fill them with white. When you've isolated the textured areas of the stone walls and everything else is white, invert the channel by pressing Command/ Ctrl+A and then Command/Ctrl+I (Figure 12.34).

Figure 12.33 Create a high-contrast matte of the Green channel to isolate wall detail.

Figure 12.34 Inverted high-contrast channel to add snow to the sides of the buildings

With the inverted channel still selected, copy and paste it into SnowGroup in the Layers panel. Name the layer **SnowBuildingFront**. Change the blending mode to Screen. The building fronts now look like they've been dusted with snow (Figure 12.35).

Figure 12.35 *Screen snow detail from a high-contrast matte onto your buildings.*

Use this same high-contrast channel technique to dust the other surfaces with snow, such as the bridge and abutments, chimneys, and any other textured surfaces (Figure 12.36).

Using a high-contrast matte again, add snow to the trunk of the tree (Figure 12.37).

Figure 12.36 *Add more snow to textured surfaces throughout the scene.*

Figure 12.37 *Add snow to the tree trunk.*

Hand Painting

You must add some of the final snow details by hand-painting. Select the Snow layer, and paint snow on the tops of all the chimneys. The brush BrokenLineSolid, the seventeenth brush in the custom brush set included on the DVD called `Custom Brush Examples.abr`, is very good for adding lines of snow while retaining texture in the painted areas (Figure 12.38).

Use a new custom brush to add icicles dripping down from overhanging surfaces. From the same custom brush set, choose HardRoundSolid5, and set the size to 3. Open the Brush panel, and select Shape Dynamics. In the Control drop-down menu on the right under Size Jitter, choose Fade. In the box directly to the right of Fade, type **20**: this is the distance the brush will paint until the size drops to 0 pixels. Select Scattering, and set the amount to 10% and Control to Off. Scattering gives the icicle some texture (Figure 12.39).

Figure 12.38 Hand-paint snow on the tops of the chimneys.

Go to one of the chimneys, and paint a stroke straight down from a surface that needs an icicle (Figure 12.40). You should vary the number to the right of Fade—smaller numbers produce shorter icicles. Save the custom brush for future use, and call it **Icicles**.

Figure 12.39 Custom brush fade settings

Here are some more suggestions where hand-painting will enhance the winter version of the scene:

Figure 12.40 Paint icicles using a fading custom brush.

- Turn the LampPosts layer back on, and add snow to the top and any upward-facing surfaces of the lampposts.
- Any surface that faces the sky should have snow on it, including the cathedral spire.
- Paint snow on the edges of the peaked roofs facing away from the viewer.
- Some of the bushes are unevenly covered with snow and need to be smoothed out. Add a sprinkling of snow to the top of each bush.
- You can add more snow on the roofs if you want a heavier snowfall.
- Above the CanalWinterGroup, create a new layer named **FrontReeds**, and paint in the reeds on the right side that overhang the canal.
- Make the background trees into winter trees using the same technique you used for the large tree (Figure 12.41).

Figure 12.41 More details added with hand-painting

Final Details

Because this is winter, it would be a nice touch to add smoke curling out of the smokestacks.

This section requires Photoshop Extended, a more expensive version of Photoshop that includes some additional features. If you don't have that version, you can do the same thing by taking a screen shot of the frame of the movie you want to use. Then, copy the frame into Photoshop, and follow the same procedure.

If you have Photoshop Extended, you can open a QuickTime sequence for editing in Photoshop. Choose File → Open, and select HDfog03.mov from the Chapter 12 section on the DVD. This footage is courtesy of www.detonationfilms.com, a stock-footage website with a huge selection of explosions, smoke, and flames.

Next, choose View → Animation to open the Animation panel. A timeline appears at the bottom of the Photoshop interface. Drag the slider to the right to review the clip and find a frame with smoke that will work in the chimneys. Go to the Channels panel, and look through the RGB channels. Because the clip is gray, there isn't a lot of variation between them, but the Blue channel has a bit more contrast. You'll use this channel to extract the smoke from the background. Shift+Command/Ctrl+click the Blue channel twice to load the channel as a selection. By clicking the channel twice, you grow the selection and get more of the smoke (Figure 12.42).

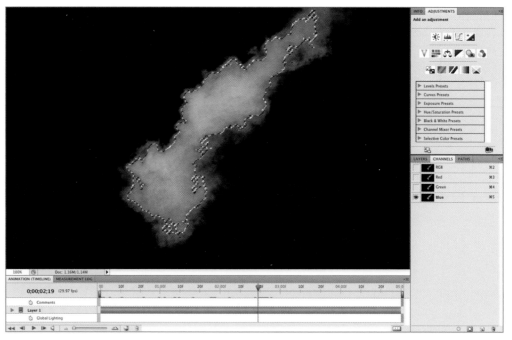

Figure 12.42 *Opening a QuickTime clip in Photoshop and using the Blue channel to extract a smoke element*

Press Command/Ctrl+C to copy the smoke out of the movie, and paste it into your project. Distort and scale it into place. Do this with several frames to add different plumes of smoke to several chimneys (Figure 12.43).

Figure 12.43 *Smoke added to the chimneys*

You can also use some of the smoke to add more depth to your composition by adding haze in front of the cathedral and in front of the houses at the far end of the canal. When you're finished adding smoke and haze, select all of those layers and place them in a group called **Smoke+Haze.**

With snow added to all the surfaces, the sky now looks too saturated as well as overly dark. In the Layers panel, select WinterSkyGroup. Apply a Hue/Saturation adjustment layer, name it **DesaturateSky,** and make the sky grayer. Then, add a Curves adjustment layer, name it **LightenSky,** and pull the middle of the curve up to lighten the sky.

When you're finished, your scene should look like Figure 12.44.

Figure 12.44 *Finished daytime winter scene*

Bonus Section: Dusk

All the hard work is finished. Let's have some fun and take this scene one step further to make it look like dusk, just after the lamplighter has lit the street lights. We'll review the techniques you used to tone the castle earlier in the book and to take a scene from day to night in the previous chapter.

Adding a Multiply Layer

Create a selection with the buildings, trees, chimneys, cathedral, pathways, and canal—everything but the smoke and the sky. At the top of the project, add a new adjustment layer, this time choosing Solid Color. Choose a dark blue with the RGB settings 55, 85, 115. Because you had a selection made when you added the adjustment layer, the layer mask shows the color only in the selection. Set the layer blending mode to Multiply, and change the name of the layer to **BlueMultiply**. Doing so makes the scene too dark, so adjust the layer's opacity to 50%.

With the foreground darkened, the sky now looks too light. In WinterSkyGroup, turn off both the DesaturateSky and LightenSky adjustment layers that you added. . Your sky will now look suitably darker and more saturated (Figure 12.45).

Figure 12.45 Toning the daytime winter image with a solid-color adjustment layer and darkening the sky

Adding an Overlay Layer

Select the glass lamps on all the lampposts. Above the BlueMultiply layer, add another solid-color adjustment layer, and pick an orange color with RGB settings 255, 195, 70.

Set the layer blending mode to Overlay, and rename the layer **OrangeOverlay**. The orange color is confined to the area of the glass lamps by the layer mask. Paint white into the layer mask around the base of each lamppost to show a circle of illumination. The lamp on the right would cast light onto the nearby bushes, so hand-paint some warm light onto the hedge.

Load the selection from the OrangeOverlay layer mask, and add another solid-color adjustment layer—this time a light yellow with RGB settings 255, 245, 205. Set the blending mode to Overlay, and rename the layer **YellowOverlay**. Paint black into the layer mask so that the lighter yellow only appears at the bottom of the lamplight where the flame would be burning. Still in the layer mask, paint black around the circle of light at the base of the lamps to constrain this brighter color to the center of the circle of illumination (Figure 12.46). Select all the toning layers—BlueMultiply, OrangeOverlay, and YellowOverlay—and place them in a new group named **Toning**.

Figure 12.46 Cast warm illumination from the lamppost.

The shadows around the base of the house and in the canal would be darker at this late hour. Select the CanalCurves adjustment layer, and duplicate it. (You should keep the original version for the daytime winter scene.) Turn the original CanalCurves off, and select the copy. Rename the duplicated layer **CanalCurvesDusk**. Pull the adjustment layer curve down to Output 90 to darken the shadows. Paint white into the adjustment layer mask with a soft brush to deepen and soften the shadows, and add shadows around the base of the left-side building.

Adding Illuminated Windows

You're almost finished, but one last detail remains—lights in the houses. Create another layer called **LitWindows** in the Toning group, and add some warm light coming from a few of the background windows using the same techniques you learned in the last chapter. Your finished project will look like Figure 12.47. You can compare your project to the final one on the DVD named SeasonsChangeFinal.psd.

Figure 12.47 *Final dusk scene*

The three versions of this scene—the summer version, the winter version, and the bonus dusk version—will be used for the next lesson on adding motion to your matte paintings using After Effects.

Assignment: Take Your Own Photo From Summer to Winter

Use the skills you learned in this chapter and apply it to an image that you select, or use a subject that you photographed yourself.

Starting with a summer photograph, do the following:

1. Duplicate your original plate so that all changes are made to a copy.
2. Add a one-inch black mask around your image to add some workspace.

3. Replace or paint out any details in your image that are incompatible with your vision of the scene. You can replace the sky, unattractive sections of buildings, or incongruous elements.

4. Place all of the layers comprising your summer scene in a group.

5. Duplicate the summer scene group, and rename the duplicate to indicate it is the winter version.

6. Remove any green from the scene, and replace it with snow using the techniques described in the chapter.

7. If you are also taking your scene to dusk, add a blue multiply layer to darken it, and add illuminated windows.

thirteen

Getting Started in After Effects

Nothing reinforces the reality of *a matte shot better than adding motion to the camera filming the shot. In the predigital days, most matte shots were stationary, because the camera had to be locked off; even a wiggle of movement would destroy the illusion when the plate and the painting shifted against each other. Because the painting and the camera were stationary, the only motion in the final shot was the live-action footage.*

In contrast, matte shots today move in order to blend with the production footage. This can be accomplished in two ways: either the plate is filmed from a moving camera, or the motion is added in post-production. You'll learn the latter technique in this chapter.

Today, you'd be hard pressed to find any shots filmed with a stationary camera in the works of contemporary directors such as Michael Bay, Steven Spielberg, Martin Scorsese, and David Fincher. Movies today move more than ever, and After Effects allows you to add motion to your matte paintings.

You'll learn about After Effects by adding motion to the summer to winter painting created in the last chapter. In this exercise, you'll cross-dissolve between the three states of the painting: summer, winter, and winter dusk. Additionally, you'll move the sky, animate the lights and smoke, and push in with the camera to enlarge the entire scene in the frame.

Preparing a Painting for After Effects

If you take all the layers in the Photoshop file into After Effects, it will make the task of turning the painting into an animation more complicated. Therefore, you must reduce your file to as few layers as possible while maintaining a good representation of the scene. Any item you plan to animate must be on a separate layer. If you would like to try this process yourself, use the final file from the end of Chapter 12, "Changing Seasons." When you have reduced the file to only eight layers, it should match SeasonChangeForAE.psd in the Chapter 13 section of the DVD in Photoshop. The Layers panel for the reduced Photoshop file looks like Figure 13.1.

All the alpha channels and paths have also been deleted. The black Mask layer was eliminated, but the composition still has the work area around the edges (Figure 13.2). This allows you to see what you're doing when you animate the clouds.

Getting Into After Effects

There are many different ways to set up the After Effects interface and project settings. In order for your project to match the figures, open SeasonsChange_01_Start.aep from the Chapter 13 DVD materials. This file is set up properly for the current project, but it has nothing in it.

After Effects' native format is .aep, which stands for *After Effects Project*. All After Effects project files bear that suffix. Throughout this chapter, I've included .aep files that correspond to the progression of the project. If you get lost, you can always open one of the files on the DVD to catch up.

Close Photoshop so that all your computer resources can be devoted to After Effects.

An older version of After Effects won't open a file created in a newer version of the program, so you must have After Effects CS5 to use the .aep files included on the DVD. CS5 runs only on 64-bit Windows systems and Intel-based Macs, so using this latest version of After Effects may require a computer update. Don't worry: if you have an earlier version, you can follow along without those files, but some of your settings may be different from what is shown in the demonstration.

Figure 13.1 Eight layers to be used in After Effects

Figure 13.2 The reduced summer to winter matte painting in Photoshop

Importing the Composition

You need to import the Photoshop composition that will be the basis of the moving matte shot. In order for the names and organization to match what is shown in the figures, you will use the demonstration file on the DVD while working through this chapter. Choose File → Import → File to open the Import File dialog box. Select SeasonsChangeForAE.psd on the DVD, and, in Import As, choose Composition - Retain Layer Size. Click Open, and a second dialog appears. Make sure that in the Import Kind drop-down menu, Composition – Retain Layer Sizes is selected (Figure 13.3). Leave the other options as they are, and click Open.

Figure 13.3 *Import File dialog box*

Interface Panels

The After Effects interface is divided into panels similar to Photoshop. There are several preset workspaces to choose from at the upper-right in the interface. For this chapter, make sure Standard is chosen from the Workspace drop-down menu `Workspace  Standard`.

On the left side, in the Project panel, double-click SeasonsChangeForAE. Your interface will now look like Figure 13.4.

Figure 13.4 *After Effects panel layout*

Let's look at some important aspects of each of these panels.

The exact location of the panels and which panels are visible depends on how the interface was left from the previous session using After Effects. Because of that, your interface may differ from what is shown in the figures.

The Project Panel

The Project panel holds pointers/links to all the elements that will make up your animation. Make sure you always keep the original files that make up the project on your drive in the same place. In order to keep .aep files small, After Effects references these files and doesn't store the actual Photoshop files, movies, still images, sound files, or any other outside file associated with the project. After Effects .aep files internally retain only elements created in the program, such as solid layers of color, text, adjustment layers, and intermediate compositions. Everything else is saved as links to outside files.

Figure 13.5 Information and preview for any item selected in the Project panel

Compositions, known from here forward as *comps*, are the containers that hold the elements of your animation and also determine the resolution of your work. SeasonsChangeForAE is the comp you opened in the Viewer panel by double-clicking it.

In the Project panel, all comps are identified by this icon: . When you select a comp or layer, After Effects shows information about your selection at the top of the Project panel, including a thumbnail preview of the contents. In this case, you'll see that the comp is 3672 × 2648 pixels, the size of the Photoshop file you imported (Figure 13.5).

Figure 13.6 All the layers and comps displayed in the Project panel

Just below the comp is a folder called SeasonsChangeForAE Layers. When you click the arrow next to the folder, the arrow reorients facing downward, revealing all the layers that were imported from Photoshop (Figure 13.6).

The Viewer Panel

Any item you double-click in the Project panel opens in the Viewer panel. This works for comps and for individual layers. When you have a comp open in the Viewer panel, you can add animation and effects to any layers in the comp.

At the bottom of the Viewer panel are two important drop-down menus for working with your comp. First, at far left in the Viewer window, is the Magnification Ratio pop-up, which displays the percentage that you're zoomed in or out of the Viewer panel. To the right of that is the Resolution/Down Sample Factor pop-up, which displays the resolution of the comp. Resolution is based on how many pixels After Effects is required to compute to display the image. If the magnification ratio is set to 25%, and the resolution is set to Full, the program is computing 16 times as many pixels as are required to produce an accurate representation of the scene at that size. Why? Because at one-quarter size, After Effects is displaying only every fourth pixel; but at full resolution, it's forced to compute every pixel, or 4 × 4 more pixels than are needed.

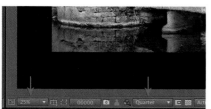

Figure 13.7 Magnification Ratio pop-up and Resolution/Down Sample Factor pop-up

Conversely, if the magnification ratio is set to 100% to view the image detail, but the resolution is set to Quarter, the image will look blurry. In general, you'll want to have the magnification ratio and resolution in synch. After Effects is more responsive and updates are faster with the resolution set lower. However, when you do the final output, After Effects automatically renders at full resolution unless you set it specifically not to do so.

The source Photoshop file for this project is quite large, so set the resolution for the scene to Quarter. For most of this project, you'll work at a 25% magnification ratio (Figure 13.7). You can, from time to time, look at the scene at full or half res to preview how things are shaping up. When you do, you should adjust the resolution to match.

The Timeline Panel

At the bottom of the interface is the Timeline panel, where layers are keyframed and animated. In the upper-left corner is the current time, displayed in yellow `00000`. To the left of the Timeline are the layer names, with layer controls on both sides of the layer names (Figure 13.8).

To the right of the layer names is the Time Graph. Let's look at the main controls. At the top is a slender gray bar called the Time Navigator that allows you to control how many frames are displayed in the Time Graph. Below that is the Time Ruler, showing the frame numbers. Above the frame numbers is the yellow Current Time Indicator, marking what frame you're on in the animation. Just below that is the Work Area bar, a thicker gray bar that controls what frames are rendered. Under that are colored Layer Duration bars, showing when each layer is visible. Whenever a layer is selected, its Layer Duration bar is highlighted (Figure 13.9).

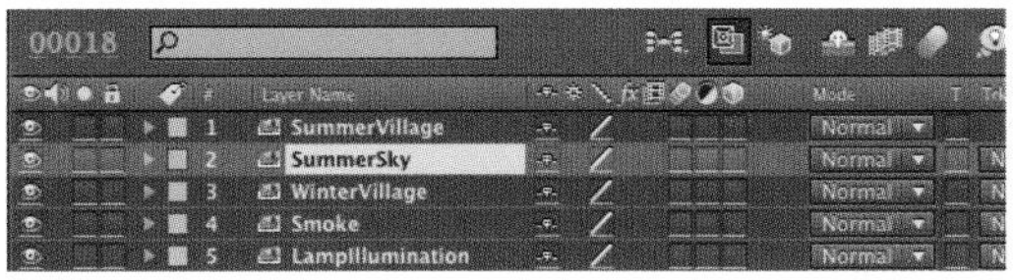

Figure 13.8 Timeline layer names and controls

The Tool Panel

Here are three important tools with which you'll work in both the Viewer and Timeline panels. To the right of the name is the keyboard shortcut to access each tool:

Figure 13.9 Time Graph components, with the currently selected layer highlighted

- The Zoom tool (Z) ⌕ enlarges and reduces the size of the comp in the Viewer panel. Click with the tool to zoom in; Option/Alt click to zoom out. You can also zoom in and out using Command/Ctrl+ the (+) or (–) key.
- The Hand tool (H) ✋ repositions what is displayed in the Viewer and Timeline panel without disturbing the layers. You can also access the tool by holding down the spacebar.
- You use the Selection tool (V) ▶ to select, move, and scale layers in the Viewer panel. It does the same thing with keyframes in the Timeline panel.

Setting the Duration of the Animation

Now that you're familiar with the location of After Effects panels and controls, you can begin to animate the project. First, you need to set the duration of your animation by adjusting the composition settings. Because After Effects defaults to the length of the previous comp, the length of the current comp may be different from the one shown here.

Let's make this animation 20 seconds long. This composition is currently 400 frames long, but 20 seconds at 29.97 frames per second equals 599.4 frames, which we'll round up to 600 frames. To change the length, choose Composition → Composition Settings. Set Frame Rate to 29.97 and Duration to 600 (Figure 13.10). These settings make the animation 20 seconds long.

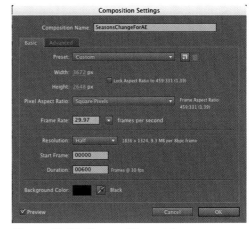

Figure 13.10 Composition settings

With the duration adjusted, you need to display the additional frames. At the top of the Time Graph is the Time Navigator. Pull the right end of the Time Navigator bar to the extreme right to show all the frames in the animation (Figure 13.11).

Frames 0 through 599 now show in the Time Ruler. Because the comp starts at frame 0, 599 is the last frame. Drag the Current Time Indicator 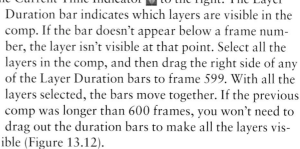 to the right. The Layer Duration bar indicates which layers are visible in the comp. If the bar doesn't appear below a frame number, the layer isn't visible at that point. Select all the layers in the comp, and then drag the right side of any of the Layer Duration bars to frame 599. With all the layers selected, the bars move together. If the previous comp was longer than 600 frames, you won't need to drag out the duration bars to make all the layers visible (Figure 13.12).

Figure 13.11 Pull the Time Navigator bar to the right.

Figure 13.12 Drag the Layer Duration bars to the right.

You can check your work up to this point by opening SeasonsChange_02_Import.aep on the DVD.

Animating the Sky

With your project set up, you're ready to begin animating. The first layer to which you'll add motion is SummerSky. Move the Current Time Indicator to 00000 in the Timeline panel. Select the SummerSky layer, and click the arrow to the left of the name. Doing so displays the Transform group. Click the arrow next to the Transform group to display the animateable properties: Anchor Point, Position, Scale, Rotation, and Opacity (Figure 13.13).

Figure 13.13 Click the arrow next to the SummerSky layer name to reveal the animateable properties.

In After Effects, it isn't possible to know whether the arrow to the left of a property is open (pointing down) 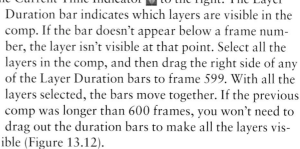 or closed (pointing to the right) ▶ in the user interface. In this chapter, if you're asked to click an arrow to reveal additional properties, and the properties are already showing, do nothing and proceed with the lesson.

Setting Keyframes

With the Current Time Indicator at frame 0, click the stopwatch next to Position in the Transform properties 🕐. Clicking the stopwatch sets a keyframe for that property. As in Maya, you set a keyframe whenever you want to change something over time. Notice that a yellow diamond shape appears at frame 0 in the Timeline to the right of the Position property, indicating where the keyframe was set.

The sky should move from right to left over the course of the animation. You don't want to move it too dramatically—only enough to give the scene some life. To the right of Position are the X and Y coordinates of the layer: 1966.0, 642.0. X represents the position of the layer horizontally, or to the right or left in the Viewer panel. Y represents the position of the layer vertically, or up or down in the Viewer. Move the Current Time Indicator

Figure 13.14 *Two keyframes set to move the sky between frame 0 and frame 599.*

to frame 599. Click the X (horizontal) coordinate position, and change it to 1843 to move the sky to the left. You don't need to set another keyframe manually. After you've set one keyframe for a property, when you move to another frame and change that property, a new keyframe is automatically set (Figure 13.14).

Move the Current Time Indicator back and forth—an action known as *scrubbing*—between frame 0 and frame 599, to see the motion (Figure 13.15).

Figure 13.15 *Subtle motion of the sky*

RAM Preview

To preview the motion as it will appear in the final animation, select the Preview panel at right in the interface. On the right side of the panel is the RAM Preview button (Figure 13.16). When you click it, or press the 0 key on the numeric keyboard as a shortcut, After Effects begins to load the animation into RAM. When as many frames as the memory can hold are loaded, the frames automatically begin to play in real time. If it's taking too long to load, and you only want to see part of the sequence in real time, click the RAM Preview button or press 0 on the numeric keyboard again. Only the frames already loaded will play. If this motion is too subtle for your taste, feel free to move the sky more.

Figure 13.16
RAM Preview button

Bear in mind that After Effects' ability to load in all the frames in the animation depends on how much RAM is in your computer. A green line appears below the Time Ruler to show how many frames were successfully loaded into RAM (Figure 13.17).

Figure 13.17 *Frames loaded into RAM preview*

The number of frames you can RAM-preview is directly related to the resolution setting. You can preview 16 times as many frames when Resolution is set to Quarter as you can when it's set to Full.

You can check your progress by opening SeasonsChange_03_Sky.aep on the DVD.

Precomposing the Summer Version

Precomposing, or *precomping*, is a key concept in After Effects. Think of a precomp as a container to hold the attributes of several layers so they can be animated together. In this case, you want to cross-dissolve between the summer and winter versions, but you need to keep the animated sky and summer village together.

To precomp the summer version, select both the SummerVillage and SummerSky layers in the Timeline, and choose Layer → Precompose. The Pre-Compose dialog box appears. Name the new composition **SummerVersion**, and select Move All Attributes Into The New Composition (Figure 13.18).

Click OK, and look down in the Timeline panel. The two summer layers have been replaced by a new comp named SummerVersion in your current composition (Figure 13.19).

Double-clicking the SummerVersion precomp in the Timeline replaces the SeasonsChangeForAE comp and opens SummerVersion in both the Timeline and Viewer. This comp contains the two summer layers, complete with the animation on the sky you just added.

When you open a comp for the first time, After Effects adds a tab at the top of the Timeline panel. All open comps are tabbed

Figure 13.18 Pre-Compose dialog box

Figure 13.19 SummerVersion comp in the SeasonsChangeForAE comp

, and clicking the tabs is a handy way to switch between comps. Return to the SeasonsChangeForAE comp by clicking the tab for that comp.

Cross-Dissolving to the Winter Version

Working in the Timeline panel of the SeasonsChangeForAE comp, click the arrow next to the Transform properties for the SummerVersion precomp. Move the Current Time Indicator to frame 100; or, for greater accuracy, type **100** in Current Time in the upper-left corner of the Timeline panel. Click the stopwatch next to Opacity to keyframe it at 100% . To dissolve to the winter version, move to frame 200 and change the number to the right of Opacity to 0% . Click the RAM Preview button again to view your animation (Figure 13.20).

You can check your work against SeasonsChange_04_CrossDissolve.aep on the DVD.

Figure 13.20 Cross-dissolve between the summer and winter versions

Animating the Winter Sky

You still need to animate the WinterSky layer. Rather than animating it by changing the position coordinate numbers as you did for the SummerSky layer, let's try an alternate approach. This time, you'll use the Selection tool to move and keyframe the layer. Make sure you're still on frame 200. In the Viewer panel, click the WinterSky layer to select it. Be aware that there can be several layers under the Selection tool, which can make it difficult to select the layer you want. The solution is to lock the layers you aren't working on currently so you can't select them. Click the box in the SummerVersion lock column to make the layer unselectable until you unlock it (Figure 13.21).

Figure 13.21 *Lock the SummerVersion layer.*

With the WinterSky layer selected, set a Position keyframe at frame 200. You can't see the WinterSky layer at this point in the animation because the SummerVersion precomp is covering it. Move to frame 599, and drag the sky to the left while holding down the Shift key to constrain the movement and set a second keyframe.

Just as in Photoshop, holding the Shift key constrains movement to 90-degree increments, either horizontally or vertically.

Scrub the Current Time Indicator through the entire sequence to watch the motion. The movement of the winter sky doesn't begin until frame 200, but the sky starts to become visible before that. Move the Position keyframe at frame 200 to frame 0 using the Selection tool. Scrub through the sequence again, particularly watching for the transition from summer to winter. Match the movement of the winter sky to the summer sky so the transition doesn't appear disjointed in the cross-dissolve. If the winter sky is moving more quickly than the summer sky, adjust the timing by going to frame 599 and dragging the winter sky to the right. If it's moving too slowly, drag it to the left some more.

Dissolving to the Winter Dusk

You've now cross-dissolved between the summer and winter scenes, and you've moved the skies in both seasons. For a third part of this animation, you'll dissolve to the winter dusk version of the scene and have the street lamps and house lights come on.

Select the WinterVillage layer in the Timeline, move to frame 300, and set an Opacity keyframe at 100%. Move to Frame 400, and set Opacity to 0%. Run a RAM preview of the animation to see a cross-dissolve between the three versions.

Effects

They don't call it After *Effects* for nothing. The program ships with hundreds of built-in effects for color correction, image distortion, and animation. All filters in After Effects are nondestructive and don't alter the original image. You can come back at any time and change or delete a filter you've added. Also, all parameters on all effects can be animated. In this animation, you'll get practice working with four of them: Curves, Hue/Saturation, CC Snow, and Displacement Map.

Figure 13.22 Apply a Curves effect to WinterSky.

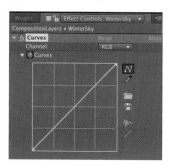

Figure 13.23 Curves effect control panel

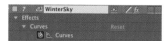

Figure 13.24 Set a keyframe on Curves.

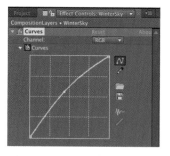

Figure 13.25 Pull up the middle of the curve.

Figure 13.26 Desaturate the sky.

Curves Effect

The sky for the winter village looks too dark and saturated when it first appears behind the summer sky. You'll use a Curves effect to lighten the sky. With the WinterSky layer selected in the Timeline, choose Effect → Color Correction → Curves. Notice that when you apply the Curves effect, a new parameter called Effects appears in the Timeline just below WinterSky. Click the arrow to the left of Effects to show the Curves effect, which you just applied (Figure 13.22).

When you apply an effect, it automatically opens in the Effect Controls panel, which is tabbed in the upper-left corner with the Project panel. If an effect isn't open in the Effects panel, you can double-click the effect in the Timeline panel to display all the parameters in the Effect Controls panel. Because the Project and Effects panels are tabbed to share the same space and are on top of each other, panels can sometimes get lost behind one another. If that happens, choose Window and select either Project or Effect Controls to have that panel appear at the top of the tabbed area.

The curve the Effects Controls panel displays should be familiar—it's similar to the Curves dialog box in Photoshop (Figure 13.23).

With WinterSky still selected in the Timeline, go to frame 400, where WinterVillageDusk is at 100% opacity. The sky looks good here, so you need to set a keyframe on Curves. To the left of Curves, under Effects in the WinterSky layer, is another arrow. Click it to reveal the animateable parameter of Curves—also called Curves—with a stopwatch beside it. Click the stopwatch to set a keyframe (Figure 13.24).

A yellow diamond appears in the Timeline, showing that a keyframe has been created at frame 400. Move to frame 300. In the Effect Controls panel, pull up the middle of the curve to lighten the sky (Figure 13.25). Because a keyframe was already set at frame 400, this sets another keyframe automatically.

Hue/Saturation Effect

Now the sky darkens over 100 frames as the WinterVillage layer cross-dissolves to the WinterVillageDusk layer, but the color is over-saturated at the start of the cross-dissolve. You'll apply a second effect after Curves to take out some of the color.

With WinterSky still selected, return to frame 400 and choose Effect → Color Correction → Hue/Saturation. In the Effect Controls panel, Hue/Saturation appears. Set a keyframe for the Channel Range parameter in the Hue/Saturation controls. Move to frame 300, and change Master Saturation to -17 (Figure 13.26). Because a keyframe was created at frame 400, a second keyframe is automatically set, animating the saturation of the sky over 100 frames.

Adding a Snow Effect

The scene goes from summer to winter, but where is the snow? In the next step, you'll add a falling snow effect to enhance the wintery feel. First, you need to learn about solids.

Solids

Solids are layers composed of solid colors created in After Effects. You'll use a solid to add snow to the composition.

Choose Layer → New → Solid. The Solid Settings dialog box appears. Change the name to **SnowSolid**, click the color swatch in the Color area to open the Color Picker, and choose black. Click the Make Comp Size button to make the solid the same size as the comp on which you're working. Click OK to accept these parameters (Figure 13.27).

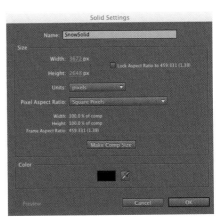

Figure 13.27 *Solid Settings dialog box*

Blending Modes

Drag the SnowSolid layer to the top of the Timeline panel so it's above the SummerVersion precomp. The SnowSolid layer has blackened the entire comp. You need to change the blending mode so you can see the scene again. Depending on how your interface is set up, the blending mode controls in the Timeline panel may not be visible. To turn them on, go to the Panel Menu icon ▤ in the upper-right corner of the Timeline panel, and click it. From the pop-up menu, choose Columns, and make sure Modes is checked (Figure 13.28).

Now, when you look at the layer names in the Timeline, you see a control column called Mode. The drop-down menu to the right of SnowSolid reads Normal; change it to Screen (Figure 13.29). Blending modes in After Effects work the same way they do in Photoshop. Because the solid was black, setting the blending mode to Screen doesn't change the comp.

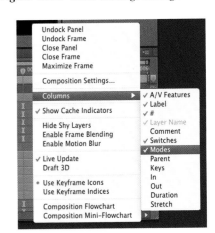

Figure 13.28 *Columns menu*

Figure 13.29 *Set the SnowSolid blending mode to Screen.*

CC Snow

One of After Effects' built-in effects is a powerful snow generator. With SnowSolid selected, choose Effect → Simulation → CC Snow. Scrub through the Timeline to see the effect. Applying this filter with the defaults produces a reasonable snowfall. However, you can make some changes to get an even better result.

You applied the CC Snow effect to the SnowSolid layer, and that layer is at the top of the Timeline panel. This makes the CC Snow effect visible in the summer section of the animation, which is clearly not what you want. Move the Current Time Indicator to frame 100.

Figure 13.30 *CC Snow properties*

After Effects offers two ways to change any of the animateable properties. You can click+release on a property to highlight it, and then type in the new numeric property. Alternatively, you can click+hold and drag right and left on most property numbers to change the amount interactively. Try it on the CC Snow Amount property: click 1000, and drag to the left until it reads 0 and all the snow disappears. It may take a few tries to get the hang of this. If you click+release, you can't drag to change the setting, you can only enter a numeric amount. You must click+hold to be able to drag left or right to change the setting.

Click the stopwatch next to Amount and change Flake Size to keyframe those properties. Lower Flake Size to 1 (Figure 13.30).

Move to frame 200, and change Amount to 1000 and Flake Size to 2.5. Now, move to frame 400, and change Amount to 2000. As a result, the snow builds up slowly as summer fades to winter, and then it becomes more intense and heavy as dusk darkens the village.

Figure 13.31 *Layer controls open*

By now, the Timeline panel is getting crowded with all the Transform and Effects controls open (Figure 13.31).

If you aren't working on a layer, you can click the arrow to the left of the name to close all the controls (Figure 13.32). In order to preserve screen real estate, you should get into the habit of leaving the controls open only for layers on which you're working.

Figure 13.32 *Layer controls closed*

While you're working on a composition, you may sometimes want to turn off the visibility of some layers in order to concentrate on others. Just as in Photoshop, you can do that by clicking the eye to the left of the layer name ![eye icon] .

Varying the Lights

From frame 300 to 400, several changes occur simultaneously: the city gets darker, the street lamps illuminate, and lights in the homes are lit. It would add charm to the scene if these events happened at different intervals. Let's change it so the street lamps don't come on until the dissolve to dusk is almost complete.

Select the LampIllumination layer, and move to frame 375 in the Timeline. Change Opacity to 0, and set a keyframe. Move to frame 425, and set Opacity to 100.

Masks

It would be good to stagger the times at which the window lights inside the houses come on. There is a problem with this, however: all the lights are on the same layer (WindowLights). You'll need to use masks to cut the WindowLights layer into different sections, and you'll need to animate the lights coming on at different times. In the top Tool panel, select the Pen tool (G) . Make sure you're still working in the SeasonChangeForAE comp, and move to frame 400 where all the lights are on. In the Viewer panel, with the WindowLights layer selected, draw a square around the top lit dormer window on the left house to create a mask. Notice how all the lights outside of the mask disappear (Figure 13.33).

Figure 13.33 Use the Pen tool to mask off the top left window.

In the Timeline, click the arrow to the left of the WindowLights layer to show a new category, Masks. Click the arrow next to Masks, and you'll find Mask 1, which you just added to the layer (Figure 13.34).

To the right of Mask 1 is the Mask Modes drop-down menu, labeled Add. If you select Subtract from the menu, it shows the opposite of Add: subtracting the area you've masked, showing all of the layer except for what is covered by the mask. If you select Inverted to the right of the Mask Modes menu, the choice in the menu is inverted. Add with Inverted selected is the same as Subtract, and Subtract with Inverted selected is the same as Add. Checking and unchecking Inverted is a convenient way to view what you've masked off. Set the mask mode to Add, and uncheck Inverted.

Figure 13.34 Masks appears under the WindowLights layer.

Move to frame 485, set the WindowLights layer's opacity to 0% so the window doesn't show, and set a keyframe. Move to frame 500, and set the WindowLights layer's opacity to 100%. Now the light comes on over 15 frames.

Masking New Layers

You'll now duplicate the WindowLights layer in order to animate more of the lights coming on. Duplicate WindowLights by pressing Command/Ctrl+D. Delete the mask from the duplicate layer, and draw a new mask around the lit window below the dormer window. With the Selection tool, move the WindowLights layer Opacity keyframe that's set to 0% in the Time Graph to frame 448, and move the Opacity keyframe that's set to 100% to frame 460 (Figure 13.35). Now you have two copies of the WindowLights layer, each with a different masked area and each animated to appear at a different time. When you scrub through the animation, the second-floor lights appear shortly before the third-floor lights illuminate.

Figure 13.35 Move a keyframe in the Time Graph using the Selection tool

Duplicate the WindowLights layer several more times, and separately mask off the other lights in the background. Assign each a slightly different time to come on.

Transforming Masks

You can also transform a mask by double-clicking it with the Selection tool. Doing so gives you a transform box much as in Photoshop, where you can grab the corners to scale and rotate the mask (Figure 13.36).

You can check your work to this point by opening SeasonsChange_05_Effects.aep on the DVD.

Figure 13.36
Transform a mask by
double-clicking it.

Moving the Smoke

The scene is coming alive, but there is a discordant note: the smoke from the chimneys doesn't move, and it looks painted on the sky. An advanced technique will add motion to the plumes.

Fractal Noise

Add a new black solid just above the Smoke layer by choosing Layer → New → Solid. Make it the same size as the comp, and name the solid **FractalNoise**. With the layer selected, choose Effect → Noise & Grain → Fractal Noise. Doing so creates a big cloud of chunky noise that you'll use to displace and move the smoke (Figure 13.37). Move the solid with the Fractal Noise effect applied to it down in the Timeline so it's just above the Smoke layer.

Figure 13.37 Fractal noise over a black solid

Displacement Maps

Turn off the visibility of the FractalNoise solid by clicking the eye to the left of the layer. Select the Smoke layer just below it. Choose Effect → Distort → Displacement Map. Click the arrow to the left of Smoke and, under Effects, select Displacement Map.

What Is a Displacement Map?

The Displacement Map effect uses the differences in grayscale tonal values from an image to shift the location of pixels on a target layer. If the control image is white, pixels on the target layer are shifted the maximum amount. If the image is black, pixels on the target layer are shifted the negative of the maximum amount. If the image is gray, the pixels don't move at all. All the other grayscale values between black and white affect the image accordingly. Generally, the visibility of the displacing image is turned off and only used to shift pixels on the target layer.

In the Effect Controls panel, you need to choose the layer the Displacement Map effect should use to displace the smoke. Set the control properties as follows (Figure 13.38):

- Displacement Map Layer: FractalNoise
- Max Horizontal Displacement: 5
- Max Vertical Displacement: 5
- Use for Horizontal Displacement: Luminance
- Use for Vertical Displacement: Luminance

Figure 13.38 Settings for the Displacement Map effect

Leave the rest of the properties at the defaults. Scrub through the animation. Nothing happens!

Precomping the Fractal Noise

You need to do two more things to get the displacement to occur. First, you can't displace a layer using an effect applied directly to another layer. You must precomp the FractalNoise solid so the effect occurs in the precomp and not in the layer being used to displace the smoke.

Earlier, you turned off the visibility of the FractalNoise solid. You need to turn it back on by clicking the visibility control (currently blank) ■ to turn the layer visibility back on ◉. Now, select the FractalNoise layer, and choose Layer → Precompose. Name the precomp **SmokeComp**, and select Move All Attributes Into The New Composition.

Animating the Displacement Map

Next, you need to animate the FractalNoise solid so the displacement is moving. Double-click SmokeComp to open it in the Timeline and the Viewer. Go to frame 0, and set a Position keyframe for the X and Y coordinates of the FractalNoise solid at 1836, 1324. Go to frame 599, and move the solid up to 1836, 277. Doing so mimics the motion of rising smoke. In the FractalNoise Effect Controls panel, change Contrast to 300. This enhances the difference between light and dark in the noise and causes a more vivid displacement. Click the arrow next to Transform in Effect Controls, and change Scale from 100 to 60 to make the chunks smaller and in scale with the smoke (Figure 13.39).

Finally, to add some churn to the smoke, set a keyframe on Evolution at 0, move to frame 599, and set it to 1x +0.0, or rotate the dial once around (Figure 13.40).

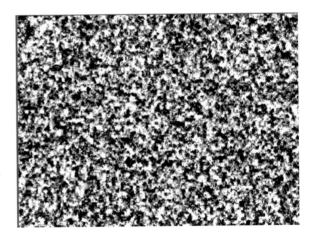

Figure 13.39 Fractal noise with higher contrast and smaller scale

Figure 13.40 Evolution settings

Return to the SeasonsChangeForAE comp, select the Smoke layer, and open Displacement Map in the Effect Controls panel again. Set the Displacement Map Layer selection to SmokeComp if that option isn't already chosen `15. SmokeComp ▾`.

Scaling the Displacement

Scrub through the Time Graph. Although the smoke looks good on the left, it appears too large and chunky on the right because the houses are further away. Draw a mask around the left side of Smoke layer using the Pen tool. As a result, smoke is only visible on the left side. Duplicate the Smoke layer, select the mask on the duplicate layer, and click Inverted to the right of the mask mode. Now, the Smoke layer shows on both sides of the comp. Make a new solid with fractal noise for that layer, precomp it, and create a smaller, slower-moving fractal pattern for the houses on the right.

The smoke appears rather abruptly, and it would be more realistic if it faded in over a longer period of time. Move to frame 200, set Opacity to 0% on the Smoke layer, and set a keyframe. Move to Frame 400, and move Opacity up to 100%. Do the same for the duplicate of the Smoke layer on the right side.

You're almost finished! You can check your work by referring to SeasonsChange_06_Lights+Smoke.aep.

Final Camera Move

Have you been wondering when you'd get rid of the border around the edge of the image? You'll remove it when you select the final resolution for the animation, and add a camera move to tie the entire piece together.

Select all the layers in the SeasonsChangeForAE comp, and choose Layers → Pre-Compose, or use the keyboard shortcut Shift+Command/Ctrl+C. Name the new comp **AllLayers**, and choose Move All Attributes Into The New Composition. Now the SeasonsChangeForAE comp contains only the new AllLayers comp.

Reformatting the New Comp

The current composition is 3672 pixels × 2648 pixels—much too large for a usual render. You'll reformat this comp to produce a more reasonably sized render and give it a more cinematic aspect ratio.

Choose Composition → Composition Settings, or press Command/Ctrl+K. From the Preset drop-down menu, choose HDV/HDTV 720 29.97. Leave everything else as is, and click OK. Now only the center of the composition is visible, because you've chosen a smaller format for the comp (Figure 13.41).

Select AllLayers, and zoom out by pressing Command/Ctrl+ the (–) key several times in the Viewer until you see a rectangle surrounding the comp (Figure 13.42).

Figure 13.41 *Comp formatted to the final render dimensions*

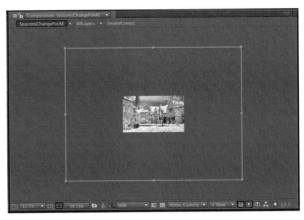

Figure 13.42 *Zoom out to show the edges of the rectangle surrounding the comp.*

Scaling the Precomp

Move to frame 0, and, using the Selection tool, click one of the boxes at the corners of the rectangle surrounding the comp. Hold down the Shift key to constrain the precomp to a uniform scale, and then pull a corner toward the center until the scene fits into the new rendering resolution. Somewhere around 42% works fine, with none of the border visible. Move AllLayers up in the Viewer so you see most of the bridge (Figure 13.43).

Set keyframes for both Scale and Position on frame 0. Move to frame 599, move AllLayers down so you see more of the sky, and crop off the bridge. Scale AllLayers up to 48%, and center the cathedral as much as possible without showing the work area (Figure 13.44).

Figure 13.43 *Scale to fit in the new resolution.*

Figure 13.44 *Move up, and push in to frame the cathedral.*

Easing Out, Easing In

The camera starts and stops abruptly, without any of the natural ramping up and down that would occur with a human cameraperson. This makes the camera move look unnatural and computer generated. Luckily, After Effects has a built-in provision to emulate a natural camera move, known as *ease in* and *ease out*. You can apply these to any animated property; they're particularly important on camera moves.

Select AllLayers in the Timeline, and select the keyframes for Position and Scale at frames 0 and 599. Right-click one of the keyframes, and, from the pop-up menu, choose Keyframe Assistant → Easy Ease (Figure 13.45). The keyframe changes from a diamond shape ◆ to the eased shape 🗵 .

Run a RAM preview again, and see how the camera begins moving slowly, speeds up in the middle, and slows to a gentle stop at the end.

Figure 13.45 Add Easy Ease to the Position and Scale keyframes.

Figure 13.46 The Render Queue panel

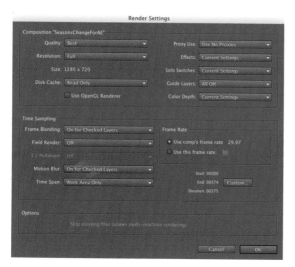

Figure 13.47 The Render Settings dialog

The Render Queue

It's time to render out your animation. Press Command/Ctrl+M (I remember it as "M" for "Make movie"), and the Render Queue panel opens, tabbed with the Timeline panel (Figure 13.46).

Render Settings

Before rendering, you need to decide on the render settings and the format to which you're outputting. To the right of Render Settings, click Best Setting to open the Render Settings dialog. Select Quality: Best and Resolution: Full. Leave the rest of the parameters as they are, and click OK (Figure 13.47).

Output Module

To the right of Output Module, click Lossless to open the Output Module Settings dialog. For Format, choose QuickTime. In the Video Output area, click Format Options to open the QuickTime Options dialog box. For final output, under Video Codec, select H.264 from the drop-down list. This format compresses the file so it will play smoothly on your computer while maintaining good image quality. Under Advanced Settings, select Key Frame Every __ Frames, and enter **10**. Leave Quality at 100. Click OK in both the QuickTime Options and Output Module Settings dialogs (Figure 13.48).

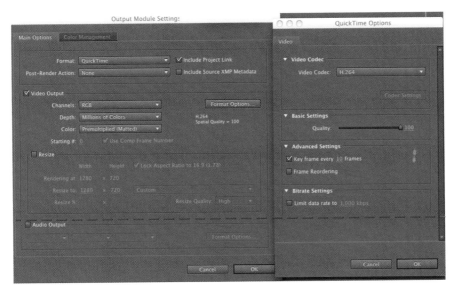

Figure 13.48 *Choose H.264 for Video Codec.*

To the right of Output To, click SeasonsChangeForAE.mov, and select where the movie will be outputted. In the upper-right corner of the Render Queue panel, click Render. Go get a cup of coffee, because the render will take a few minutes.

You can check your work against the final file for this project, SeasonsChange_07_CameraMove.aep.

Time Remapping

Ahhhh! Bliss! The project is finished. You've turned in your final animation, and you can relax...

What the !?@#! The director needs it to be exactly 12.5 seconds long instead of 20 seconds. That's terrible! You'll have to adjust all the keyframes. It will be hours of work!

Relax! After Effects comes to the rescue.

Open SeasonsChange_07_CameraMove.aep. Double-click the SeasonsChangeForAE comp to open it in the Timeline and the Viewer. In the Timeline, select AllLayers, and choose Layer → Pre-Compose. Name the new precomp **Retime**, and select Move All Attributes Into The New Composition.

Select the new Retime layer, and choose Layer → Time → Enable Time Remapping. Doing so immediately adds a new property named Time Remap to the AllLayers precomp. The Layer Duration bar also has two keyframes, one at each end of the Time Graph. Drag the right keyframe to frame 375, which is 12.5 seconds into the take. This change crushes all the animation that used to take 20 seconds into only 12.5 seconds.

Next, drag the right end of the Work Area bar—the thicker gray bar below the Time Graph—to the left, to frame 375 (Figure 13.49). Doing so tells After Effects that you only want to render that area.

Figure 13.49 Time-remap the animation.

Press Command/Ctrl+M, set the rendering parameters as you did before, and render out the time-remapped version. Finished—and your coffee is still warm!

The Final Animation

The final version shows gentle transitions through the seasons, all in 12.5 seconds (Figure 13.50).

Figure 13.50 Final animation

You can check your work against the final file for this project, `SeasonsChange_08_Final`
`.aep`. A rendered-out version of the movie, `SeasonsChangeForAE.mov`, is also on the DVD.

Assignment: Create an Animation Changing Summer To Winter Using Your Own Painting

Create an animation of your summer to winter painting completed in the last chapter using
After Effects. Here are the steps to follow:

1. Reduce the number of layers in your matte painting to the minimum necessary to complete the animation. For this project, if you are bringing more than ten layers into After Effects, you need to reduce your file.
2. Import your painting into After Effects, and choose Composition – Retain Layer Sizes.
3. Animate the sky in your summer version.
4. Precompose the summer version, and cross-dissolve it with your winter version.
5. Animate the sky in the winter version to match the movement of the summer sky.
6. Add a CCSnow effect.
7. If you also prepared a dusk version of your file, cross-dissolve to that, and bring the building lights on at different intervals.

fourteen

Working over a Moving Plate

In the past chapters, you've worked on
stationary images for your matte paintings and then added motion using
After Effects and camera projection. However, in studio work, many matte
shots are added to moving images.

In this chapter, you'll have the opportunity to experience working
on a moving plate. To make the assignment interesting, you'll use footage
taken from the roof of a skyscraper in New York City's Times Square.
Your mission is to create a vision of this globally recognized landmark 100
years from now, with futuristic structures and technological developments
far beyond what currently exists. You can add megastructures, mile-high
buildings, and fantastic new forms of transportation—whatever strikes
your fancy!

There is one other novel feature to this exercise. Before this, you've
worked solo. Now, you'll act as part of a movie studio team: your plate
will have been prepared by the Matchmoving department. You'll use that
information to add your matte painting to the scene.

The Plate

Open After Effects, and drag the folder `FutureNYC_Plate` from the Chapter 14 DVD materials into the Project panel. After Effects recognizes this as a `.jpg` sequence, or a movie. In the Project panel, drag the sequence `FutureCityNYC.[000-599].jpg` to the Create A New Composition icon at the bottom of the Project folder. Doing so creates a new comp the same size as the sequence. Run a RAM preview to look at the plate as a moving image. You'll create your matte painting over this sequence. No doubt you're now wondering how you'll paint on a moving image, when the camera pans and you never see the entire scene at the same time.

Merging Frames into a Panorama

The answer to the dilemma is that you'll patch together a temporary plate over which you'll paint that is comprised of frames taken from different times in the sequence. Close After Effects without saving, and open Photoshop. In the source folder for the plate `FutureCity_Plate` on the DVD, open frame `FutureNYC.000.jpg`. In the same sequence, open frames `FutureNYC.200.jpg`, `FutureNYC.300.jpg`, `FutureNYC.400.jpg`, and `FutureNYC.599.jpg`. Make a new Photoshop file with width 4500 by height 1400, and name the file **FutureNYC_All.psd**.

Return to frame 000, select all, copy the frame, paste it into `FutureNYC_All.psd`, and move it from the center to the left side of the file. Copy frame 200, and paste it on top of the first frame. Set Opacity to 50%, and move frame 200 around until the area of overlap is lined up with frame 000 (Figure 14.1). Use the large building in the foreground as a reference to match the two frames as closely as possible.

Figure 14.1 Line up frames 000 and 200, with 200 set to 50% opacity

The frames won't line up precisely because of distortion at the edges of the frame. The camera pans higher during the course of the shot, so `frame 000` is lower in the file than `frame 200`. When you have the frames in alignment, set the opacity of `frame 200` back to 100%. This is a temporary plate over which to paint. It won't be used in the actual shot, so you don't need to worry about a perfect match.

Softening the Transition Between Frames

Repeat the process with frames 300, 400, and 599—align 300 to the edge of 200, then 400 to the edge of 300, and then 599 to the edge of 400—until you have all five frames roughly lined up with overlapping edges. Each frame will have a soft area of transition created between the frames on the left side. Look for areas where the disjointedness between the various frames is least obvious, such as areas with lights but without any distinctive details, like a building edge.

Choose the Rectangular Marquee tool, and give it a feather of 28 pixels. Select around the entire left side of frame 200, to the left of the purple W sign. Delete that section, and you'll have a smooth blend between frame 000 and frame 200. Do the same thing for frames 300 and 400, until you have a smooth panorama of the entire shot (Figure 14.2).

Figure 14.2 *Blend the five frames together by deleting the left side of frames 200, 300, 400, and 599 with the Rectangular Marquee tool.*

Cropping the File and Removing White in the Background

Crop the file as tightly as you can without deleting any of the frame edges. Because the camera pans up and the later frames are positioned higher, there are white spaces at top and bottom of the plate. Change the Rectangular Marquee tool feather to 2 pixels, and select a sliver of each frame nearest the white areas that you need to patch. For the top section, you'll fill in the white with sky from each frame; for the bottom area with the lower section of the buildings, you'll use the dark ground tones. For each frame, press Command/Ctrl+J to duplicate the section of the frame nearest the white area you need to patch, and press Command/Ctrl+T to transform and stretch the section to cover the white (Figure 14.3). It doesn't have to be perfect; you just need to get rid of the distraction of the white background.

Figure 14.3 *Get rid of the white at top and bottom by scaling a sliver of the frames to fill the white space.*

Merging the Layers

Select all five layers and the Background layer, and press Command/Ctrl+E. Now only one layer remains, named Background. Voila! The entire sequence is shown in one file, over which you're ready to paint (Figure 14.4). Save the file to your hard drive as `FutureNYC_Plate.psd`. You can check your work against `FutureNYC_Plate.jpg` in the Chapter 14 section of the DVD.

Figure 14.4 Final plate ready for painting

The Painting

At the end of this chapter, you'll be asked to prepare your own version of this project. You will learn how to add painted elements to a moving plate using a demonstration file so that your layer names and elements will match the figures. If you want to jump right into working over the moving plate, you can skip this section on creating the painting, and go to "Compositing the Painting over a Moving Plate" later in this the chapter. Be sure to come back and check out the techniques described in this section when you create your own version of New York 2100.

For this project, you won't be changing the color or tone of the plate. The futuristic elements will be added to what is already there and melded seamlessly with the original cityscape. Here are a few techniques used to create the futuristic structures in this demo.

Megastructures

Take a moment to study the prepared plate, and envision what New York in the far future will look like. Surely it will have huge buildings to house the ballooning population of 2100. The left side of the plate has a big open area that is a great spot to add a megastructure. Working over the `FutureNYC_Plate.psd` file or over the `FutureNYC_Plate.jpg` from the DVD, create a new layer above the Background layer, and name it **LfMegastructure**. Remember that the painted additions must match their neighbors. Where a new element is placed will determine its tonal properties. Owing to atmospheric perspective, nothing in the distant background will be as light or as dark as objects closer to the viewer. In other words, the megastructures you add to the far background will have less contrast than those in front. The exceptions are lights shining from far-off buildings, but you'll deal with those later.

Drawing a Selection for the Megastructure

You'll start by creating a megastructure on the opposite side of the river. Do a sketch using the Rectangular Marquee tool and the Lasso tool, with the feather on both set to 0.

First, create a large blocky shape in the background on the left side of the plate with the Rectangular Marquee tool. The outline should delineate the desired contours of the megastructure. As a general rule, the main mass of a large building shows a myriad of smaller details that help to establish scale. Use the Lasso tool to refine the architecture by adding, subtracting, and intersecting from the initial shape, and create a selection something like the one shown in Figure 14.5.

Figure 14.5 *Complex marquee selection for a distant megastructure*

Filling the Selection With the Gradient Tool

Fill the selection with the Gradient tool set to Foreground To Transparent in the Gradient Editor. Select tones from the ground beneath the structure to fill the selection from the bottom up. Now, choose a slightly darker version of the same tone, and fill the selection from the top down. Doing so makes the highest part of the building slightly darker (Figure 14.6).

Figure 14.6 *Gradient-fill the selection with tones from the background.*

Adding Abstract Detail

On a huge structure like this, you can use abstract detail garnered from a similar structure to begin creating forms. This demo uses a photo of an oil refinery from CGTextures.com. Open Buildings0149_L .jpg from the Chapter 14 folder on the DVD, and look through the RGB channels. Choose a channel in the Channels panel that shows the refinery details clearly—in this case, the Red channel—and duplicate it. Use a curve on the Red copy channel to make a very high-contrast version of the structure (Figure 14.7).

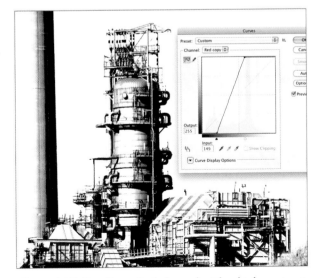

Figure 14.7 *Duplicate Red channel with a high-contrast curve applied to it*

Cover the Megastructure With High-Contrast Detail

Copy out interesting sections from the Red copy channel, and return to the Layers panel. Paste the high-contrast black and white information into a new layer on top of the LfMegastructure layer. Rename the new layer **HighContrastDetails**. Take different sections from the refinery, and reposition, scale, and distort them to match the large forms of the megastructure (Figure 14.8). Make sure most of the structure is covered by the black and white texture from the refinery.

You won't use the details from the refinery directly—you'll create a selection to paint into based on the tones from the image.

Loading Selections From Alpha Channels vs. Layers

When you load a selection from an alpha channel, Photoshop bases the selection on the grayscale tones. White pixels load as 100% selected, black pixels as 0% selected, and intermediate tones with corresponding selection values. This differs from the Layers panel in that loading a selection from a layer (Command/Ctrl+click the layer preview icon) doesn't create a selection based on the tones, but rather creates a selection based on where pixels are present. To understand the difference, try it here. Command/Ctrl+click the layer preview icon for the HighContrastDetails layer. Doing so loads a selection based on where pixels are present on the layer (Figure 14.9).

Now, open the Channels panel, and Command/Ctrl+click into one of the channel preview icons. Doing so loads a complex selection based on the grayscale tones of the alpha channel. This intricate selection is what you'll use to create abstract forms in the megastructure (Figure 14.10).

In black and white images like the high-contrast refinery reference, the RGB channels look the same, so it didn't matter which channel you clicked into to create the selection. You'll paint into the dark areas from the refinery selection, the opposite of what you currently have selected: press Command/Ctrl+Shift+I to invert the selection.

Intersect with the Layer Selection

Return to the Layers panel, and Command/Ctrl+Option/Alt+Shift+click into the LfMegastructure layer. This command intersects the existing selection with the selection from the LfMegastructure layer and allows you to paint only into the area of the structure. You won't be using the HighContrastDetails layer any more, so you can either delete it or turn off its visibility. Now you can see the silhouette of the megastructure with the selection contained within it (Figure 14.11).

Paint Into the Selection

Choose the LfMegastructure layer, and paint into the selection with a darker tone to add random detail from the refinery to the megastructure (Figure 14.12).

Using the random patterns as a starting point, paint into the structure, looking for interesting forms and shapes to enhance. If the building were this distant, the detail would be at a very low contrast level. However, it's hard to paint at low contrast, because the tones aren't clearly defined. Go ahead and paint at higher contrast so you can see what you are doing. You will reduce the contrast later (Figure 14.13).

Figure 14.8 *Cover the structure with high-contrast detail.*

Figure 14.9 *Selection loaded from a layer in the Layers panel*

Figure 14.10 *Selection loaded from a channel in the Channels panel*

Figure 14.11 *Selection loaded from the Channels panel, inverted, and intersected with the LfMegastructure layer selection*

Figure 14.12 *Random industrial texture added to the megastructure by painting into the selection*

Figure 14.13 *Paint into the random detail to discover new forms.*

Lights

The painted forms are shaping up nicely; now you can add lights. Create a new layer called **MegastructureLights**. Lights are less affected by atmospheric perspective than non-illuminated building surfaces. You can see that when you look out of an airplane at night: you see the lights of distant cities long before you can see any structural details. Why? Because the lights from buildings and streets cut through the atmosphere.

But you must be careful about the scale of the lights. The megastructure you're painting is miles away, so the windows will be extremely small. If you painted the windows the size of those in the foreground, they would have to be hundreds of feet high, making your futuristic structure look fake. In contrast, lots of tiny windows will reinforce the tremendous scale of the building.

At this point, you may want to seek out the artwork of two pioneers in visualizing futuristic megastructures: Syd Mead and Robert McCall. Mead brought huge structures into the popular consciousness through his concept painting for the film *Blade Runner* (1982). Note particularly how he utilizes many minute windows to emphasize the immensity of distant structures. McCall, another visionary artist, specialized in futurist cities, including dazzling floating megastructures. If you're at a loss for inspiration, these artists should get your imaginative juices flowing.

Painting Randomized Windows With a Custom Brush

Figure 14.14 Make a selection around the 15- by 10-pixel window shape.

Rather than individually hand-painting thousands of windows in the megastructure, you can create a custom brush to do the job. Make a new Photoshop file, 50 × 50 pixels. Using the Rectangular Marquee tool with no feather on it, make a selection 15 pixels high by 10 pixels wide, and fill it with black. Select an area slightly larger than the black rectangle (Figure 14.14) and, with the Brush tool selected, choose Edit → Define Brush Preset. Name the new brush **Window**.

Adding Dynamics to the Brush

Choose a bright yellow color from the Color Picker. Open the Brush panel. Click the check box next to Color Dynamics, and open the Color Dynamics controls by clicking the name. Set Hue Jitter to 10% and Brightness Jitter to 5%. Doing so adds some color variation to the windows. Turn on Scattering, and set Scatter to 800%. That's not a typo—you want a lot of scatter. Set the Control drop-down menu to Off. Click Brush Tip Shape, and set spacing to 900%. Again, that's not a typo; you want distance between each window. Don't be afraid to try extreme settings for the parameters to get the results you want.

Create a new layer on top of the LfMegastructure layer, and call it **MegaWindows**. Try the brush by painting some windows over the megastructure. The randomness is great, but the windows are too big. Undo to get rid of the windows you painted. Now, set the brush size to 1 pixel, and begin populating the building with windows (Figure 14.15). Because the windows are on a separate layer, you can be sloppy with the first pass and erase any areas that should be windowless. Remember, the original Window brush you saved had none of the dynamics you've added. If you want to use this much more complex brush in the future, be sure to save it under a different name, such as **WindowsDynamic**.

Many large structures are lit from the bottom by the glow of the surrounding city. Use the Gradient tool to

Figure 14.15 Populate the building with tiny windows.

brighten the bottom of the megastructure, with the illumination dropping off as it gets higher. You can add some larger lights on the structure to illuminate other parts of the building for dramatic effect (Figure 14.16). Add more lights for the surrounding city and support buildings to taste.

Reducing the Contrast of the Building

Now you need to reduce the contrast of the building. Distant buildings are typically lighter at the base, because there is more smog and haze near the ground. Add a new layer called **MegastructureHaze**. Place it below MegastructureLights but above LfMegastructure. Load the LfMegastructure layer selection to create a selection into which you can paint. Choose the Gradient tool, set it to Linear Gradient, and select Foreground To Transparent in the Gradient Editor. Set the tool opacity to 30% so you can use it repeatedly to build up lighter tones.

Sample the sky color from near the top of the structure, and use the Gradient tool from the top of the composition down to decrease contrast on the building. Select the sky color from near the base of the building, and use the Gradient tool from the ground up to add the lighter tone to the base of the structure. The selection confines the gradient to the area of the megastructure. The gradient tone shouldn't cover all the detail you added, just obscure it enough to place the building in the far background (Figure 14.17). Because you're adding the haze on a separate layer, you can adjust the amount you need as your composition comes together.

Figure 14.16 Lighten the building base and selected sections.

Figure 14.17 Hazed megastructure in the far distance

Extending an Existing Building

Let's try another approach to creating futuristic structures, this time by adding to the top of one of the buildings in Times Square. Select the building situated near center-right on the plate with a small yellow/orange dome sticking up from the top (use Figure 14.18 to help locate the building). Use the Rectangular Marquee tool to draw the building extension. Cut into the selection symmetrically on the sides to add some variety to the profile (Figure 14.18).

Fill the selection with the Gradient tool using the dark façade color of the structure being extended (Figure 14.19).

Add surface detail to the structure, remembering to follow the curve of the building. You can use the ellipse technique you learned when you worked on the castle project (Figure 14.20).

Rather than painting in the lights, you can grab lit sections from other buildings in the plate. When you use existing lights in the plate, you know they will match the tone and color of what is already there. Use the copied sections to create a flat row of lights, and contour the lights with the Warp tool to fit the circular building (Figure 14.21).

With one row of windows distorted, duplicate them all over the structure. Erase and paint into the windows to add variety, and change the color of some levels (Figure 14.22).

Taking detail lifted from more industrial structures, add some landing pads and other ornaments to finish the building (Figure 14.23).

Figure 14.18 Draw the outline of the riser using the Rectangular Marquee tool.

Figure 14.19 Fill the selection with the Gradient tool, using color from the façade of the building.

Figure 14.20 Add surface detail.

Figure 14.21 Extending an existing building using lights from the plate

Figure 14.22 Duplicate and colorize the windows.

Figure 14.23 Finish the building with additional details.

If you're working over the FutureNYC_Plate.jpg file from the DVD, or if you created your own base plate, save the file to your hard drive as FutureNYC_Painting.psd. Put this file aside for now, and use the demo file FutureNYC_AE.psd from the Chapter 14 materials on the DVD for the rest of the chapter to learn about compositing over a moving plate. It will be easier to follow along if you're using the same file shown in the demonstration. At the end of this chapter, you'll have a chance to create your own painting and place it into this scene.

Compositing the Painting over a Moving Plate

As part of this "team" project, you'll work on a file prepared by the Matchmoving department. Matchmoving programs automatically position tracking points that follow what is in the moving image. Typically, the best points to track are areas of high contrast. Through an extremely complex series of mathematical computations, the tracking program places the points in space and creates a digital camera that exactly reproduces the motion of the camera that photographed the live-action plate.

> I won't cover how to do motion tracking, or matchmoving, because it's a book-length topic in itself. If you want to learn more, I recommend *Matchmoving: The Invisible Art of Camera Tracking* by Tim Dobbert (Sybex, 2005).

Open the file FutureNYC_Start.aep from the Chapter 14 DVD materials. If it isn't already open, double-click the FutureNYC_Track comp in the Project panel to open it in the Viewer panel. The first thing you'll notice is the constellation of small squares outlined in red, created by the matchmoving program. Scrub through the timeline to view the footage with the trackers over it. Notice how these small trackers, known as *nulls* in After Effects, precisely follow many points in the footage.

> SynthEyes, an affordable tracking program used for this project, is available for purchase at www.ssontech.com/.

Importing the Painting

Import the painting, FutureNYC_AE.psd, by dragging and dropping the Photoshop file into the After Effects Project panel. A dialog appears; choose Import Kind: Composition – Retain Layer Sizes. Leave Layer Options as they are, and click OK.

You now have two comps in the Project panel. The first comp is FutureNYC_AE, which was created by the import of the Photoshop file. Double-click this comp in the Project panel to open it in the Viewer. The project appears just as it did in Photoshop (Figure 14.24). You'll use this comp as a reference for positioning the elements in 3D space.

Figure 14.24 *FutureNYC_AE comp that contains the original layout of the painting from Photoshop*

The second comp, FutureNYC_Track, contains the tracked footage. This is where you'll position the painted elements in the 3D space. Double-click this comp to open it in the Viewer. This comp contains the live-action plate and 120 tracking points (Figure 14.25).

Figure 14.25 *FutureNYC_Track comp, containing the footage and null tracking points*

In the Project panel, click the arrow next to the folder `FutureNYC_AE Layers` to display all the individual layers imported from Photoshop. Notice that the layers have the same names as the layers in the Photoshop document, followed by a slash mark and then the name of the original Photoshop document. This is where carefully naming the layers in Photoshop pays off in managing the project.

Look in the Timeline panel. You'll find 120 trackers in the scene, represented by null shapes. *Null shapes* are empty points in After Effects that represent the tracking points. Back in the Project panel, in the `FutureNYC_AE Layers` folder, select the `SmallFloatingBalls/FutureNYC_AE.psd` layer, the last layer in the folder; then, Shift+select the `BigBall/FutureNYC_AE.psd` layer, the second layer in the folder. You'll have all the layers selected except the `Background/FutureNYC_AE.psd` layer (Figure 14.26)

Now, drag the layers into the Timeline panel for the FutureNYC_Track comp, dropping them just above the top null shape, `null_Tracker120Shape` (Figure 14.27).

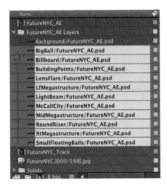

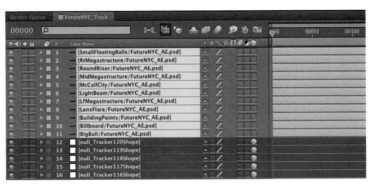

Figure 14.26 *Select all the layers except* Background/FutureNYC_AE.psd.

Figure 14.27 *Drag the layers into the top of the FutureNYC_Track comp Timeline panel*

Layers come into the Timeline in the order you selected them in the Project panel, so if the layer order in your project is different from Figure 14.27, it's because you selected them in a different order. If you accidently brought in the `Background/FutureNYC_AE.psd` layer, select it in the Timeline panel and delete it.

Deselect all the layers in the Timeline by choosing Edit → Deselect All. Look in the Viewer panel: the layers appear on top of each other. Yet as you scroll through the Timeline, the painted elements don't move (Figure 14.28), because the painting is still in the 2D workspace. Before you place the elements in 3D, you need to learn how to navigate the After Effects 3D world.

From here on, layer names will be shortened to dispense with the name of the Photoshop file that After Effects appends to every layer. For example, `BigBall/FutureNYC_AE.psd` will be referred to as BigBall.

Figure 14.28 Layers in the Viewer panel

Navigating After Effects' 3D Workspace

In Chapter 13, "Getting Started in After Effects," you used After Effects in the traditional 2D mode. When you're using After Effects' 3D workspace, you can view the scene from multiple angles in the Viewer panel, just like a 3D object. At the bottom of the Viewer panel is the 3D View pop-up menu; it currently reads Active Camera . The Active Camera view is where the scene will be rendered, and it has the background plate showing behind it. Similar to the views in Maya, a camera controls every view in After Effects' 3D workspace.

There are six orthographic views: Front, Left, Top, Back, Right, and Bottom. The angles of these views are set and can't be altered. You can zoom in or out and move the view right and left, but you can't rotate around the scene from these set views. To rotate around the scene and examine it from any angle, click the 3D View pop-up menu and choose Custom View 1 to open it in the Viewer panel (Figure 14.29).

With the Viewer panel displaying Custom View 1, the background plate and the city elements disappear, and all you see are the tracking points and the camera. When you scrub through the Timeline, the 3D tracking nulls form a partial cylindrical shape (Figure 14.30).

Press C on the keyboard to choose the Camera Manipulation tool, which lets you rotate the view. Click+drag the cursor in the Viewer panel to rotate around the partial cylinder of tracked points. The camera created by the matchmoving program is in front of the tracked points. If you scrub through the Timeline now, you'll see the camera rotate on the Y-axis to pan over the tracked points, reproducing the movement of the camera that photographed the scene.

Figure 14.29
Use the 3D View pop-up menu to select the view.

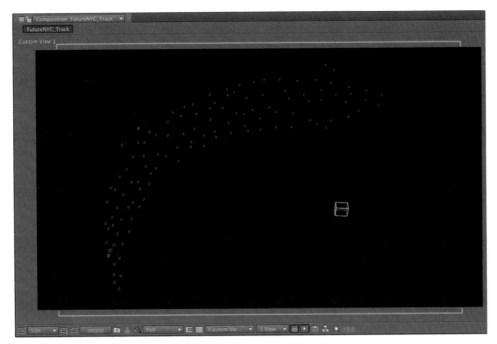

Figure 14.30 *Nulls form a partial cylinder shape in Custom View 1.*

The Camera Controls

If you repeatedly press C again, you'll sequence through the three camera controls:

- Orbit tool ◉ to rotate around the 3D scene
- Track XY tool ◉ to move up, down, right, or left in the 3D scene
- Track Z tool ◉ to push into or out of the 3D scene

Experiment with navigating the 3D workspace using this trio of tools. You may find yourself getting lost in 3D space, when suddenly everything is off the screen and you're unable to figure out where the elements are. If so, press Command/Ctrl+Option/Alt+Shift+\ (backward slash key) to center what you've selected in the Viewer panel. If you have nothing selected, the keyboard shortcut centers everything—very useful!

The Unified Camera Control

There is one final tool for navigating the 3D workspace (available in CS 4 and 5): the Unified Camera tool. The icon looks like a camera ◎. It comes up first when you press C to access the camera controls, but it requires a three-button mouse to function. In the Viewer panel, the Unified Camera tool can perform all three of the camera controls:

- Left-click+drag to make it the Orbit tool.
- Press the middle mouse button to make it the Track XY tool.
- Control+left-click+drag to make it the Track Z tool.

Return to the Viewer panel, and, from the 3D View pop-up menu, choose Active Camera again. The background plate and city elements return. All these elements are currently still 2D, and 2D elements show up only in the Active Camera Viewer panel. Next, you'll make all the painted elements into 3D layers.

Making the Painting 3D

Make sure you're still in the FutureNYC_Track comp. In the Timeline, select all the layers containing painted elements from your Photoshop file, and click the 3D Layer icon to the right of one of the layer names ![icon]. With all the layers with painted elements selected, turning one layer 3D does the same to all the others (Figure 14.31).

The city elements disappear. What just happened?

You made the 2D painted layers into 3D layers that can be manipulated in 3D space, and they're out of view of the camera. Choose Custom View 1 again, and orbit the view. All the nulls in

Figure 14.31 *Click the 3D layer icon to turn on 3D for all selected layers.*

the project were set to 3D, which is why they showed up previously in the 3D views. The painted layers have now joined the nulls in 3D space. You'll see the new layers in the middle of and slightly below the nulls. However, they're in the wrong position (Figure 14.32). You need to reposition the 3D layers around the cylinder of null points to match the original painting in Photoshop.

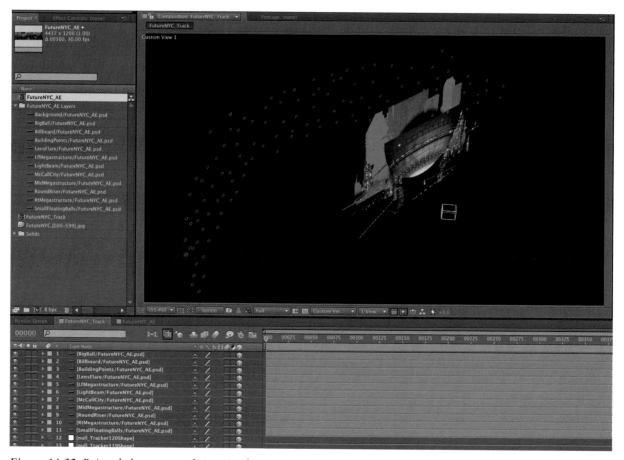

Figure 14.32 *Painted elements made into 3D layers*

Positioning Layers in 3D Space

Return to the Active Camera view. The painted elements are out of frame and not visible in this view. You must bring them to the center. Go back to Custom View 1, and select all the painted layers. It's important not to select the camera or the nulls in the project, only the painted layers. Use the Selection tool  (keyboard shortcut V) to move the elements into the center of the nulls. To see the project from several different views simultaneously, you can select 4 Views from the Select View Layout drop-down menu (Figure 14.33).

In the Timeline, scrub to frame 300 so you're in the middle of the sequence. You can set each of the four views to a different angle using the 3D View pop-up menu. The Top and Front views assist you in getting the painted layers into position. Scale down the layers so you can see them all in the view; try around 80% (Figure 14.34).

Figure 14.33
Select the 4 Views option.

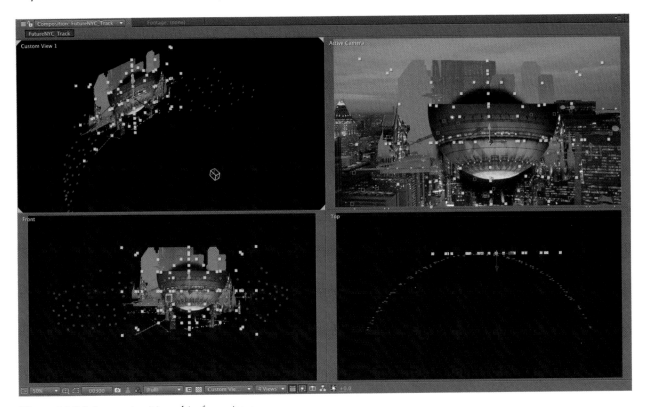

Figure 14.34 Layers positioned in four views

The layers should now be visible in the Active Camera view at frame 300. Return to one view so you have more room to work. Set the view to Active Camera from the 3D View pop-up menu. The Active Camera view is the only one where the 2D live-action plate is visible, which can present a problem while you're working in that view. To position the new layers, you need to be able to select 3D layers and nulls in the Active Camera view. However, if you click in the Active Camera view, you'll constantly select the 2D layer with the live-action plate.

Figure 14.35 *Lock the live-action plate.*

Scroll to the bottom of the list of layers in the Timeline, and lock the 2D background plate, `FutureNYCity.[000-599].jpg` (Figure 14.35). Now you can work in the Active Camera view without accidentally selecting the plate.

You can check your work to this point by opening `FutureNYC_LayersCentered.aep` from the Chapter 14 DVD materials.

In the Timeline, scroll back to the top where the painted layers are located. To avoid getting confused by the multiple layers on top of each other, you should position the layers, one by one, in 3D space. Turn off the visibility of the painted layers in the Timeline, with the exception of the BigBall layer. In the Active Camera view, only the live-action plate and BigBall are visible (Figure 14.36).

Figure 14.36 *Turn off visibility of the other layers so only BigBall is in the Active Camera view.*

The BigBall layer needs to be positioned above the foreground building visible in frames 0–300. Because you're on frame 300, that building is out of frame to the left. Scrub through the Time Graph to frame 000. Now the ball is off screen on the right. You need to move the ball to the left so it's visible with the building.

Manually Positioning Layers

There are several ways to get the layer into the correct position. The first technique is to move the layer manually by working back and forth between the Active Camera view, the orthographic views, and the three different custom views. You can set each custom view to a different angle on the scene.

From the Select View Layout drop-down menu, switch to 2 Views Horizontal. Select the right view, and, from the 3D View pop-up menu, select Active Camera. Select the left view, and set it to Custom View 1. Now, select the BigBall layer with the Selection tool (V) in the Active Camera view. With the layer selected, the 3D Axes control appears. This control, represented by three colored arrows, is used to move and rotate the layer on the axes: red for X, green for Y, and blue for Z. By default, it appears in the middle of the layer. You select one of the colored arrows with the Selection or Rotation tool to transform the layer. After Effects gives you a preview of the axis you're about to select when you hover over one of the arrows (Figure 14.37).

Figure 14.37 Axis-selection icon indicating which axis you're about to select

Using the 3D Axes control, move the BigBall layer to the left on the X-axis and up on the Y-axis. You want to position the element on top of the foreground building (Figure 14.38). Note that your custom view may differ from what is shown here, depending on how you've set the view.

Figure 14.38 Manually position a layer above the left foreground building.

Move to frame 80 so the ball and building are in the middle of the frame. The position is better, but the ball still needs to be aligned along the cylinder of points and rotated to face the camera. In the custom view, move the ball closer to the nulls. It will help to switch to the Top view to achieve a more precise alignment.

Press the W key to access the Rotation tool. The 3D Axes control remains the same, but the cursor changes into a pointer with a circular arrow below it ▣. Click the 3D Axes control to rotate the BigBall layer on the Y-axis so it directly faces the camera. You'll need to work back and forth between the three axes to get the layer precisely aligned.

You'll use the Selection and Rotation tools a lot, and V and W aren't the most intuitive keyboard shortcuts. A mnemonic trick I use is to think of them as "mooV" and "Wotate" while working in After Effects.

While aligning a layer, you may forget where it was positioned in the original painting. If so, double-click the FutureNYC_AE comp in the Project panel, and you'll see the original layout from Photoshop. When you've checked the position, return to the FutureNYC_Track comp.

The ball is larger than in the painting. Uniformly scale the ball by selecting a corner of the layer and holding down the Shift key while you pull the corner in or out. As a final check, examine the layer from several views to make sure it's right on top of the nulls on the cylinder of tracking points (Figure 14.39).

Figure 14.39 *BigBall layer aligned with the nulls, facing the camera*

The camera is at the bottom of the Timeline, named Camera01Shape in the comp; it provides the Active Camera view. It's important not to move this camera, so take this opportunity to lock it. The matchmoving program has placed a keyframe on every frame for the camera. If you move Camera01Shape accidently, you'll notice that the camera hops to a new position when you reach that frame in the animation.

Using Nulls to Position Layers

Let's position the McCallCity layer using a different method. Double-click the CityFutureNYC_AE comp to see the original layout, and note where the floating city is positioned.

Click the tab for the FutureNYC_Track comp at the top of the Timeline to return to the main project. Select the null in the Active Camera view closest to where McCallCity is to be positioned, null_Tracker54Shape. You'll copy the null's position and use it to place the McCallCity layer. Click the arrow next to null_Tracker54Shape to open the Transform attributes. Notice that the tracking program has set Position, Scale, and X, Y, and Z Rotation keyframes on every frame of the sequence (Figure 14.40).

All you want from this null is its position, not all those keyframes. Select the null's Transform attributes, and click the stopwatch to the left. When you click the stopwatch on an attribute that has keyframes, it removes all the keyframes, changing the stopwatch next to each attribute from keyframed 🕑 to not keyframed 🕑. Click the word *Position* in the Position attribute, and press Command/Ctrl+C to copy the position at -119.7, -237.4, -16.7 (Figure 14.41).

Figure 14.40 *Keyframes have been set on every frame of null_Tracker54Shape.*

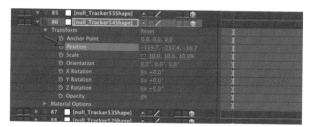

Figure 14.41 *Click the Position attribute, and copy it.*

If you click an attribute that has keyframes and then copy it, all the keyframes are copied. If you copy an attribute that has no keyframes, only the current value is copied, without the keyframes.

Turn on the visibility of the McCallCity layer, select it, and press Command/Ctrl+V to paste the position of null_Tracker54Shape on the floating city. McCallCity jumps to the same position as the null (Figure 14.42). Now it's positioned on top of the half cylinder of nulls. All you need to do is scale the floating city, move it up, and rotate it toward the camera.

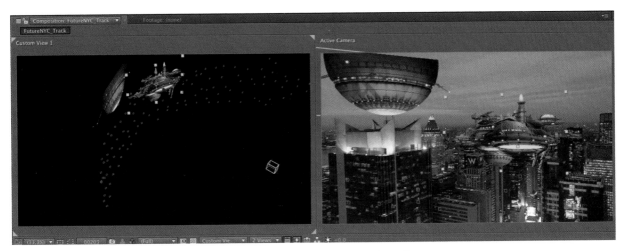

Figure 14.42 *Copy the position of a null near where you want to position a layer, and paste that position value onto the layer.*

Checklist for Positioning Layers With Nulls

In positioning the other elements in your comp, you'll follow the same procedure you used for the floating city. The following checklist can guide you through the process:

1. Select the null closest to where you want the layer to end up.
2. Click the arrow next to the layer name to see all the Transform attributes.
3. Select all the attributes, and click one of the stopwatches that have keyframes to remove the keyframes.
4. Select the Position attribute on the null, and copy it.
5. Select the layer you want to reposition, and paste the Position attribute from the null onto it.
6. The layer jumps to the new position, but isn't scaled or oriented properly. Position, rotate, and scale the layer so it matches the original painting imported from Photoshop.
7. Use different views to check that the layer lines up with the cylinder of tracking points.

Parenting Layers Together

The LensFlare layer should go on top of the McCallCity layer. Select the Position, Scale, and Orientation Transform properties from McCallCity, and copy them. Select the LensFlare layer, and paste the aforementioned Transform properties onto it. The flare hops on top of the flying city in exactly the same position in 3D space. Select the Z-axis with the Selection tool, and move the flare slightly in front of the city. The flare was set to Screen in Photoshop, and the blending mode for the layer was imported with the layer, so the flare brightens the ship. Move it down to the bright anti-gravity thruster under the floating city. Create a mask to confine the flare under the ship, and feather the mask by 20 pixels to soften the transition (Figure 14.43). For organizational purposes, position the LensFlare layer above the McCall city layer in the Timeline panel.

Figure 14.43 *Mask off the flare under McCallCity.*

Don't be concerned if the layer order in the Timeline of your project differs from what is shown in the figures. In 2D space, the layer order is very important, because any layer that is higher in the Timeline is visible over a lower layer. In 3D space, which layer is visible to the camera is determined by its position on the Z-axis, or whether a layer is closer or further away from the camera. The position of a 3D layer in the Timeline doesn't matter, except that all 3D elements must be higher in the Timeline than the live-action plate, FutureNYC.[000-599].jpg. Any layers below the 2D live-action plate in the Timeline aren't visible to the active camera.

You'll animate the ship later in this chapter, and it will be helpful to have the ship and the flare move as one. To parent the flare to the ship, you need the Parent column to be visible in the Timeline. If it isn't, open the Timeline Panel menu in the upper-right corner of the Timeline ▥, and be sure Columns → Parent is selected. Select the LensFlare layer in the Timeline, and, in the Parent column, click the drop-down menu. Change it from None to McCallCity (Figure 14.44).

Now the LensFlare layer is parented to the McCallCity layer and will move anywhere it moves. Lock LensFlare so you don't accidently move it. In order to test the parenting, select McCallCity and move it with

Figure 14.44 Parent LensFlare to McCallCity.

the Selection tool to make sure the flare moves with it. You'll animate the flare so the light will pulse. However, even when independently animated, it will still move with its parent.

Adding Moving Spotlights to a Building

At old Hollywood premiers, special high-intensity spotlights called *klieg lights* would rotate back and forth, shooting piercing beams of light into the night sky. You'll add animated klieg lights to the RoundRiser building to heighten the drama of the scene. Place the RoundRiser building using the null position technique you just learned (Figure 14.45).

Figure 14.45 RoundRiser layer positioned

Move the LightBeam layer above the RoundRiser layer to keep the Timeline vorganized. Copy the Position, Scale, and Orientation attributes from the RoundRiser layer, and paste them onto the LightBeam layer. The light beam appears on top of the RoundRiser layer. Move the spotlight slightly in front of the RoundRiser layer on the Z-axis. Choose a location on the RoundRiser layer that could have a klieg light on it, and move the base of the spotlight there (Figure 14.46).

Figure 14.46
LightBeam
positioned in front
of RoundRiser

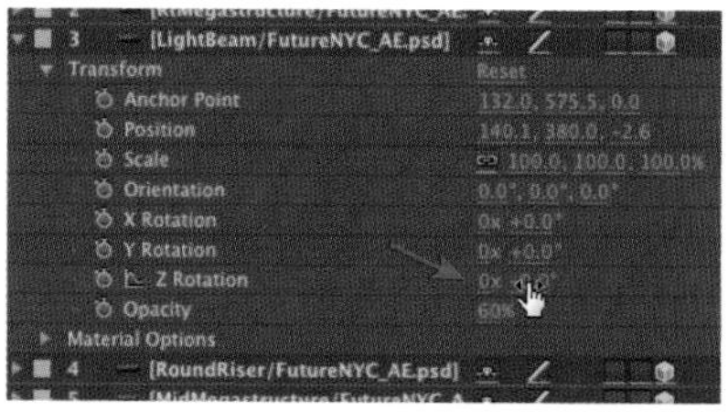

Figure 14.47 *Click and drag the Z Rotation degree value.*

You can animate the Z-axis of LightBeam to show it moving back and forth in the sky. Click+hold+drag the underlined degree value to the right of the Z Rotation Transform attribute where it says +0.0°. As you drag the value back and forth, the light beam layer rotates on the Z-axis (Figure 14.47).

Relocating the Anchor Point of a Layer

The beam rotates from the center of the layer, but you want it to rotate from the base. The rotation originates from the location of the anchor point, represented by a crosshairs icon ✦ at the center of the 3D Axes control's green, red, and blue arrows. You need to resituate the anchor point to rest at the base of the beam. Anchor Point is first on the list of Transform attributes for each layer. By default, the anchor point is located at the center of a layer. To reposition it, you'll adjust the X, Y, and Z attributes listed to the right of Anchor Point in the Transform attributes. To change the X attribute and move the beam to the right, click and drag the first of the three underlined values listed to the right of Anchor Point. Now, click and drag the second underlined value—the Y attribute—to move the beam of light up. The Z attribute adjusts the depth of the anchor point. In this instance, you don't want to move it.

Note that the anchor point stays in the same position while you're adjusting the X, Y, and Z coordinates—only the layer moves. After changing the anchor point, you need to readjust the position of the beam with the Selection tool, because the layer was moved. With the anchor point now at the base of the beam, you can animate the spotlight. Go to the Z Rotation Transform attribute for the beam, and Click+hold+drag the second underlined value to move the beam back and forth from its base.

Animating the Motion of the Light Beam

Go to frame 300, and set a Z Rotation keyframe at 27°. Move to frame 400, and rotate the spotlight to the right 55°. Move to frame 500, and set another keyframe at 27°. Move to frame 600, and set a keyframe at 55° again. The spotlight appears at frame 200, so set another 55° keyframe there. Run a RAM preview of the light. The motion isn't smooth, so you need to add an ease-in and ease-out on the keyframes. Select all the Z Rotation keyframes, Control+click any one of them, and choose Keyframe Assistant → Easy-Ease. To make the beam blend transparently, Control+right-click the LightBeam layer name in the Timeline and, from Blending Mode, choose Screen. This is an alternative way of assigning a blending mode to a layer without having to open the Modes column in the Timeline. Set the layer opacity to 60%. RAM preview the comp again. Now the beam eases in and out of the rotation fluidly (Figure 14.48).

Duplicating the Beam

With one spotlight set up, let's duplicate it and have several beams shooting into the night sky. Duplicate the LightBeam layer by selecting it and pressing Command/Ctrl+D. Move the beam up in the Y-axis using the Selection tool, and find another area on the building where a beam could originate. Because you only changed the position, the duplicate retains the same rotation as the original. The movement of the beams will look better if they are not synchronized, so select all the

Figure 14.48 *Anchor point for the light beam moved to the base of the beam and animated*

Z Rotation keyframes, and move them 50 frames to the right to offset the movement from the first beam. You should also change the initial Z orientation of the duplicated beam. That way, the initial orientation of the beam will be different from the first one but still retain the animation on the Z rotation.

Orientation and rotation are confusingly similar in After Effects: they both rotate a layer around the anchor point. For your purposes, it's best to animate the Z rotation for the beam and leave the orientation with no keyframes. This allows you to use Z orientation to change the initial angle of the beam on the RoundRiser building.

Duplicate the beam a third time, and find another building location for it. Select all the Z Rotation keyframes on the new layer, and offset them from the two other beams. You can also move individual Rotation keyframes around to vary the intervals of beam movement (Figure 14.49).

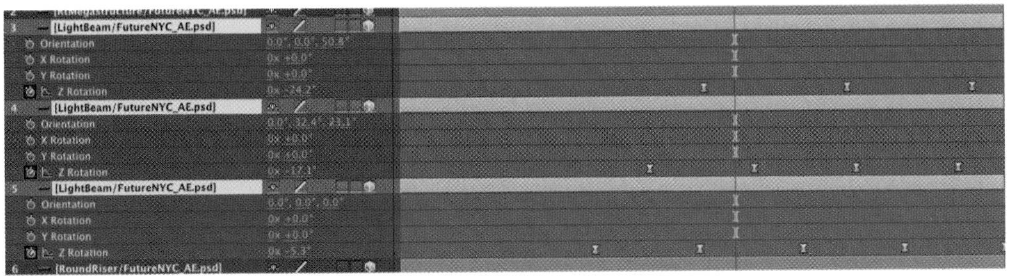

Figure 14.49 *Offset keyframes for three sets of light beams*

Adding a Flare to the Beams

The source of the spotlights should evidence a bright flare where the light faces the camera. You can use the LensFlare layer you already imported and that is currently parented to McCallCity. Select the LensFlare layer, and duplicate it. Rename the new layer SmLensFlare. Move SmLensFlare on top of the first LightBeam layer copies, just above the RoundRiser layer; doing so keeps all the layers associated with the RoundRiser layer together. Select RoundRiser, and copy the Position attribute. Select SmLensFlare, and paste the position. The flare is much too large, and it has a mask leftover from McCallCity. Select just the mask for the layer, and delete it. Scale the flare so it fits at the base of the first LightBeam layer, and move it forward in Z space so that it's slightly in front of the beam. In the Parent column, unlink it from the floating city and set Parent to None. Duplicate the SmLensFlare layer two more times to add flares to the base of the other light beams (Figure 14.50); and, to stay organized, move the duplicate SmLensFlare just above the LightBeam layer with which it's associated.

Figure 14.50 Light beams with flares

Parenting the Beams to the RoundRiser Building

You now have six layers that should be linked to the RoundRiser building. In the Timeline, select the three LightBeam layers and the three SmLensFlare layers. In the Parent column, select RoundRiser from the drop-down menu. If you're satisfied with the animation, lock the six parented layers so you won't accidently move them.

Adding a Video Billboard

Next, you'll add a video billboard to the side of a building. Find `David_HenryMorph.mov` in the Chapter 14 DVD materials. Drag it into the Project panel, and from there into the Viewer panel for the FutureNYC_Track comp. Doing so creates a new layer in the Timeline named `David_HenryMorph.mov`. Click the 3D Layer box to make the layer 3D. Refer back to the CityFutureNYC comp to find the location of the billboard. Return to the FutureNYC_Track comp and, from the Active Camera view, select the null closest to where the billboard will be placed: null_Tracker89Shape. Delete the keyframes on the null, and

Figure 14.51 Video billboard positioned on a building

select and copy the Position attribute. Paste the position onto `David_HenryMorph.mov`. The movie jumps close to the correct position. Scale and rotate to get it better oriented on the building; use the building windows in the plate as a guide for lining up the billboard in proper perspective (Figure 14.51).

Moving the Layer Duration Bar

Scrub through the comp. Because the video is only 396 frames and the comp is 600 frames, the footage runs out before the comp is complete, and the billboard disappears. Select the Layer Duration bar for the video billboard, and drag it to the right until the end of the layer coincides with the last frame (Figure 14.52).

Figure 14.52 Drag the `David_HenryMorph.mov` *Layer Duration bar to the right.*

Time-Remapping the Video

There is enough video to cover where the billboard is visible in the comp, but the best part of the video—where the morph occurs—isn't seen at the beginning of the camera pan. Let's time-remap it to show off the cool parts. Choose Layer → Time → Enable Time Remapping. Now you can change the timing of how the frames are displayed. Choose the last keyframe at frame 598, and drag it to the left to frame 400 (Figure 14.53). When you scrub through the take, the video shows the man morphing into the cat for the first 200 frames and then holds on a frame of the man for the last 198 frames.

Figure 14.53 Drag the right Time Remapping keyframe to the left.

Time remapping allows you to play with time like putty, so you can make the image run backward, forward, and anything in between. Let's make the video run in reverse for the last 198 frames so the man morphs back into the cat. Go to frame 200, select the Time

Remapping keyframe, and copy it (Command/Ctrl+C). With the David_HenryMorph.mov layer still selected, move to frame 598, and paste the keyframe (Command/Ctrl+V). Now the morph occurs in 200 frames, reverses itself, and plays backward until the end frame (Figure 14.54).

Figure 14.54 *The time-remapped morph plays in 200 frames and then plays backward.*

Adding a Black Boarder to the Billboard

The video billboard needs a dark border to integrate with the side of the building. Select David_HenryMorph.mov, and choose Layer → Pre-Compose. This time, select Leave all Attributes In 'FutureNYC_Track' so you don't lose the time remapping on the layer. After Effects automatically names the new comp David_HenryMorph.mov Comp. Click OK to accept these settings. Double-click the David_HenryMorph.mov comp in the Timeline to open it in the Viewer. You'll see that it contains the original video clip but none of the time remapping. The time remapping is still applied in the FutureNYC_Track comp. Choose Layer → New → Solid, and make a new black solid the size of the comp. Drag the black solid below the video layer, and set the opacity to 50%. Select the video layer, and scale it down a bit so the billboard has a black border.

Click the tab for FutureNYC_Track, and view the results. The time remapping remains unchanged, but the billboard has a black border around it. The border is partially transparent, because the opacity is set to 50% in the precomp. You need to mask off the right side of the billboard where it intersects the building in front of it. With the billboard layer selected, draw a mask around the edge of the building, and set Masking Mode to Subtract. Feather the mask 1 pixel to soften it (Figure 14.55). Scrub through the Timeline to see the results.

With the video billboard in place, you can delete the Billboard layer in the comp; it was simply a placeholder for the movie version.

Figure 14.55 *Black border added to the video billboard*

Preparing the Project for Animation

Before you begin animating the scene, you should make sure all the stationary elements are set up correctly so you can concentrate exclusively on motion. You must attend to four remaining details.

Breaking Up the SmallFloatingBalls Layer

The SmallFloatingBalls layer contains four flying spherical vehicles that will be animated independently. Because they were imported on a single layer, you need to break this layer into four parts.

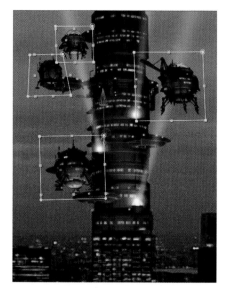

Figure 14.56 SmallFloatingBalls layer duplicated four times, and each flyer masked separately

Position the layer on top of the RoundRiser building, and move it slightly in front of the building and spotlights on the Z-axis. With SmallFloatingBalls selected, use the Rectangle tool in the Toolbar panel ▣ to draw a rectangular mask around one of the balls. Duplicate the layer and, on the duplicate, move and scale the mask so it shows another of the flying balls. Repeat this process two more times until each flying ball is on a separate layer with its own mask (Figure 14.56).

Positioning the Remaining Layers

Position the remaining layers of your composition on your own. When you're finished, all the layers should be seamlessly attached to the video footage. You can compare your work so far to `FutureNYC_LayersPositioned.aep` on the DVD.

Making the Nulls "Shy"

Because you're finished using the nulls, you can hide them so they don't take up space in the Timeline while you animate. There is a switch to the right of each layer to mark a layer as *shy*; the switch looks like a little man peering over a fence ▣. If you click the icon, it changes to look as though the little man has ducked down behind the fence ▣. At the top of the Timeline, clicking the Hides All Layers For Which The 'Shy' Switch Is Set icon ▣ hides all marked layers until you click the switch again. For this project, select all the null layers and click the Shy switch next to one of the layers. Now, click the master Shy switch at the top of the Timeline (Figure 14.57). All the null layers are hidden, freeing up a lot of room in the workspace and making it easier to see at a glance the layers with which you're working. You can always unshy the switch, if you need to go back and work with a shy layer.

Figure 14.57 Hide the null layers using the Shy switch.

Rotating the Layers to Minimize Lens Distortion

With all the layers in place, you'll notice a problem when you scrub through the Timeline: some of the layers, such as the BigBall layer, distort dramatically as the camera pans and moves near the edge of the frame. At frame 35, the BigBall layer looks fine (Figure 14.58).

However, by frame 225, the ball looks stretched and distorted, plus the edge of the layer is visible because the layer is no longer facing the camera (Figure 14.59). This is due to lens distortion from the wide-angle lens used to photograph the original footage.

To minimize that distortion, you'll animate the layer orientation to keep it straight on to the edge of the comp. This isn't a perfect solution—the best solution requires an advanced technique that maps the painting onto 3D geometry in the comp, as was done in the camera-projection project. However, this cheat works reasonably well.

Figure 14.58 *The BigBall layer shows no distortion on frame 35.*

Figure 14.59 *The BigBall layer shows considerable distortion on frame 225.*

Figure 14.60 *Edge of the layer not aligned*

Figure 14.61 *Edge of the layer aligned*

Scrub between frames 0 and 50, and note when the camera begins to pan. The camera starts to move somewhere around frame 35. Select the BigBall layer, and set an Orientation keyframe at frame 35 to establish a starting point for the rotation of the layer. You can make sure the layer is aligned to the camera by checking that the layer edges are aligned with the edge of the comp. You can easily do this by checking the edges of the layer visible outside of the View window (Figure 14.60 and Figure 14.61).

Next, move to frame 225, where the BigBall layer begins to exit the comp. Rotate the layer so it's flat on to the camera, or about 22° on the Y-axis. Scrub through the comp again. The distortion on the layer is significantly minimized (Figure 14.62).

Figure 14.62 *The BigBall layer keyframed to face the camera on frame 225*

Scrub through the Timeline to see what layers show the most distortion. The RoundRiser layer will also look better if it's animated to face the camera. Luckily, that layer has the animated beams and lens flares parented to the building, so they will all rotate with their parent layer.

Animating the City

Let's add some life to the city by animating additional elements. The McCallCity layer should drift above the city during the sequence and illuminate the tops and sides of the buildings over which it travels. First, you'll animate its motion over the city. The McCallCity layer is off screen to the right at the start of the sequence. Scrub forward to frame 150, where the floating city is clearly within frame. Set keyframes for both the position and orientation. Rotate the city on the Y-axis so it's facing the camera (Figure 14.63).

Move to the last frame in the sequence, and reposition the floating city up and to the right so it's almost leaving the frame. Rotate it to face the camera. Keyframes are automatically set on its position and orientation (Figure 14.64).

Now McCallCity slowly floats over the city during the sequence, but it doesn't begin moving until frame 150. Select and move the Position and Orientation keyframes on frame 150 to frame 0. Check to make sure the floating city is completely off screen on frame 0; if the edge is still visible, move the layer to the right, out of frame. Use the layer edge to see that the layer is still oriented toward the camera.

Scrub to frame 300, and switch to the 2 Views - Horizontal layout. Change one of the views to Top, and move McCallCity back in Z space so it almost touches the RoundRiser layer and its associated light beams, but doesn't intersect with them. Rotate the floating city to face the camera directly (Figure 14.65).

Figure 14.63 *McCallCity on frame 150*

Figure 14.64 *McCallCity on frame 598*

Figure 14.65 *McCallCity on frame 300, in front of the RoundRiser layer elements*

Pulsing the City Flare

Let's animate the flare under the ship so that it pulses. Select the LensFlare layer parented to McCallCity, and set a keyframe for 100% opacity at 250. Move to 300, and turn the opacity down to 50%. Because you already set one keyframe, all subsequent keyframes are set automatically. With the Selection tool, select both keyframes and copy them. Move to frame 350, and paste the keyframes at the new location. You have four keyframes, with the flare going from 100% opacity to 50% twice. Copy all four keyframes, move to frame 450, and paste again. Now the pulse continues through the entire sequence.

Reactive Lighting on the City

The floating city flies right over buildings, but they show no effect from the huge flare. You'll use an adjustment layer to add reactive lighting to the buildings.

Choose Layer → New → Adjustment Layer. Move the new layer below all the layers that make up the city so it only adjusts the FutureNYC.[000-599].jpg layer that is the live-action plate (Figure 14.66).

With the adjustment layer selected, choose Effect → Color Correction → Curves, and add a curve to the adjustment layer. Pull the curve way up to brighten the plate (Figure 14.67).

Masking the Adjustment Layer

This curve lightens the entire plate, but not the painted elements. An adjustment layer adds whatever effect you apply to it to all layers below it in the Timeline.

Move to frame 400. On Adjustment Layer 1, mask off all the buildings that would be touched by the light of the floating city (Figure 14.68). Note that the masks in the following figures have been thickened for visibility; the masks in your interface will be thinner than those shown.

Figure 14.66 *Adjustment layer added above the plate but below the painted elements*

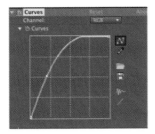

Figure 14.67 *Pull the curve up to brighten the plate.*

Figure 14.68 *Masked areas that are lit by the floating city*

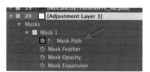

Figure 14.69 *Keyframe the Mask Path property on the masks*

Feather the masks 8 pixels, and keyframe the masks' Mask Path. If Mask Path isn't visible, you may need to click the arrow to the left of the mask name to reveal the four mask transform properties (Figure 14.69).

Move to frame 450. Because you're masking moving footage, the masks you set up don't move with the sequence (Figure 14.70). You need to keyframe the masks so they follow the building tops.

Figure 14.70 *Masked areas don't move with the sequence and must be keyframed.*

A word to the wise: keep the building areas you choose to mask off simple. Creating moving masks to isolate individual areas is tedious and difficult! If you mask off a lot of tiny details, you'll need to spend hours adjusting the masks to get an acceptable-looking result.

Keyframing the Masks

Select all the masks, move them into proper position on frame 450, and set a keyframe on Mask Path. Adjust the masks as a group first to get them into approximate position. You'll need to adjust the masks individually to make them fit as the sequence proceeds. Go forward another 50 frames, and adjust the masks again. Continue to advance in 50-frame increments until you've keyframed the masks for the entire sequence.

Next, move through in 10-frame increments, and adjust the position of the masks individually. By holding down the Shift key when you click the Next Frame or Previous Frame buttons in the Preview panel, you'll always advance/go back 10 frames; this is a great way to jump through keyframes. When you're animating masks in this fashion, work in keyframe intervals that are as widely spaced as possible, so the keyframes are smooth and won't jump noticeably. Set as few keyframes as you can while still having the masked areas follow the sequence exactly.

Adding an Intersecting Mask

When you're finished, the curve adjustment lights up only the chosen buildings. However, the masked building sections are evenly brightened: the light doesn't drop off on surfaces further away from the floating city. You need an intersecting mask to confine the adjustment to the area under the floating city.With the adjustment layer still selected, use the Ellipse tool to create a large circular mask twice the size of the floating city. Position it below the city, and give the mask a 200-pixel feather to make it very soft. The intersecting mask must be the last mask in the layer, in order for the intersection to work with the other masks. Set its Masking Mode to Intersect. Now, animate this mask to follow under the floating city. Where the round mask intersects with the building masks, those areas are illuminated. Where it doesn't intersect, the adjustment layer has no affect (Figure 14.71).

Figure 14.71 *The intersecting mask confines the adjustment layer to under the floating city.*

Expressions

You're still not finished with the lighting. Although the animated flare pulses brighter and darker during the sequence, the intensity of the light it casts on the buildings doesn't vary. You'll use an advanced After Effects technique called *expressions* to make the building illumination match the pulsing of the flare.

Expressions use a layer property from one layer to drive a layer property of another layer. This can involve complex math, and consequently many After Effects users are intimidated by it. Don't be. There are some great ways to use expressions even if you aren't a math whiz. Here's how you do it.

Move McCallCity and the LensFlare layer parented to it down in the Timeline to just above Adjustment Layer 1. Doing so keeps the project organized; the LensFlare layer will control the adjustment layer's opacity. Select the LensFlare layer just above the McCallCity layer. Make sure the pulsing Opacity attribute you animated is visible by pressing T, the keyboard shortcut to show only the Transparency attribute. This closes all the other attributes and shows only Opacity.

Using the Pick Whip to Link Attributes

Now, select Adjustment Layer 1 and press T again to show only the Opacity attribute for that layer. Select the Opacity attributes on both layers. Option/Alt+click the stopwatch next to Opacity in Adjustment Layer 1. Something unusual happens: a red bar appears at the bottom of the Viewer panel that says "Refresh Disabled (finish editing text to refresh view)." A new property appears below Opacity labeled Expression: Opacity. Next to it are four icons. On the Adjustment Layer 1 Opacity property, click+hold the icon that looks like a swirl [image], known as a *pick whip*. Still holding, drag the pick whip to the Opacity property of the pulsing LensFlare layer. A line appears between the two attributes (Figure 14.72). Release the pick whip.

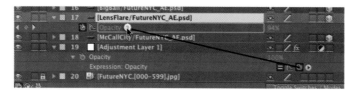

Figure 14.72 *Use the pick whip to link the opacity of the adjustment layer to the opacity of the LensFlare layer.*

In the Timeline, text appears that says `thisComp.layer("LensFlare/FutureNYC_ AE.psd 2").transform.opacity`. This is the expression that controls the opacity of the adjustment layer, based on the opacity of the LensFlare layer (Figure 14.73).

Figure 14.73 *The opacity of the adjustment layer is controlled by the opacity of the LensFlare layer.*

You can use the pick whip to connect any two properties with compatible parameters. The powerful thing about controlling the adjustment layer this way is that if you change the animation of the flare, the reactive light on the buildings will change with it, because they're linked together by the expression.

Film Grain

You're nearly finished with the futuristic vision of New York City, but you need to attend to one last detail. If you do a RAM preview of the comp at 100% and full resolution, you'll see that there is animated noise in the plate, called *film grain*. This grain dances in the background; it's an artifact of the photography process. However, the painted elements evidence none of this dancing grain, so it's easy to tell what is painted and what is part of the live shot. The painted elements also look sharper than the plate.

The last step in this project is to degrade all your beautiful work to match the footage by blurring and adding film grain. You should do this last because the Grain filter is computationally intensive, and your computer will slow to a crawl when you apply it.

Blurring the Layer

Select the BigBall layer, and choose Effect → Blur & Sharpen → Gaussian Blur. When Gaussian Blur opens in the Effect Controls panel, set Blurriness to 1. Doing so softens the painted elements to match the footage. In order to keep the film grain sharp, you must add the blur first.

Adding Grain

Now, add the film grain. Choose Effect → Noise & Grain → Add Grain. The effect of the filter appears on the layer in a preview area enclosed by a white box (Figure 14.74). This allows you to preview a small area of grain without adding it to the entire layer. If the preview area doesn't show up, make sure Viewing Mode is set to Preview in the drop-down menu in the Effect Controls panel.

Figure 14.74 *White preview box for Add Grain*

It's easy to add too much grain to a project, particularly if you don't look at it in motion (Figure 14.75).

Run a RAM preview, paying attention to the area within the white box. You won't be able to see accurately what the filter is doing unless you preview it at full resolution and 100% size in the View panel. The default grain settings look too big and fast; so, under Tweaking, change Intensity to 0.8 and Size to 0.7. Under Animation, make Animation Speed 0.6 (Figure 14.69). Run another RAM preview.

The final setting may not look much different from the original painted image when it's still, but in motion, the dancing grain matches the plate exactly (Figure 14.70).

Figure 14.75
Too much grain

Figure 14.77
Good amount
of grain

Figure 14.76 *Add*
Grain settings

Warning! Before you render, you *must* set Viewing Mode to Final Output. If you leave it set to Preview, the white box enclosing the preview area will be rendered into the final shot, which is definitely not what you want to happen.

Adding Blur and Grain to All The Layers

When you have Gaussian Blur and Add Grain looking the way you want, copy the two effects from the BigBall layer and paste them onto all your painted elements. Do this last, because they will seriously slow down the preview. If you need to work on the project after applying these effects, turn off Gaussian Blur and Add Grain by clicking the box marked *fx* next to each effect *fx* . Leave yourself a note to turn the effects back on before doing the final render.

Render out the completed project using the same setting as in the previous chapter (Figure 14.78). The final project for this demo, FutureNYC_Finish.aep, is on the DVD. A half-resolution rendered version, FutureNYC_Final.mov, with a few bits of additional animation added, can also be found on the Chapter 14 section of the DVD.

Figure 14.78 Six frames from the final render

Assignment: Create Your Own City

Now that you've tried the process of working over a moving plate with a demo file, it's time for you to create your own vision of a futuristic city. You should not change the color or tone of the moving plate, but make your painted additions seamlessly meld with what is already there. The final file should contain these basic elements, all of which you learned to set up in this chapter:

- Five or more different sections of buildings spread throughout the composition. The background should be filled with megastructures.
- An element that flies over the city, emitting a pulsing light: a floating megastructure, an air car, or a spaceship.
- A moving billboard that you can attach to the side of one of the buildings.

In the animation phase of the project, challenge yourself to do the following:

- Add movement to several elements in the composition.
- Add reactive light to the buildings over which your flying object moves.
- Use an expression to link the pulsing light on the flying object to the reactive light on the buildings.
- Add blur and noise to the painted elements so they blend better with the plate.

I'd love to see what you come up with for this project. At the end of Chapter 15, I'll give you a website where you can send your projects for critique and review.

fifteen

CHAPTER

Using After Effects' True 3D Space

You've reached the final chapter, *and you're about to put everything you've learned to the test. In the previous chapter, you got your feet wet in After Effects' 3D space by creating a scene on a set of tracked points over a moving plate. In this exercise, you'll experience the full extent of what After Effects can do as you dive headfirst into the vast ocean of 3D space. You'll venture where few mortals have been before by creating a vision of Hades out of Dante's Inferno.*

This time, you'll harness the full power of this compositing workspace and produce a scene as complex as those created at major special-effects houses. You'll bring a layered painting into After Effects and position the layers in full 3D space. Then, using a special projection technique, you'll create a horizontal plane of animated lava. Using groups imported from Photoshop, you'll animate the inside of a 2D precomp and add that to your 3D workspace. Finally, you'll extract actors who were shot against a green screen and add the moving figures to the scene to give it a dramatic focus.

The Painting

At the end of this chapter, you'll be asked to prepare your own version of this project after learning how to set up the 3D scene using a demonstration file. Before you begin working in After Effects, here are some final tips on the workflow for a complex matte painting. I'll also provide two more examples of using photography in your painting without using the photographs directly. If you want to get right into true 3D space, you can skip this section and move to the "Importing the Painting into After Effects" section of the chapter. You can come back to this section when you create your own version of Hades.

Getting Your Idea Down at Lower Resolution

For this demonstration, you'll work on a painting with multiple layers of information to show off the 3D space. This concept sketch began as a blank 1920 × 1080 Photoshop file to which were added a misty sky, distant mountains, and a succession of blocky cliffs rising up from a river of lava. Figures were sketched in to indicate the position of the actors on a foreground cliff. The two-person scene includes a sword-bearing guide with an awestruck visitor crouched at his feet. With all the elements present, the basic layout for the painting is set (Figure 15.1).

Figure 15.1 Hades concept sketch

Increasing the Resolution for the Final Painting

When you're doing a concept sketch, you'll typically begin at a lower resolution in order to work quickly and get your ideas down. When you're ready to proceed with the final matte, you should double the resolution. That way, you'll have enough pixels to add the crucial details that make a scene realistic. When you work at a higher resolution and scale it down in the final render, the painting always looks better. Here's why. When the final is composited, the file is reduced to half its original size. This process compresses the image. This sketch was enlarged by 200 percent to arrive at a final size of 3840 × 2160.

> You should add a one-inch black border around the edge of the painting to give you additional workspace. To save space, the black border is eliminated in this section's illustrations.

Working at the higher resolution, you can add more detail to the basic concept. The sketched figures were replaced by one frame of the green-screen footage you'll use later in the chapter. Photographic textures, many of which are included in the Chapter 7 ("Texturing and Color Correction") DVD materials, were used to build the crumbling city on the cliffs (Figure 15.2).

Figure 15.2 *Hades painting in progress*

Figure 15.3 *Waterfall reference photo*

Additional Painting Techniques

When you're working on a fantastic scene, you can use photographic references in creative ways. Open ViewOfHadesInProgress.psd from the Chapter 15 DVD materials. This is a much-reduced version of the work file on which you can try out these techniques.

Turning a Waterfall into a Cascade of Lava

To add the waterfalls, you can use an extreme color-correction curve to adapt a real-world photo to your purposes. Open 377027.jpg from the Chapter 15 DVD materials (Figure 15.3).

Look through the RGB channels to find a channel that isolates the waterfall from the foliage. The Blue channel shows the most contrast, so duplicate it. Apply a high-contrast curve to it to create an extraction matte (Figure 15.4).

Load the selection from the duplicated channel, and then subtract the upper waterfall and stray pixels from the main waterfall. Return to the RGB channel, and press Command/Ctrl+J to duplicate the waterfall onto a new layer. Apply this extreme color-correction curve to the waterfall (Figure 15.5).

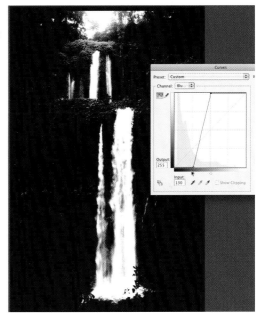

Figure 15.4 *Duplicate Blue channel with a high-contrast curve applied*

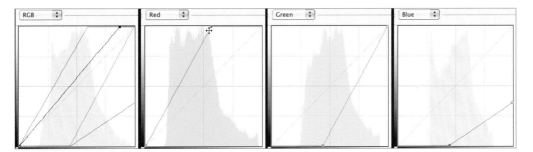

Figure 15.5 *Color-correction curves for changing the waterfall to lava*

Now the waterfall looks like lava (Figure 15.6).

Select all, and copy the color-corrected waterfall out of the file. Paste it into `ViewOfHadesInProgress.psd` above the CastleRockLf layer, and distort it into place (Figure 15.7).

Figure 15.6 Lava waterfall

Figure 15.7 Waterfall distorted into position

Painting Through a Selection Extracted from a Photograph

Adding spiky floating rocks will provide a menacing and mysterious mise-en-scène, like the dark side of *Avatar*'s floating islands in the sky. Here is a step-by-step procedure you can follow to achieve this effect:

If you don't know what mise-en-scène means, look it up. It's a term every film buff should know!

---

1. Still working over `ViewOfHadesInProgress.psd`, create a new layer called **FlyingStones** above the LfSmMountains layer, and rough in some interesting shapes (Figure 15.8).
2. Add basic lighting and texture to the shapes using the ChalkVarOpacity and Spotted Random brushes from the custom brush set on the DVD (Figure 15.9).
3. Open the photo `Background_mountains_0463.JPG` from the Chapter 15 DVD materials (Figure 15.10). You'll use this reference to add a real-world craggy surface to the floating rocks.
4. Look through the alpha channels to find the one that shows the most detail on the rocks. The Red channel looks the best, so apply a high-contrast curve to a duplicate of the channel to pull out the craggy texture (Figure 15.11).

Figure 15.8 *Blocked in flying stones*

Figure 15.9 *Paint some basic detail onto the flying stones using custom brushes.*

Figure 15.10 *Craggy mountain photo reference*

Figure 15.11 *High-contrast curve applied to the duplicate Red channel*

5. Load the selection into the duplicate Red channel, and copy the white pixels from the same high-contrast channel. Paste it into `ViewOfHadesInProgress.psd` above the FlyingStones layer, and scale and distort the pixels onto the underside of the floating rock (Figure 15.12). Name the new layer **RockTexture**.

6. Command/Ctrl+click into the RockTexture layer preview icon to load the selection containing the rock texture (Figure 15.13).

This is a variation on the technique you used in the last chapter to add base textures to the background megastructures. The difference is that, although you used the alpha channel to load the texture of the oil refinery, in this instance you copied only the white pixels, capturing the texture of the rock. Pasting the pixels into a layer allows you to load a textured selection directly from the layer pixels.

Figure 15.12 Distort the copied selection to fit the blocked-in floating stone.

Figure 15.13 Load the selection from the copied white pixels.

7. Turn off the visibility of the RockTexture layer, and return to the FlyingStones layer. Hide the selection, and paint into it to add nature-based rock texture. By painting into the selection, you get lots of happy accidents and tiny textural details that are hard to create without the assistance of photography (Figure 15.14).

Figure 15.14 *Paint into the selection.*

8. Do some freehand painting to add craters and spikes until the floating islands look suitably threatening (Figure 15.15).

Figure 15.15 *Finished flying stones*

The Finished Painting

You're finished working over ViewOfHadesInProgress.psd. If you want to save what you've painted to use when you create your own version of the scene, save it to your hard drive under another name and close it. The painting you'll use for this demonstration is in a sub-folder so it can be found by the After Effects project files that reference it. On the DVD, navigate to Chapter 15 → ViewOfHadesAfterEffects → (Footage) → ViewOfHadesForAE Layers → ViewOfHadesForAE.psd.

This final demonstration file is more finished, and it includes additional detail, such as smokestacks emerging from the cliff-side cities and integrated bits of old machinery to complete a vision of Hades (Figure 15.16).

Figure 15.16 *Finished demonstration file to be imported into After Effects*

Importing the Painting into After Effects

Take a closer look at the ViewOfHadesForAE.psd painting. It's organized differently from the painting in Chapter 14, "Working over a Moving Plate," in that many of the layers are divided into groups (Figure 15.17).

Groups from Photoshop are handled differently when they're brought into After Effects. Each group is imported as a separate precomp. You'll use these 2D precomps to do much of the animation that will appear in the 3D environment.

Turn on and off the visibility of the group RockCityLf to see what the group contains. Now, click the arrow next to the RockCityLf group to open it. This group contains all the elements that make up the left-side rock city, including the lights, waterfall, and smoke from the city (Figure 15.18). Take a moment to examine all the groups in this file as well as the individual layers that make up the composition. You'll quickly appreciate that the groups are logical divisions that contain elements that work together or are animated.

Select ViewOfHadesForAE.psd on your desktop, and drag the file into the After Effects Project panel. For Import Kind, choose Composition – Retain Layer Sizes. After Effects automatically creates a comp the same size as the Photoshop file, named ViewOfHadesForAE. Double-click the comp to open it in the View panel. All the layers are laid out exactly as they were in Photoshop. You'll use this comp for reference after you load the layers into 3D space. In the ViewOfHadesForAE comp Timeline panel, select all the layers and precomps, and copy them (Figure 15.19).

Create a new comp, and, from the preset menu, choose HDTV 1080 29.97. The dimensions of the final render are 1920 × 1080. Name it **ViewOfHades3D**. The new comp should open automatically in the Viewer panel; double-click it in the Project panel to open it. Paste all the layers and precomps you just copied into the new comp.

Figure 15.17
Painting prepared
for After Effects
with groups

In Chapter 14, you dragged all the layers from the Project panel into the Timeline. When you did that, all the layers came in on top of each other. Because you repositioned all the layers to match the tracking points, it didn't matter that you lost the layers' relative positioning to each other.

In this case, you're copying the layers out of one comp, where they're properly positioned, and pasting them into the new comp you just created. This technique retains the relative positioning of the layers to one another. You'll use this to your advantage in positioning the layers in 3D space.

Using a Null to Scale and Position Elements Together

The layers pasted into ViewOfHades3D are correctly positioned in relation to each other, but they're too large. This is because the original painting was twice as large as the new comp in which you're working. Make all the layers 3D by clicking the 3D Layer switch. The layers stay in exactly the same place in the Active Camera view. You need to scale them down to 50% of their current size to match the new comp. However, if you select all the layers and precomps and scale them, they scale around their own layer centers and no longer align with each other. To retain the original positioning, you need to create a null object to which to parent all the layers.

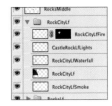

Figure 15.18
RockCityLf group

A *null object* is an empty point in space that you can use to control other layers. Choose Layer → New → Null Object. The null comes into the comp resembling a red box. When you select it, solid red squares appear at each corner and in the middle of each side (Figure 15.20).

Parenting the Layers to the Null

Deselect the null by pressing Shift+Command/Ctrl+A. Now, select all the layers and precomps in the Timeline panel, and use the pick whip to parent them to the null object. You can also choose Null 1 from the drop-down menu in the Parent column to achieve the same result (Figure 15.21).

With all the layers and precomps parented to the null, scale the null down to 50%. The layers and precomps use the null's center and stay aligned to each other. Now, move the null to center the painting in the comp.

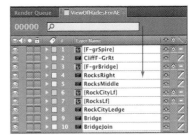

Figure 15.19 Select all the
layers and precomps in the
ViewOfHadesForAE Timeline
panel.

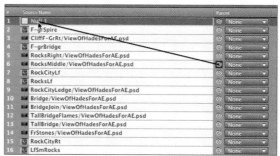

Figure 15.20 Create a null object.

Figure 15.21 Link all the layers and precomps to the null object.

Checking the Alignment

You can check the alignment and scale of the painting by switching back and forth between the ViewOfHadesForAE comp set to 25% and the ViewOfHades3D comp set to 50% in the Magnification Ratio pop-up. The two comps look exactly the same. When you have the painting scaled and positioned, delete the null.

Adding a Camera to the Comp

You must add a new camera to the comp, so choose Layer → New → Camera. Leave the camera at the default of 50mm.

The new camera appears at the top of the Timeline. There is a default active camera in the comp already, but this camera replaces it. In the timeline, it appears as Camera 1. It has two advantages: it's visible in the View panel, and it can be animated. Only cameras that you add to a project are visible in the View panel; all default cameras are invisible. The Active Camera is the only view that will render out of After Effects.

Choose 2 Views Horizontal from the Select View Layout drop-down menu. Set the left view to Custom View 1 and the right to Active Camera. Depending on how you've moved the views around, you may have a different Custom View 1 than what is shown in Figure 15.22. If this is the case, use the camera navigation tools to reposition Custom View 1 until it displays a similar angle.

Selecting the Camera to Display the Angle of View

Select Camera 1 in the Timeline panel to see the angle of view that the active camera is recording in Custom View 1. Normally, the lines delineating the camera view aren't shown, but they appear when the camera is selected. You'll need to position the layers and precomps inside the angle of view in 3D space. The right side shows the actual view that the active camera records (Figure 15.22).

Remember, if you ever get lost in a View panel, you can choose Edit → Deselect All and then press Command/Ctrl+Option/Alt+Shift+\ (backslash) to center everything in the view. You can also center a single layer, or a selection of layers, using the same shortcut.

Figure 15.22 Layers in 3D space with the camera selected to show the angle of view

Turning Off Collapse Transformations

As you look back and forth between Custom View 1 and Active Camera, there is a key difference: none of the precomps are visible in the Custom View 1 panel. This is because the Collapse Transformations switch is on ☀ for each of the precomps (Figure 15.23). The Collapse Transformations switch controls the order in which effects are applied to layers in a composition. It isn't needed in this project; click the Collapse Transformations switch for each of the precomps to turn it off ■. Now all the precomps appear.

You can check your work to this point against `ViewOfHadesPaintingImport.aep` in the Chapter 15 DVD materials.

Figure 15.23 Collapse Transformations is on for all the precomps. Click to turn it off.

Setting Up a Ground Plane Using a Solid

When you're working in 3D space, you need to think of positioning elements spatially, like pop-up cards. Therefore, you have to create one horizontal plane from which all the images stick up vertically. To create the horizontal plane, you'll use an advanced technique: you'll project the image of the GroundPlane layer onto a horizontal solid.

> Projecting an image in After Effects is a complex process because there is no utility specific to this function. However, you can use a workaround that produces the same effect. After Effects 3D space allows you to use a spotlight to cast shadows from one layer to another. Adapting this capability, you'll use the light as a projector to transfer the painting of the ground plane onto a solid white layer.
>
> Be forewarned that if you miss any of the steps, the procedure won't work. A checklist is provided at the end of this section for troubleshooting.

Rotating the Solid

Turn off the visibility of all the layers except the GroundPlane and Camera 1. Choose Layer → New → Solid, click the Make Comp Size button, and select a pure white color from the color

Figure 15.24 Position and orientation of the White Solid 1 layer

selector. Because the solid is white, After Effects names it White Solid 1. In the Timeline panel, make White Solid 1 3D, and click the arrow to the left of Transform. Under Orientation, rotate the solid on the X-axis 90°. It's now flat on to the camera and shows up in the Active Camera view as a line—it's like looking at the edge of a piece of paper. Move the plane down a small amount on the Z-axis so its position is 960, 560, 0. Rotate it two degrees more on the orientation X-axis to 92° (Figure 15.24).

The White Solid 1 layer is now visible as a sliver of white in the Active Camera view (Figure 15.25).

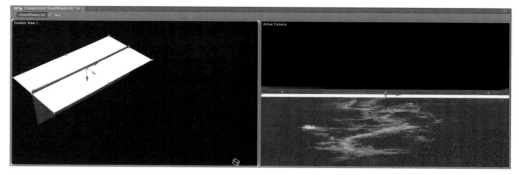

Figure 15.25 White Solid 1 visible as a sliver of white

Figure 15.26 Final Scale attributes of the White Solid 1 layer

Scaling the Solid

Scale the plane so it's large enough to cover the foreground in the Active Camera view and the horizon at the back of the GroundPlane layer. The final Scale settings should be around 250, 550, 100. Note that the Constrain Proportions box, which looks like a linked chain 🔗, has been turned off for the solid so that it can be non-uniformly scaled (Figure 15.26).

Check in the Active Camera view to ensure that the plane covers the view completely on the right and left sides. When you're finished, the ground plane should look like Figure 15.27.

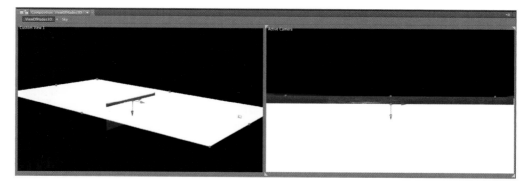

Figure 15.27 Final position of the White Solid 1 layer

Projecting a Texture onto the Ground Plane

Select the GroundPlane layer, and duplicate it. Right-click its name in the Timeline, and select Rename (Figure 15.28), or select the layer name, and press the Return/Enter key. Rename the duplicate **GroundPlaneReference**. Rename the original **GroundPlaneProjection**.

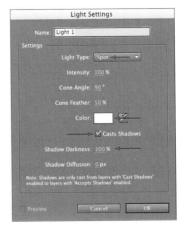

Figure 15.28 Rename the two GroundPlane layers.

Lining Up the Projection Layer

Move both ground plane layers to the top of the Timeline above Camera 1 and White Solid 1, with GroundPlaneReference first in the layer stack. Turn off 3D for the GroundPlaneReference layer to make it 2D. In the Active Camera view, use the ViewOfHadesForAE comp as your reference to make sure the GroundPlaneReference layer is positioned exactly as it was in the original painting. Because this reference layer is 2D, it's only visible in the Active Camera view. GroundPlaneProjection must still be set to 3D.

Adding a Light

Add a light to the scene by choosing Layer → New → Light. When the Light Settings dialog box appears, choose Spot for Light Type, select Casts Shadows, and make Shadow Darkness 100% (Figure 15.29). Light 1 appears at the top of the Timeline.

Figure 15.29 Settings for Light 1

Copying the Active Camera Position

Select Camera 1, twirl down the arrow to the left of Transform, and click on the word *Position* in the Transform attributes. Press Command/Ctrl+C to copy the X, Y and Z Position attributes. Select both Light 1 and the GroundPlaneProjection layer, and paste the Position attributes onto them. Both Light 1 and the GroundPlaneProjection layer jump to the camera position and are positioned right on top of it (Figure 15.30).

The GroundPlaneProjection layer isn't visible in the active camera because it's directly on top of it. Select the GroundPlaneProjection layer, and move it slightly in front of the camera on the Z-axis. Don't move it too far in front of the camera—it shouldn't intersect the horizontal solid plane. It can now be seen, but GroundPlaneProjection is much too large and blocks the view of the active camera (Figure 15.31).

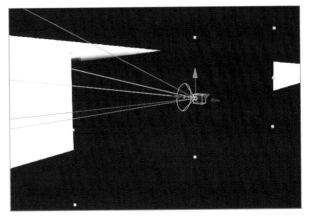

Figure 15.30 GroundPlaneProjection and Light 1 at the same position as Camera 1

Scaling Down and Positioning the GroundPlaneProjection Layer

To correct the situation, scale down the layer to make it smaller and move it down on the Y-axis until it matches the GroundPlaneReference layer. You need to turn the GroundPlaneReference layer visibility on and off to guide the positioning, because it blocks out the GroundPlaneProjection layer. Remember, the GroundPlaneReference layer is only visible in the Active Camera view, because it's 2D. When the two layers match exactly, turn off the visibility on the GroundPlaneReference layer (Figure 15.32).

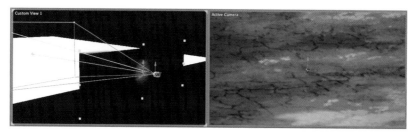

Figure 15.31 GroundPlaneProjection moved slightly in front of Camera 1

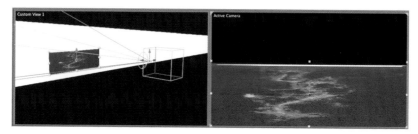

Figure 15.32 Final position of the GroundPlaneProjection layer

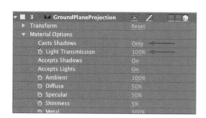

Figure 15.33 Material Options for the GroundPlaneProjection layer

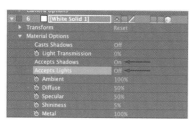

Figure 15.34 Material Options for White Solid 1

Setting the Material Options

Under GroundPlaneProjection's Material Options, set Light Transmission to 100%. There are three setting for Casts Shadows: On, Off, and Only. Click the Casts Shadows setting repeatedly until it reads Only (Figure 15.33). With Casts Shadows set to Only, it doesn't matter what Accepts Shadows and Accepts Lights are set to; the result is the same. This makes the GroundPlane Projection layer invisible, so it no longer shows up in your project. Like an invisible slide, this layer will only be used by Light 1 to cast shadows.

The White Solid 1 layer is the screen onto which the GroundPlane Projection slide will be projected. Change White Solid 1's Material Options to Accepts Lights: Off and Accepts Shadows: On (Figure 15.34).

With the viewer set to 4 Views—Custom View 1, Active Camera, Front, and Top—the projection should look like Figure 15.35.

Increasing the Resolution of the Projection

Even with everything set up correctly, the projection looks blurry in the active camera when the View panel is set to full resolution. This is because After Effects, by default, projects the image at the resolution of the comp. This comp is 1920 pixels wide, which is half the resolution of the image that is being projected. This isn't enough resolution to create a clear projection. You must turn up the resolution to get as sharp an image as possible.

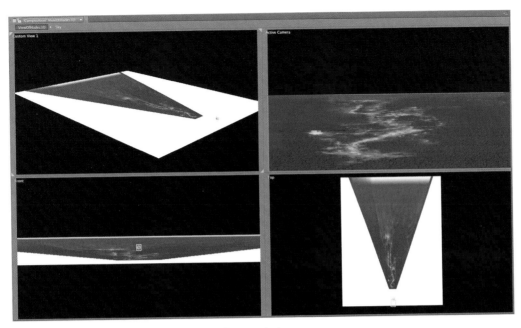

Figure 15.35 Four views of the projected ground plane

Choose Composition → Composition Settings. The Composition Settings dialog box appears. Click the Advanced tab, and on that tab, click Options; the Advanced 3D Options dialog appears. From the Shadow Map Resolution pop-up menu, choose 4000 (Figure 15.36). The projected texture will be much sharper.

With Light, White Solid 1, and GroundPlaneProjection properly aligned, lock these layers so you don't accidently move them.

Positioning the Sky

When you turn on the visibility of the Sky comp, it appears in the middle of the ground plane. Select Sky, and move it away from the camera on the Z-axis. Move Sky back so it intersects the ground plane at the horizon but doesn't show any white from the ground plane where the two meet (Figure 15.37).

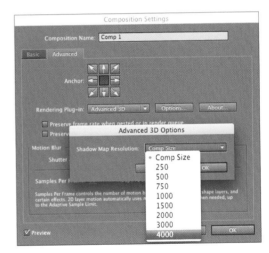

Figure 15.36 Increase the resolution of the projected image.

As it moves back, it becomes smaller in the Active Camera view. If you're careful to select only the Z-axis, and don't change the X and Y coordinates, Sky will stay in the correct relative position to the rest of the composition, and you can uniformly scale it up to fill the Active Camera view. If Sky has moved on either the X-axis or Y-axis, you'll need to do repositioning after scaling.

Scale up Sky so it matches its original position in the ViewOfHadesForAE comp. Remember, the original painting was created at double the size of the comp in which you're working. By setting the size of the ViewOfHadesForAE comp to 25% and the size of the ViewOfHades3D comp to 50%, you can click back and forth between the tabs at the top of the Timeline panel to compare the positioning of elements in the two comps.

Figure 15.37 Sky precomp positioned

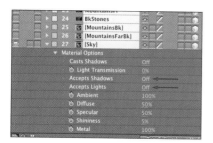

Figure 15.38 Material Options for the layers and precomps not receiving the projection

Turning Off the Projection on Other Layers

You'll notice that Sky is slightly darkened at the horizon, because it's receiving the projection of the ground plane from the spotlight. You don't want this, because only the original painting should show on all the other layers and precomps in the composition. Select all the layers and precomps in the Timeline except White Solid 1, GroundPlaneProjection, and Ground Plane Reference. Under Material Options, set Accepts Shadows to Off and Accepts Lights to Off (Figure 15.38). Because you had all the layers selected when you changed the Material Options on one layer, all the layers are affected. Now only the White Solid 1 layer will accept the projection; the other layers will remain unchanged.

Projection Plane Checklist

To set up a projection in After Effects, do the following:

1. Copy the position of the camera.
2. Paste the camera position onto the spotlight that will be projecting the texture, and onto the projection layer.
3. Move the position of the projection layer slightly ahead of the light.
4. Scale the projection layer to match the 2D reference layer in the Active Camera view.

Then, change the following parameters:

- Set the spotlight to:
  - Color: White
  - Casts Shadows: On
  - Shadow Darkness: 100%
  - Remaining settings: defaults
- Set the White Solid's Material Options to:
  - Casts Shadows: Off
  - Light Transmission: 0%
  - Accepts Shadows: On
  - Accepts Lights: Off
  - Remaining settings: defaults
- Set the projection layer's Material Options to:
  - Casts Shadows: Only

- Light Transmission 100%
- Remaining settings: defaults
- Set the Material Options on all the other layers in the composition, except the Solid that is receiving the projection and the projection layer, to:
    - Accepts Shadows: Off
    - Accepts Lights: Off
    - Remaining settings: defaults
- Set the projection resolution in the Composition Setting to 4000.

I know that this is a lot of steps, so you may want to bookmark this checklist for help if your projection isn't working. If for any reason you've gotten lost, open `ViewOfHades ProjectionPlane.aep` on the DVD materials to examine and compare the projection setup to what you have created.

Positioning the Other Layers

Turn on the visibility for the RockCityLf precomp, and move it toward the camera on the Z-axis. Watch for where the precomp intersects the ground plane. The projection of the ground plane has a bright spot where the lava waterfall meets the ground, so that layer must be positioned on top of that spot (Figure 15.39). As you move the precomp toward the camera, it becomes too large in the frame. If you carefully move the precomp only on the Z-axis, it will stay in the correct relative position to the other elements, and you can uniformly scale it down to the correct size. Refer back to the ViewOfHadesForAE comp for proper positioning.

Make sure RockCityLf intersects the ground plane and isn't raised above it. It's possible to position a layer so that it looks correct in the active camera but doesn't correctly intersect the ground plane (Figure 15.40).

Figure 15.39 *RockCityLf positioned correctly on the ground plane*

Figure 15.40 *RockCityLf incorrectly positioned so that it doesn't intersect the ground plane*

Notice that the base of the layer is cut off in a straight, flat line by the ground plane and, therefore, lacks the integration of the original painting. This is one of the limitations of working with flat planes and why the projected ground plane requires painting at the base of each layer to blend better.

Positioning the F-grBridge Precomp

Turn on the visibility of the F-grBridge precomp. This layer is trickier to position because you don't see where it intersects the ground plane. It needs to be slightly above the ground plane in its final position. Move it forward on the Z-axis until it's halfway between RockCityLf and Camera 1. Scale it down more so you can see it in the Active Camera view. The final scale should be around 6.2%. Work back and forth between the Custom view and the Active Camera view to adjust its positioning and scaling. In the Active Camera view, all layers should end up in the exact same location as they appear in the original painting (Figure 15.41).

Figure 15.41 *Position of the F-grBridge precomp*

Positioning the F-grSpire Precomp

Turn on the visibility of the F-grSpire precomp. It should be the closest layer to the camera, so move it forward on the Z-axis until it's slightly in front of the F-grBridge layer. As with the previous layer, you can't see where the layer intersects the ground plane, so you need to visualize where it would be in 3D space. When it's in the correct position in Z space, scale it down and move it in the X-axis and Y-axis to position it as it was in the original painting (Figure 15.42).

Figure 15.42 *Position of the F-grSpire precomp*

Positioning the MountainsFr Layer

Turn on the visibility of the MountainsFr layer. This isn't a precomp, but a regular layer composed of a single image with no animated elements. Move MountainsFr back on the Z-axis until it's close to the sky. There are two more layers of mountains behind this layer, so make sure you leave room for them. Scale up the MountainsFr layer, and position it on the X-axis and Y-axis until it matches the position in the original painting (Figure 15.43). Double-check that the MountainsFr layer intersects the ground plane.

Figure 15.43 *Position of the MountainsFr layer*

Position the remaining layers on your own, except for TallBridge, BridgeJoin, and Bridge. Remember, the layers are positioned in true 3D space for this project, and each layer must intersect the ground plane as it does in the original painting. When you're finished, the project should look like Figure 15.44 in these four different views. You can check your work by comparing it to ViewOfHadesAllPlanes.aep in the DVD materials.

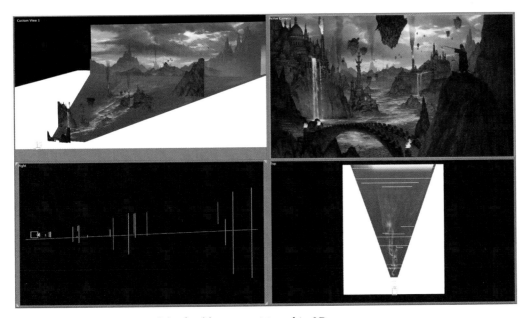

Figure 15.44 *Four views of the final layers positioned in 3D space*

Angling the TallBridge Precomp

So far, all the layers except the ground plane have been positioned facing straight on to the camera. Now you'll set up angled layers to give the composition additional dimensionality. The RockCityRt precomp and the RockCityLedge layer are connected by a tall bridge. Rotate the TallBridge comp so it connects the two layers in 3D space (Figure 15.45). Because you aren't giving the bridge an extreme rotation, it isn't distorted.

Figure 15.45 Rotating a plane to give added dimensionality

Projecting and Painting the Longer Bridge

The second bridge, named Bridge, connects the RockCityRt and RocksLf precomps. Unlike the former example, if you attempt to rotate the bridge layer to connect the two elements, the bridge becomes terribly distorted because of the severe angle of rotation (Figure 15.46).

Figure 15.46 Bridge layer rotated too much to yield acceptable results

Creating a White Solid for Projection

To create this bridge, you'll use a variation on the technique you used to project an image onto the ground plane. Create a new white solid, 1000 × 200 pixels, and make it 3D.

Rename it **WhiteSolidBridge**, and place it in position where the bridge should be between the RockCityRt and RocksLf precomps (Figure 15.47).

Figure 15.47 WhiteSolidBridge positioned where the final bridge should be

Adding the Reference and Projection Layers

Select the original Bridge layer, and duplicate it. Rename one copy **BridgeReference** and the other **BridgeProjection**. Make BridgeReference 2D, and move it to the top of the layer stack. Confirm that BridgeProjection is 3D. If it isn't, make it so. Copy the position of Camera 1, and paste it onto BridgeProjection. Now, move BridgeProjection slightly in front of the camera, and use the 2D BridgeReference layer to match the position in the original painting. This process is identical to how you projected the ground plane.

You'll now project the image from BridgeProjection onto WhiteSolidBridge, which is positioned where the bridge should be. Because you can have only one projection at a time, you must turn off the visibility of the GroundPlaneProjection layer. The ground plane turns white. Turn the ground plane visibility off as well in order to concentrate on the bridge.

Changing the Material Options

Set BridgeProjection's Material Options to:

- Casts Shadows: Only
- Light Transmission: 100%.

  Set the WhiteSolidBridge layer's Material Options to:

- Accepts Shadows: On
- Accepts Lights: Off

The spotlight should now be projecting an image of the bridge onto WhiteSolidBridge (Figure 15.48). Because you can have only one image projected in an After Effects comp, and a projection is already in use for the ground plane, you need to create a distorted version of this bridge that can be used on a rotated plane. You'll do this in Photoshop.

Figure 15.48 *Image of the bridge projected onto WhiteSolidBridge*

Take a Screen Shot of the Projected Bridge

Rotate one of the custom views around so that WhiteSolidBridge is flat on to the view, and as large as possible. The bridge image looks extremely distorted (Figure 15.49). Take a screen shot of that angle:

- In Windows, press Alt+Print Screen. Open a new file in Photoshop, and paste the screen shot in from the clipboard.
- On the Mac, a flexible screen-shot application called Grab is located in the Utilities subfolder in the Applications folder. Open Grab, press Command+Shift+A, and then click+drag over the area you want to capture. Copy the resulting file, and import it into Photoshop.

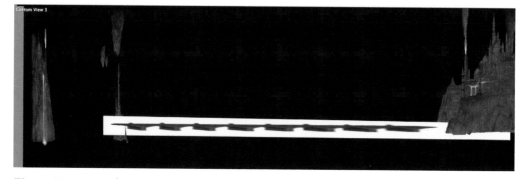

Figure 15.49 *Straight-on view of the projected bridge in the custom views*

Distort the Original Bridge to Match the Projected Bridge

In Photoshop, copy the original Bridge layer from the ViewOfHadesforAE.psd file, and paste it into the new file on top of the screen shot (Figure 15.50). Name the new layer BridgeDistort.

Transform/Distort the original bridge so it matches the distorted bridge from After Effects. It can be tricky to get the bridge to match the distorted bridge, so take your time and get it as close as possible (Figure 15.51).

Enlarge the canvas on the left, and add another section to the bridge. This allows for where the bridge extends behind the foreground layer, which comes into view when you move the camera (Figure 15.52). You can retouch any area that looks soft. Delete the reference layer, and keep just the distorted bridge on its own layer. Name the file **BridgeDistort.psd**. You can check your work on distorting the bridge against the demo file in Chapter 15 → ViewOfHades AfterEffects → (Footage) → BridgeDistort.psd on the DVD.

Figure 15.50 *Screen shot of the distorted bridge imported into Photoshop, and original bridge pasted on top*

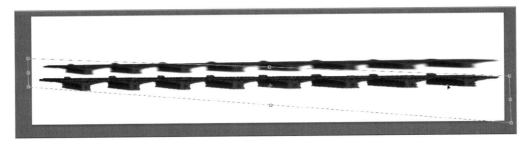

Figure 15.51 *Original bridge distorted to match the projected distorted bridge*

Figure 15.52 *Final distorted bridge with an additional section added to the left*

Import the BridgeDistort Layer Into After Effects

Import this file into After Effects, drag it into the ViewOfHades3D comp, and set it to 3D. Move, scale, and rotate the BridgeDistort layer to match the position of WhiteSolidBridge. Now, with the distorted bridge in place (Figure 15.53), do the following:

- Delete WhiteSolidBridge, onto which the bridge was projected.
- Turn off the BridgeProjection and BridgeReference layers.
- Turn the ground plane solid back on.
- Turn GroundPlaneProjection back on.

You can check your work against the file ViewOfHadesProjectedBridge.aep on the DVD.

Figure 15.53 Distorted bridge in place

Animating the Sky

Next, you'll animate the sky: as the robed figure raises his sword, rays of light will burst through the clouds. Double-click the Sky precomp. The sky is already broken into five layers. You'll animate the clouds in the precomp, and that animation will be reflected in ViewOfHades3D.

The five sky layers are shown in Figure 15.54, Figure 15.55, Figure 15.56, Figure 15.57, and Figure 15.58.

In the Sky comp, you'll move the individual layers so that the clouds part, revealing the rays of light. The clouds closest to the horizon are the farthest away and will move the least. The layer at the top of the comp, closest to the viewer, will move the most (Figure 15.59).

Figure 15.54 Sky 1: Farthest clouds near the horizon. This will be the entire original sky.

Figure 15.55 Sky 2: Background clouds just above the mountains. Notice that the bottom of the clouds should be soft, to blend with the underlying layer.

Figure 15.56 Sky 3: Right-side clouds

Figure 15.57 Sky 4: Left-side clouds

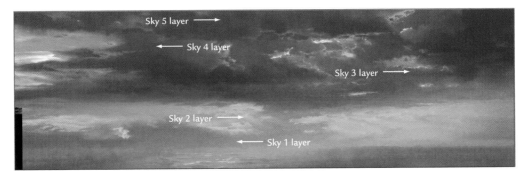

Figure 15.58 Sky 5: Top layer of clouds nearest the viewer

Figure 15.59 Sky layers closest to the horizon move the least; layers higher up move the most.

Sky 4 and 1 move in the opposite direction of Sky 5, 3, and 2 so the sky can part (Figure 15.59 and Figure 15.60).

Figure 15.60 *The clouds part to reveal the light.*

Using the Solo Switch

In order to concentrate on an effect you'll add to the Sky precomp, you need to turn off visibility of all of the other layers. You could manually turn off each layer, but there is an easier way. You can use the Solo switch to turn off all the layers except Sky. In the ViewOfHades3D comp,

Figure 15.61 *Solo switch clicked for the Sky comp to make it the only visible layer*

click the switch to the right of the Visibility eye for Sky; a round shape fills the box, indicating that the Solo switch is set for that layer (Figure 15.61). All the other layers disappear. You can click the Solo switch for other layers to add it to the visible layers, but the other layers without the Solo switch set won't be visible until the Solo switch is turned off for all layers.

Figure 15.62 *Setting for CC Light Rays*

Creating Light Rays

Create a new adjustment layer above the Sky precomp by choosing Layer → New → Adjustment Layer. The adjustment layer comes in at the top of the layer stack; move it down so it's just above Sky. Choose Effect → Generate → CC Light Rays, and set the parameters as follows (Figure 15.62):

- Intensity: 50
- Radius: 50
- Warp Softness: 10
- Transfer Mode: Add

Position the Source of the Light Rays

At frame 0, click the crosshair icon to the right of the Center attribute in the CC Light Rays controls, and click the screen just above where the light will appear. Set a keyframe for the intensity of the effect. Doing so generates a flare and some tiny light rays streaming out of the clouds (Figure 15.63).

Move to frame 300, and change the intensity to 200. Notice how the light rays change as you scrub through the animation. This creates a dramatic "godrays" effect that is driven by the underlying information in the painting (Figure 15.64).

Click the Solo switch on both the adjustment layer and Sky to turn it off, and make all the other layers visible. Remember, if the Solo switch is on for any layer, the non-Solo layers won't be visible.

Figure 15.63 *Position of the CC Light Rays effect at frame 0*

Figure 15.64 *Position of the CC Light Rays effect at frame 300*

Animated Lava

The river of lava on the ground plane will look more ominous when it's animated. To do that, you'll use an animated fractal noise pattern tinted to look like molten lava and combine it with the existing ground-plane painting. Select the GroundPlaneProjection layer, which the spotlight uses to project the ground-plane image, and precompose it. Name the new comp **GroundPlaneProjectionComp**. Double-click the new comp to open it in the viewer.

Adding a Fractal Noise Effect

Create a new white solid the same size as the comp, and name it **MovingLavaSolid**. Choose Effect → Noise & Grain → Fractal Noise, and set the parameters as follows at frame 0 (Figure 15.65):

- Fractal Type: Basic
- Noise Type: Soft Linear
- Contrast: 160
- Brightness: 0
- Overflow: AllowHDR Results
- Under Transform:
  - Deselect Uniform Scaling
  - Scale Width: 80
  - Scale Height: 10

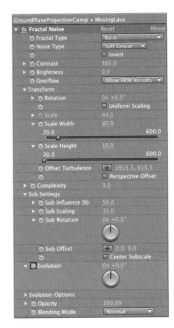

Figure 15.65 *Settings for Fractal Noise*

- Complexity: 3
- Under Sub Settings:
  - Sub Influence: 50
  - Sub Scaling: 15
- Set a keyframe on Evolution.

Leave everything else at the defaults.

The Tritone Effect

Figure 15.66 Tritone effect

The comp is now filled with black and white fractal noise. You need to tint the noise to look like lava. Choose Effect → Color Correction → Tritone, and set the three color swatches to bright orange, smoldering red, and very dark red (Figure 15.66).

Now you have a comp full of stretched, tinted fractal noise (Figure 15.67).

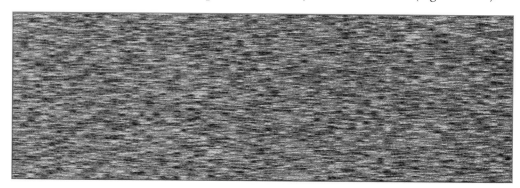

Figure 15.67 Tritone effect applied to the fractal noise

The Corner Pin Effect

Figure 15.68 Corner Pin effect

You need to distort the lava into perspective using a Corner Pin effect. Still in GroundPlaneProjectionComp, with MovingLavaSolid selected, choose Effect → Distort → Corner Pin (Figure 15.68).

The Corner Pin effect lets you choose new positions for the corners of the layer to which it's applied. Zoom out in the Viewer panel so there is a lot of room around the comp. Click the crosshairs for each of the four corners, and place them as shown in Figure 15.69. The white lines were added to make the corner pin clearer; they won't show up in the viewer.

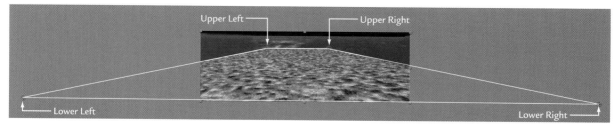

Figure 15.69 Position for the four corner-pin points

Scrub to frame 300, and open the Fractal Noise effect controls for the MovingLavaSolid. Change Evolution to 1x+180° (Figure 15.70). This setting makes the lava churn and move.

Figure 15.70
Evolution animation

Creating an Alpha Channel

Still working in the GroundPlaneProjectionComp, you need to confine the lava to the areas where it appears in the painting. The painting has no alpha channel for the lava, so you'll have to create one in After Effects. Turn off the solid with the animated lava, and select the GroundPlane layer. Duplicate it, and name the new layer **GroundPlaneAlpha**. Move it to the top of the Timeline panel.

The Shift Channel Effect

With GroundPlaneAlpha selected, choose Effect → Channel → Shift Channels. This allows you to swap one channel, RGB or alpha, into another channel. You can use this effect to create an alpha channel in footage that doesn't contain one. In the Show Channel And Color Management pop-up menu ▨ at the bottom of the viewer, look through the Red, Green, and Blue channels to find which one has the most contrast in the river of lava. The Red channel is the most distinct. Under Shift Channels, choose Red from the Take Alpha From drop-down menu (Figure 15.71). The GroundPlaneAlpha layer now has an alpha channel from its own Red channel.

Figure 15.71 *Shift channels to use the Red channel for the alpha channel.*

The Invert Effect

Turn off GroundPlane and MovingLavaSolid so only the GroundPlaneAlpha layer is visible. Now the area around the river is blocked out, leaving just the lava. This is the inverse of what you want. Choose Effect → Channel → Invert, and, from the Channel drop-down menu, choose Alpha (Figure 15.72).

The lava disappears, leaving only the surrounding plane (Figure 15.73).

Figure 15.72 *Invert effect on the alpha channel*

Adding Contrast to the Alpha Channel

Choose Effect → Color Correction → Curves to add a curve to the layer. From the Curves Channel drop-down menu, choose Alpha. Use a high-contrast curve to clean up the alpha channel, totally excluding the river of lava (Figure 15.74).

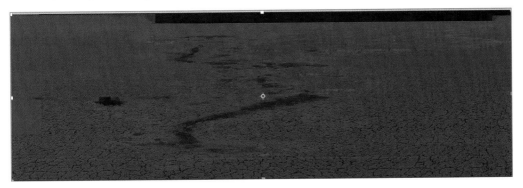

Figure 15.73 *The lava is removed by the alpha channel.*

Figure 15.74 *High-contrast curve to the alpha channel*

Turn the GroundPlane and MovingLavaSolid layers back on. With the GroundPlaneAlpha layer on top with the new alpha channel, the fractal lava takes the place of the painted lava.

Masking the Top of the Moving Lava

One last detail: you need to mask off the fractal noise near the horizon because the movement would be minimal in the far distance. With this technique, all the motion will be confined to the foreground. With MovingLavaSolid selected, draw a mask over the top of the layer (Figure 15.75). Set Mask to Subtract and Mask Feather to 260.

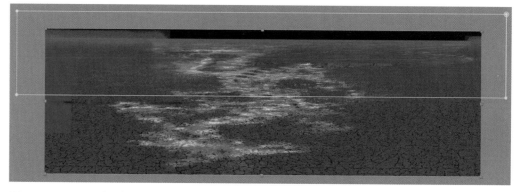

Figure 15.75 *Mask off the top of the MovingLavaSolid layer.*

Run a RAM preview of the comp. The effect is subtle, but it adds motion to the scene. Return to the ViewOfHades3D comp. The animation you added is now reflected in the 3D scene, with the animated GroundPlane precomp being projected onto the ground plane.

Extracting Figures from Green Screen

There is currently a placeholder for the actors in the scene, but now you'll extract the live-action figures from the background and add them to the project. This section will give you a quick and dirty look at how to extract or *key* figures shot against a green screen.

For a more complete rundown on how to work with green-screen footage, consult *The Green Screen Handbook* by Jeff Foster (Sybex, 2010).

Open the file Guide+Visitor.mov from the Chapter 15 DVD materials. The green-screen footage shows two actors: one portraying a guide to Hades and a second portraying a visitor. In this 10-second clip, the guide brandishes his sword at the landscape of Hades while the visitor looks on in despair (Figure 15.76).

Drag the footage Guide+Visitor.mov into the Project panel. You won't drop the footage into the comp directly, but rather precomp it and prepare the footage in 2D; only then will you bring it into your 3D project. Drag the footage down to the Create A New Composition icon at the bottom of the Project panel ▣. After Effects automatically names the comp the same as the footage, Guide+Visitor.

Creating a Garbage Matte

First you should mask off as much of the green screen as you can. This footage has already been cropped to remove much of the unneeded background; but with a quick application of a RotoBezier, you can get rid of even more of the green screen and make the extraction process easier. Because you're getting rid of extraneous material with this mask, it's referred to as a *garbage matte*.

Keyframe the RotBezier Mask

Choose the Pen tool, and select the RotoBezier check box in the Tools panel ☑ RotoBezier . RotoBezier curves automatically calculate the direction of the curve for you, and they're extremely fast to work with. Move to frame 000, and draw a mask around the edges of the figures without an excessive number of points; six to eight should be enough. Set a keyframe on Mask Path. Scrub forward in the footage to frame 15, and you'll notice that the actor's robe moves to the left side of the frame. Change the position of the mask to accommodate this motion. Since you already set a keyframe on the mask, a new keyframe is added whenever you make a change to the RotoBezier. At frame 75, the

Figure 15.76 *Green-screen footage*

With thanks to School of Visual Arts student Carolina Amaral for portraying the visitor.

actor starts to lift his sword, so move the top-right keyframe to allow for that. Go through and move the Bezier points where needed to get rid of as much of the background as possible without masking off any part of the figures (Figure 15.77).

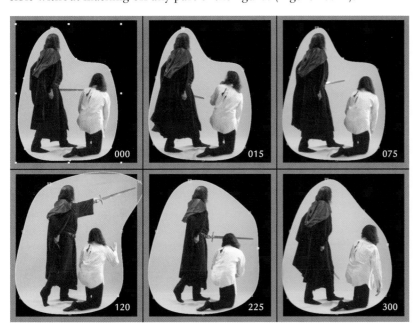

Figure 15.77 *Create a garbage matte to get rid of as much extraneous information as possible.*

Applying the Keylight Effect

In preparation for keying your figures, you should turn off the visibility of the mask in the view by clicking on the Toggle Mask and Shape Path Visibility icon 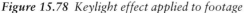. Scrub to frame 75 to begin the keying process. Keying removes the background from subjects that were shot against either a blue- or green-colored screen. The keyer looks for a particular color in the footage and removes that color. After Effects ships with a superb keyer called Keylight. Select the footage in the Timeline, and choose Effect → Keying → Keylight. Keylight opens in the Effect Controls panel. Go to Screen Color, select the eyedropper next to the color swatch, and click into the footage in an area where the green screen is showing. Choose an area that is in the middle of the green tones: neither the darkest green in the background nor the lightest in the foreground, but rather in the middle. Most of the green instantly disappears (Figure 15.78).

Keylight creates an alpha channel for the footage. You can view it by clicking the Show Color And Color Management Settings icon at the bottom of the Viewer panel. From the pop-up menu, choose Alpha; the icon changes to the Alpha Icon. You're now viewing the alpha channel for the footage, with white opaque and black transparent. There are a lot of areas where the alpha isn't completely white, causing the figures to be semitransparent, as indicated by gray pixels (Figure 15.79).

Figure 15.78 Keylight effect applied to footage

Figure 15.79 Alpha channel after the Keylight effect is applied

Adding a Red Solid Behind the Figures

Scrub to frame 120. Switch the Show Color And Color Management Settings icon back to RGB so again you're seeing the color version of the actors. Choose Layer → New → Solid, click the Make Comp Size button, and choose a bright red color. Click OK to accept those settings. Drag the new solid below the footage (Figure 15.80). The red background makes it easier to see what areas need work on the keying.

Adjusting the Keylight Effect Parameters

Open the Keylight controls in the Effect Controls panel. Keylight offers a large selection of controls for keying the footage. For this project, change the following (Figure 15.81):

- Clip Black: 30
- Clip White: 65
- Screen Softness: 3
- Replace Method: Hard Colour
- Replace Colour: Choose a dark red

These settings clean up the edges of the matte. There are some shadows at the actors' feet, but you'll place the figures on top of a rock, so you don't need to worry about that (Figure 15.82).

Restoring a Semi-transparent Element

Around frame 250, you'll notice that the sword becomes semitransparent. Because the sword is reflecting the green of the background, the keyer is removing part of the blade along with the green screen. Duplicate the Guide+Visitor.mov layer, and remove the Keylight effect from the duplicate. Roto around the sword for the last 100 frames, and keyframe the mask to match the movement of the blade (Figure 15.83). Place the duplicate layer behind the original keyed version. Now the sword is opaque throughout the 300 frames.

Figure 15.80 *Keyed figures against a red background*

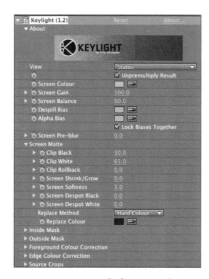

Figure 15.81 *Keylight controls*

Figure 15.82 *Cleaned-up matte*

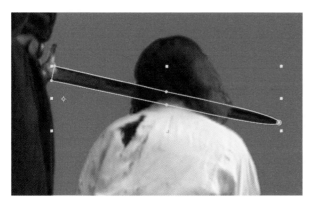

Figure 15.83 *Rotoscope around the sword for the last 100 frames*

Because you removed the keyer from the sword layer, you may see some green. Apply an Effect → Color Correction → Hue/Saturation effect, and drag the Master Saturation slider all the way to the left to -100 to remove all color from the blade. At frame 200, where the masking starts, keyframe the opacity from 0% to 100% over 20 frames to prevent the masked blade from popping on.

Adding the Keyed Figures to the Scene

Now that the keying is complete, you can delete the red solid. Double-click the F-grSpire comp to open it in the Viewer panel. Next, drag the Guide+Visitor comp into the F-grSpire comp. The figures need to be facing in the opposite direction, so scale the precomp -100% on the X-axis. Position the Guide+Visitor precomp on top of the placeholder from the Photoshop file. When the precomp and placeholder are aligned, turn off the visibility of the Figures layer. Only the live-action footage remains. Return to the ViewOfHades3D comp to preview the actors in the scene (Figure 15.84).

Figure 15.84 *Green-screen footage in ViewOfHades3D*

Color Correcting the Keyed Figures

In the context of the entire painting, the figures are too bright and not red enough for the environment. Return to the F-grSpire comp, and add a curve to the Guide+Visitor precomp. Adjusting the R, G, and B channel curves individually, darken and add red to the figures (Figure 15.85).

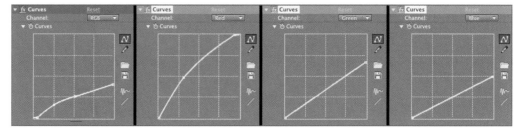

Figure 15.85 *Color correction for the Guide+Visitor precomp*

The color-corrected figures now fit into the scene (Figure 15.86).

You can compare your work to this point to `ViewOfHadesAnimation&Figures.aep` in the Chapter 15 DVD materials.

The Camera Move

With the 3D scene set up, it's time to move the camera to take advantage of the 3D environment and show off the parallax between the planes. Set a keyframe for the camera at frame 299, the final frame of the sequence, for Position, Orientation, and Point Of Interest. This will be the final position of the camera to show the entire scene (Figure 15.87).

Figure 15.86 *Final color-corrected actors*

Scrub to frame 0, and, in the Active Camera view, place the camera closer to the figures and to the right (Figure 15.88). The camera movement from 0 to 299 shouldn't be extreme. If you rotate off axis too much, it will become obvious to the viewer that the scene is composed of flat planes. However, if the camera move is conservative, the project will hold up well over a 10-second sequence. Take a moment to experiment with the limitations of the camera and to discover at what point the flat planes become apparent.

You can view this final camera move in `ViewOfHadesCameraMove.aep`.

Figure 15.87 *Camera position at frame 299*

Figure 15.88 *Camera position at frame 0*

More Details

This is the end of this chapter, but you can finish much more in this project. As in the previous chapter, adding blur and film grain on the layers will make the painting appear more film-like. If you're feeling ambitious, comping in video footage of flames on the bridge and in the background cities will take this piece to another level. Similarly, you can animate the motion of the lava waterfalls and chimney smoke, and add rising steam from the lava deposits to add to the realism.

Remember, because this piece was set up using precomps, all the video elements can be added into the 2D comps, and their contribution will update in the final scene. The sky is the limit!

A more complex version of the scene, named ViewOfHadesMoreAnimation.aep, with more animation but no video footage, is available on the DVD. A more complex version of this project, which includes the aforementioned fire and smoke footage, ViewOfHadesFinal.mov, is also on the DVD. It's at half resolution to save space.

Assignment: Create Your Own Vision of Hades

Now that you've worked through this process with a demonstration file, it's time to create your own vision of the underworld. You can either begin with the half-finished file you worked over at the beginning of the chapter and make it your own, or you can start from scratch and let your imagination run wild.

Your final painting should contain the following elements, all of which you learned to set up in this chapter:

- Five more layers of information that can be placed on planes at different depths in space.
- A ground plane onto which you can project an image to be used as the base of the project.
- Moving figures. You can use the footage provided on the DVD that you used in the demo project. If you have access to a video camera, consider dressing up some of your friends and creating your own scene.

In the animation phase of the project, challenge yourself to do the following:

- Set up your project so that all elements on the same plane are contained in precomps. Add animation to the elements in the precomps.
- Use fractal noise to add motion to water, smoke, or lava. It's a very efficient way to add motion to elements without the overhead of video footage.
- Add some video footage to your projects in the precomps. Some elements, like fire, can't be done well with fractal noise, and you'll have to add video footage to create the effect convincingly.
- Animate the sky. Based on what was demonstrated in this chapter, break the sky into layers, and animate the layers against each other to bring life to the clouds.

A Final Note

I would be happy to critique your work on any of the projects contained in this book. Feel free to email me at david@digitalmattepaintinghandbook.com. If you want formal training, I teach a matte painting course at the School of Visual Arts and Pratt Institute. I also offer weekend seminars throughout the country, and you can find information about upcoming workshops at www.digitalmattepaintinghandbook.com.

In this book, I've taught you the basic skills required to be a matte painter: perspective, form, texturing, Maya camera projection, and using the After Effects workspace. I've given you a comprehensive introduction to digital painting, but the one ingredient required to become a great matte artist is something only you can give yourself: time.

Paint! Paint every day. The more time you devote to honing your skills, the closer you'll come to realizing your vision. Masterpieces await you in the future, so get busy!

APPENDIX

About the Companion DVD

- What You'll Find on the DVD
- System requirements
- Using the DVD
- Troubleshooting

This appendix summarizes the content you'll find on the DVD. If you need help with copying the items provided on the DVD, refer to the installation instructions in the "Using the DVD" section of this appendix.

What You'll Find on the DVD

In the Chapters directory, you'll find all the files for completing the tutorials and understanding concepts in this book. This includes sample files, as well as video files that provide screen recordings of selected projects in progress.

Working with files directly from the DVD isn't encouraged because Maya and After Effects scenes link to external files such as texture maps, images, video files, and dynamic caches. Copy the entire Chapter folder for each chapter that involves Maya or After Effects to your local drive to ensure that the demonstration files function properly.

Videos are provided for selected projects. In many cases, seeing the project completed as a movie can help to clarify the processes described in the book.

System Requirements

This DVD doesn't include the Photoshop CS5, After Effects CS5, or Maya 2011 software.

You'll need to have After Effects CS5 and Maya 2011 installed on your computer to use the Maya scene files and After Effects project files included with the DVD. Earlier versions of these programs won't open files created in later versions.

Photoshop is more forgiving about what files it will open, and earlier versions of the program will open the files on the DVD. Photoshop CS5 Extended is recommended to complete all the projects, but it isn't required for most of the book.

Make sure your computer meets the minimum system requirements shown in the following list. If your computer doesn't match up to these requirements, you may have problems using the files on the companion DVD. For the latest information, please refer to the ReadMe file located at the root of the DVD-ROM:

- A computer running Microsoft Windows XP (SP2 or newer), Windows Vista, or Windows 7; or Apple OS X 10.5.2 or newer
- An Internet connection
- A DVD-ROM drive

For the latest information on the system requirements for Maya, go to www.autodesk.com/maya. Although you can find specific hardware recommendations there, the following general information will help you determine whether you're already set up to run Maya: you need a fast processor, a minimum of 2 GB RAM, and a workstation graphics card for the best compatibility.

For the most up-to-date information about system requirements for Photoshop CS5 and After Effects CS5, go to www.adobe.com/products/creativesuite/mastercollection/systemreqs/. This site provides the most current system requirements for running the CS5 Master Collection, which includes both programs.

You should also have a Wacom tablet. There is a reason artists paint with a brush rather than a brick; and for the same reason, digital artists choose to use a digitizing tablet rather than a mouse. Although it's possible to paint using a mouse, a Wacom tablet or other digital tablet should be your first purchase if you're planning to pursue digital matte painting.

Using the DVD

For best results, copy the files from the DVD to your computer. To copy the items from the DVD to your hard drive, follow these steps:

1. Insert the DVD into your computer's DVD-ROM drive. The license agreement appears.

Windows users: The interface won't launch if Autorun is disabled. In that case, choose Start → Run (for Windows Vista, choose Start → All Programs → Accessories → Run). In the dialog box that appears, type **D:\Start.exe**. (Replace D with the proper letter if your DVD drive uses a different letter. If you don't know the letter, see how your DVD drive is listed under My Computer.) Click OK.

---

2. Read the license agreement, and then click the Accept button if you want to use the DVD.

The DVD interface appears. The interface allows you to access the content with just one or two clicks. Alternately, you can access the files at the root directory of your hard drive.

Mac users: The DVD icon will appear on your desktop. Double-click the icon to open the DVD, and then navigate to the files you want.

Troubleshooting

Wiley has attempted to provide programs that work on most computers with the minimum system requirements. Alas, your computer may differ, and some programs may not work properly for some reason.

The two likeliest problems are that you don't have enough memory (RAM) for the programs you want to use or that you have other programs running that are affecting the installation or running of a program. If you get an error message such as "Not enough memory" or "Setup cannot continue," try one or more of the following suggestions and then try using the software again:

Turn off any antivirus software running on your computer. Installation programs sometimes mimic virus activity and may make your computer incorrectly believe that it's being infected by a virus.

Close all running programs. The more programs you have running, the less memory is available to other programs. Installation programs typically update files and programs; so if you keep other programs running, installation may not work properly.

Add more RAM to your computer. This is, admittedly, a drastic and somewhat expensive step. However, adding more memory can really help the speed of your computer and allow more programs to run at the same time.

Customer Care

If you have trouble with the book's companion DVD, please call the Wiley Product Technical Support phone number at (800) 762-2974. Outside the United States, call +1 (317) 572-3994. You can also contact Wiley Product Technical Support at http://sybex.custhelp.com. John Wiley & Sons will provide technical support only for installation and other general quality-control items. For technical support on the applications themselves, consult the program's vendor or author.

To place additional orders or to request information about other Wiley products, please call (877) 762-2974.

Please check the book's website at www.sybex.com/go/digitalmattepainting, where we'll post additional content and updates that supplement this book should the need arise.

Contact the Author

The author would be happy to review and critique projects completed by the readers of this book. Feel free to contact him through his personal website: www.digitalmattepaintinghandbook.com.

Index